The British War Blue Book

MISCELLANEOUS No. 9 (1939)

White Paper Supplement

GERMANY No. 1 (1939)

DOCUMENTS

CONCERNING

GERMAN-POLISH RELATIONS

AND THE

OUTBREAK OF HOSTILITIES BETWEEN

GREAT BRITAIN AND GERMANY

ON SEPTEMBER 3, 1939

AND

FINAL REPORT

BY THE RIGHT HONOURABLE

SIR NEVILE HENDERSON, G.C.M.G.

SEPTEMBER 20, 1939

Presented by the Secretary of State for Foreign Affairs
to Parliament by Command of His Majesty

TORONTO

THE MUSSON BOOK COMPANY LTD.

1 9 3 9

PRINTED AND PUBLISHED IN CANADA BY PERMISSION OF THE
CONTROLLER OF HIS MAJESTY'S STATIONERY OFFICE

Cmd. 6106
Cmd. 6115

CONTENTS

CONTENTS

CONTENTS

Further deterioration in the situation at Danzig.

Treatment of German minority in Poland.

Developments leading immediately to the outbreak of hostilities between Great Britain and Germany on September 3, 1939.

CONTENTS

CONTENTS

CONTENTS

CONTENTS

The Prime Minister's Broadcast Talk to the German People on September 4, 1939.

White Paper Supplement.

SUMMARY OF CONTENTS.

German-Polish relations from January, 1934 to January, 1939.

The governing factor in the relations between Germany and Poland during this period was the German-Polish Agreement of the 26th January, 1934 (No. 1, pp. 1-2). This agreement, which was valid for ten years, provided that in no circumstances would either party "proceed to the application of force for the purpose of reaching a decision" in any dispute between them. In the five years after the signature of this pact Herr Hitler made a number of speeches friendly to Poland (Nos. 2-8, pp. 3-5). Poland was "the home of a great, nationally-conscious people" (21st May, 1935). It would be "unreasonable and impossible," so Herr Hitler acknowledged, "to deny a State of such a size as this any outlet to the sea" (7th March, 1936). The agreement "has worked out to the advantage of both sides" (30th January, 1937).

Deterioration in the European situation resulting from German action against Czecho-Slovakia on March 15, 1939.

The position after the German occupation of Czecho-Slovakia was summarized in speeches by the Prime Minister at Birmingham on the 17th March (No. 9, pp. 6-11) and by Viscount Halifax, Secretary of State for Foreign Affairs in the House of Lords on the 20th March, 1939 (No. 10, pp. 11-18). Mr. Chamberlain described the German occupation as "in complete disregard of the principles laid down by the German Government itself," and asked: "Is this the end of an old adventure, or is it the beginning of a new? Is this the last attack upon a small State, or is it to be followed by others?" Lord Halifax stated that the action of the German Government was "a complete repudiation of the Munich Agreement and a denial of the spirit in which the negotiators of that agreement bound themselves to co-operate for a peaceful settlement." On the 23rd March the Prime Minister stated in the House of Commons that His Majesty's Government, while not wishing "to stand in the way of any reasonable efforts on the part of Germany to expand her export trade," was resolved "by all means in our power" to oppose a "procedure under which independent States are subjected to such pressure under threat of force as to be obliged to yield up their independence" (No. 11, pp. 18-19). In a conversation of the 27th May between Sir Nevile Henderson, His Majesty's Ambassador in Berlin, and Field-Marshal Göring, the Ambassador warned the Field-Marshal that Great Britain and France would be involved in war with Germany if Germany attempted to settle German-Polish differences "by unilateral action such as would compel the Poles to resort to arms to safeguard their independence" (No. 12, pp. 19-21).

German-Polish discussions (April-May, 1939).

In a speech to the Reichstag on the 28th April, Herr Hitler announced that he had made proposals to the Polish Government that Danzig should return as a Free City into the framework of the Reich, and that Germany should receive a route and railway with extra-territorial status through the Corridor in exchange for a 25-years' pact of non-aggression and a recognition of the existing German-Polish boundaries as "ultimate." On the same day a memorandum to this effect

xiii

was given to the Polish Government. The German proposals, which had been presented for the first time on the 21st March, 1939, *i.e.*, less than a week after the German occupation of Prague, were now described as "the very minimum which must be demanded from the point of view of German interests." Herr Hitler also claimed that the German-Polish Agreement of January, 1934 was incompatible with the Anglo-Polish promises of mutual assistance and therefore was no longer binding (Nos. 13 and 14, pp. 22-28).

On the 5th May the Polish Government replied to the German Government with an explanation of their point of view. The Polish note repeated the counter-proposals which the Polish Government had put forward as a basis for negotiation in reply to the German proposals, and refuted the German argument that the Anglo-Polish guarantee was in any way incompatible with the German-Polish Agreement (No. 16, pp. 33-36). The Polish Minister for Foreign Affairs elaborated his country's case in a speech made in the Polish Parliament on the 5th May. The Minister said that the Polish Government regarded the German proposals as a demand for "unilateral concessions." He added that Poland was ready to approach "objectively" and with "their utmost goodwill" any points raised for discussion by the German Government, but that two conditions were necessary if the discussions were to be of real value: (1) peaceful intentions, (2) peaceful methods of procedure (No. 15, pp. 28-33).

The Polish memorandum reminded the German Government that no formal reply to the Polish counter-proposals had been received for a month, and that only on the 28th April the Polish Government learned that "the mere fact of the formulation of counter-proposals instead of the acceptance of the verbal German suggestions without alteration or reservation had been regarded by the Reich as a refusal of discussions" (No. 16, p. 35).

The Anglo-Polish Agreement.

On the 31st March, 1939, the Prime Minister announced the assurance of British and French support to Poland "in the event of any action which clearly threatened Polish independence, and which the Polish Government accordingly considered it vital to resist" (No. 17, p. 37). An Anglo-Polish communiqué issued on the 6th April recorded the assurances of mutual support agreed upon by the British and Polish Governments, "pending the completion of the permanent agreement" (No. 18, p. 38). The Agreement of Mutual Assistance was signed on the 25th August. The articles defined the mutual guarantee in case of aggression by a European Power (No. 19, pp. 38-40).

Developments in Anglo-German relations and in the general British attitude towards the international situation (April-June, 1939).

Anglo-German as well as German-Polish relations deteriorated after the German occupation of Czecho-Slovakia. On the 1st April Herr Hitler made a speech at Wilhelmshaven in which he attacked Great Britain and British policy towards Germany, and attempted a justification of German policy (No. 20, pp. 41-49. Herr Hitler spoke in the Reichstag on the 28th April announcing the denunciation by Germany of the Anglo-German Naval Agreements (No. 21, pp. 49-53). On the 27th April a memorandum to this effect was sent to the British Government (No. 22, pp. 53-54). On the 16th June Viscount Halifax again denied to the German Ambassador in London that Great Britain or any other Power was "encircling" Germany (No. 23, p. 55). A week later (23rd June) His Majesty's Government sent a reasoned protest to the German Government denying the validity of the German unilateral denunciation of the Anglo-German Naval Agreements, and also refuting the arguments of fact (*i.e.*, persistent British hostility to Germany) by which Herr Hitler attempted to justify his denunciation of the Naval Agreements (No. 24, pp. 55-60).

In view of these facts and of the increasing international tension, Viscount Halifax took the opportunity, in a speech at Chatham House on the 29th June, to define at some length the attitude and policy of Great Britain. He explained the reason for the obligations which Great Britain had undertaken in the Continent of Europe. He discussed Anglo-German relations and stated that Great Britain had no wish to isolate Germany, and that, if Germany wished, "a policy of co-operation" could be adopted at once. "British policy rests on two foundations of purpose. One is determination to resist force. The other is our recognition of the world's desire to get on with the constructive work of building peace" (No. 25, pp. 60-67).

Deterioration in the local situation at Danzig (June 3-July 3, 1939).

With the increase of agitation in the Reich the local situation at Danzig rapidly became worse. On the 3rd June the President of the Danzig Senate made accusations against Polish customs inspectors (No. 26, pp. 68-69). The Polish Government on the 10th June replied with a denial of the accusations and a statement of the legal rights of Poland in relation to Danzig (No. 27, pp. 69-70). On the 27th June the Polish Vice-Minister for Foreign Affairs told Sir H. Kennard, His Majesty's Ambassador in Warsaw, that a Freicorps was being formed in Danzig (No. 28, pp. 70-71), and on the 28th and 30th June, and on the 1st July, Mr. Shepherd, His Majesty's Consul-General in Danzig, reported upon military preparations in the city (Nos. 29, 31, 33, pp. 71, 73, 75). On the 30th June, in view of the gravity of the situation, Viscount Halifax suggested consultation between the British, French and Polish Governments for the co-ordination of their plans (No. 30, pp. 72-73). Meanwhile, the Polish Government maintained a restrained attitude (Nos. 32 and 34, pp. 74 and 75).

British Attitude towards developments in Danzig (July 10-15, 1939).

On the 10th July, while the situation at Danzig appeared to be becoming critical, the Prime Minister defined the British attitude towards the Danzig problem in a statement in the House of Commons (No. 35, pp. 76-78). He pointed out that it was before Poland had received any guarantee from Great Britain that the Polish Government, fearing to be faced with unilateral German action, had replied to the German proposals, by putting forward certain counter-proposals, and that the cause of the Polish refusal to accept the German proposals was to be found in the character of these proposals and in the manner and timing of their presentation and not in the British guarantee of Poland.

On the 14th July Sir Nevile Henderson discussed with Baron von Weizsäcker, German State Secretary at the Ministry for Foreign Affairs, a statement by one of the German Under-Secretaries that "Herr Hitler was convinced that England would never fight over Danzig." Sir Nevile Henderson repeated the affirmation already made by His Majesty's Government that, in the event of German aggression, Great Britain would support Poland in resisting force by force (No. 36, pp. 78-80).

Temporary easing in the Danzig situation (July 19-August 2).

After the tension in Danzig at the end of June there was a temporary lull in the situation. The Acting British Consul-General at Danzig reported on the 19th July that Herr Forster, the leader of the National Socialist party in Danzig, had stated, after an interview with Herr Hitler, that "nothing will be done on the German side to provoke a conflict," and that the Danzig question could "wait if necessary until next year or even longer" (No. 37, pp. 81-82). On the 21st July

Viscount Halifax instructed Mr. Norton, His Majesty's Chargé d'Affaires at Warsaw, to impress upon the Polish Government the need for caution (No. 38, pp. 82-83). M. Beck replied, on the 25th July, that the Polish Government was equally anxious for a *détente* (No. 39, pp. 83-84). On the previous day Herr Forster had again stated that "the Danzig question could, if necessary, wait a year or more" (No. 40, p. 84). On the 31st July and the 2nd August, however, Sir H. Kennard reported less hopefully about the position (Nos. 41 and 42, pp. 84-85).

Further deterioration in the situation at Danzig (August 4-16).

On the 4th August M. Beck told His Majesty's Chargé d'Affaires at Warsaw that the Danzig Senate had that day informed Polish customs inspectors at four posts in Danzig that henceforward they would not be allowed to carry out their duties. The Polish Government took "a very serious view" of this step (No. 43, p. 86). Similar news came from Mr. Shepherd at Danzig (No. 44, pp. 86-87). On the 9th August Sir H. Kennard reported that the Polish attitude was "firm but studiously moderate"; (No. 45, p. 87). A day later, Sir H. Kennard reported to His Majesty's Government a communication made by the German Government to the Polish Chargé d'Affaires at Berlin on the Danzig question, and the Polish reply to this communication. M. Beck drew the attention of Sir H. Kennard to "the very serious nature of the German *démarche* as it was the first time that the Reich had directly intervened in the dispute between Poland and the Danzig Senate" (No. 46, p. 88). The Polish Government in their reply to the German *note verbale* stated that they would "react to any attempt by the authorities of the Free City which might tend to compromise the rights and interests which Poland possesses there in virtue of her agreements, by the employment of such means and measures as they alone shall think fit to adopt, and will consider any future intervention by the German Government to the detriment of these rights and interests as an act of aggression" (No. 47, pp. 89-90).

Sir Nevile Henderson on the 15th August discussed with Baron von Weizsäcker the deterioration in the Danzig position, and pointed out that if the Poles "were compelled by any act of Germany to resort to arms to defend themselves, there was not a shadow of doubt that we would give them our full armed support . . . . Germany would be making a tragic mistake if she imagined the contrary." Baron von Weizsäcker himself observed that "the situation in one respect was even worse than last year, as Mr. Chamberlain could not again come out to Germany." Baron von Weizsäcker also discounted the character of Russian help to Poland and "thought that the U.S.S.R. would even in the end join in sharing the Polish spoils" (No. 48, pp. 90-93).

Meanwhile, on the 11th August, M. Burckhardt had a conversation with Herr Hitler at Berchtesgaden at the latter's request, in which the question of Danzig and the general European situation were discussed (No. 49, p. 93). Viscount Halifax, who still hoped that Herr Hitler might avoid war, advised the Polish Government to make it clear that they remained ready for negotiations over Danzig (Nos. 50 and 51, pp. 93-94).

Treatment of the German Minority in Poland (August 24-27).

During the course of the correspondence outlined in this section, Sir H. Kennard reported that the German press campaign about the persecution of the German minority in Poland was a "gross distortion and exaggeration of the facts" (No. 52, pp. 95-96). On the 26th August Sir H. Kennard reported frontier incidents which had been provoked by the Germans. They had not caused the Poles to change their "calm and strong attitude of defence" (No. 53, p. 96). Reports of unfounded German allegations against the Poles were also sent by Sir H. Kennard on the 26th and 27th August (Nos. 54 and 55, p. 97).

SUMMARY OF CONTENTS

Developments leading immediately to the outbreak of hostilities between Great Britain and Germany (August 24-September 3).

The Prime Minister's letter to Herr Hitler (August 22) and Herr Hitler's interview with Sir Nevile Henderson (August 23).

On the 22nd August, after the publication of the news of Herr von Ribbentrop's visit to Moscow to sign a non-aggression pact with the U.S.S.R., the Prime Minister sent a personal letter to Herr Hitler. Mr. Chamberlain once again gave a clear statement of the British obligations to Poland, and stated that "whatever may prove to be the nature of the German-Soviet Agreement, it cannot alter Great Britain's obligation." He added that "it has been alleged that, if His Majesty's Government had made their position more clear in 1914, the great catastrophe would have been avoided. Whether or not there is any force in that allegation, His Majesty's Government are resolved that on this occasion there shall be no such tragic misunderstanding" (No. 56, pp. 98-99). On the 23rd August Sir Nevile Henderson reported his first interview with Herr Hitler earlier in the day. Herr Hitler was "excitable and uncompromising"; his language was "violent and exaggerated both as regards England and Poland." Herr Hitler observed, in reply to His Majesty's Ambassador's repeated warnings that direct action against Poland would mean war with Great Britain, that "Germany had nothing to lose, and Great Britain much; that he did not desire war, but would not shrink from it if it was necessary, and that his people were much more behind him than last September (No. 57, pp. 99-101).

Herr Hitler was calmer at a second talk, but no less uncompromising. He put the whole responsibility for war on Great Britain, and maintained that Great Britain was "determined to destroy and exterminate Germany. He was, he said, 50 years old; he preferred war now to when he would be 55 or 60." He said that "England was fighting for lesser races, whereas he was fighting only for Germany" (No. 58, pp. 101-102).

The German reply to the Prime Minister's letter was given to His Majesty's Ambassador on the 23rd August. Herr Hitler stated that the British promise to assist Poland would make no difference to the determination of the Reich to safeguard German interests, and that the precautionary British military measures announced in the Prime Minister's letter of the 22nd August would be followed by the mobilisation of the German forces (No. 60, pp. 103-105).

Text of the German-Soviet Non-Aggression Pact (August 23) (No. 61, pp. 105-106).

Appointment of Herr Forster as Head of the State of the Free City of Danzig (August 23).

Herr Forster was declared by decree of the Danzig Senate, on the 23rd August, Head of the State (Staatsoberhaupt) of the Free City of Danzig (No. 62, pp. 106-107). The Polish Government protested to the Senate against the illegality of this appointment (No. 63, p. 107).

Speeches by the Prime Minister and Viscount Halifax on the Danzig and general German-Polish situation and the determination of Great Britain to honour British obligations to Poland (August 24) (Nos. 64 and 65, pp. 108-119).

Attempts by the Polish Government to establish contact with the German Government (August 24).

In view of the increasing tension in Danzig, M. Beck told Sir H. Kennard that he considered the situation "most grave," and that he had asked the Polish Ambassador in Berlin to seek an immediate interview with the German State

Secretary (No. 66, pp. 119-120). This interview could not, however, be arranged, since Baron von Weizsäcker was at Berchtesgaden, but the Polish Ambassador had an interview in the afternoon of the 24th August with Field-Marshal Göring. The Field-Marshal regretted that "his policy of maintaining friendly relations with Poland should have come to nought, and admitted that he no longer had influence to do much in the matter." The Field-Marshal hinted that Poland should abandon her alliance with Great Britain, and left the Polish Government with the impression that Germany was aiming at a free hand in Eastern Europe (No. 67, pp. 120-121).

Interview between Sir N. Henderson and Herr Hitler, and German "verbal communication" of August 25.

On the 25th August Herr Hitler sent for Sir Nevile Henderson and asked him to fly to London to "put the case" to His Majesty's Government. The "case," which included an offer of friendship with Great Britain, once the Polish question had been solved, was contained in a verbal communication made to His Majesty's Ambassador (No. 68, pp. 121-123). During the discussion with Herr Hitler, Sir Nevile Henderson stated once more that Great Britain "could not go back on her word to Poland," and would insist upon a settlement by negotiation. Herr Hitler refused to guarantee a negotiated settlement on the ground that "Polish provocation might at any moment render German intervention to protect German nationals inevitable" (No. 69, pp. 123-124).

Correspondence between the British and Polish Governments, August 25-27.

On the 25th August Viscount Halifax suggested to the Polish Government the establishment of a corps of neutral observers, who would enter upon their functions if it were found possible to open negotiations (No. 70, p. 124). He also suggested the possibility of negotiating over an exchange of populations (No. 71, p. 124). M. Beck raised no objection in principle to either proposal (No. 72, p. 125).

Reply of His Majesty's Government, dated August 28, to Herr Hitler's communications of August 23 and 25 (No. 60, pp. 103-105 and No. 68, pp. 121-123):- interview of August 28 between Sir Nevile Henderson and Herr Hitler: speech of the Prime Minister in the House of Commons on August 29.

On the 28th August Viscount Halifax informed the Polish Government through Sir H. Kennard that in the British reply to Herr Hitler "a clear distinction" would be drawn between "the method of reaching agreement on German-Polish differences and the nature of the solution to be arrived at. As to the method, we (His Majesty's Government) wish to express our clear view that direct discussion on equal terms between the parties is the proper means" (No. 73, p. 126).

The reply of His Majesty's Government, suggesting direct discussion between the German and Polish Governments, was presented to Herr Hitler by Sir N. Henderson on the 28th August (No. 74, pp. 126-128). His Majesty's Government stated they had "already received a definite assurance from the Polish Government that they are prepared to enter into discussions," and that, if such direct discussion led, as they hoped, to agreement, "the way would be open to the negotiation of that wider and more complete understanding between Great Britain and Germany which both countries desire." In his interview of the 28th August with Herr Hitler, Sir N. Henderson repeated the British readiness to reach an Anglo-German understanding, "but only on the basis of a peaceful and freely negotiated solution of the Polish question." Sir Nevile Henderson pointed out to Herr Hitler that "it lay with him (Herr Hitler) as to whether he preferred a unilateral solution which would mean war as regards Poland, or British friendship. Herr Hitler, who said that "his army was ready and eager for battle," would not answer at once whether he would negotiate directly with Poland (No. 75, pp. 129-131).

On the 29th August the Prime Minister once more explained in the House of Commons the British standpoint (No. 77, pp. 132-136).

Interview of August 29 between Sir N. Henderson and Herr Hitler, and German demand for the arrival of a Polish representative in Berlin by August 30.

At 7.15 p.m. on the 29th August Sir N. Henderson received from Herr Hitler the German answer that the German Government was prepared to accept the British proposal for direct German-Polish negotiations, but counted on the arrival of a Polish plenipotentiary by the 30th August (No. 78, pp. 136-138). The British Ambassador remarked that the latter demand "sounded like an ultimatum," but, after some heated remarks, both Herr Hitler and Herr von Ribbentrop assured the Ambassador "that it was only intended to stress the urgency of the moment" (No. 79, p. 138). The interview was "of a stormy character." Sir N. Henderson thought that Herr Hitler was "far less reasonable" than on the 28th August (No. 80, p. 139).

At 4 a.m. on the 30th August Sir N. Henderson, on instructions from His Majesty's Government, informed the German Government that it would be "unreasonable to expect the British Government to produce a Polish representative in Berlin" by the 30th August, and that "the German Government must not expect this" (Nos. 81 and 82, p. 140).

Exchange of correspondence between His Majesty's Government and the Polish Government on August 30.

Sir H. Kennard also reported his opinion that the Polish Government could not be induced to send a representative immediately to Berlin to discuss a settlement on the basis proposed by Herr Hitler. "They would certainly sooner fight and perish rather than submit to such humiliation, especially after the examples of Czecho-Slovakia, Lithuania and Austria" (No. 84, p. 141). On this same day the Polish Government gave their assurance, in reply to advice from Viscount Halifax, to avoid any kind of provocation (No. 85, p. 141), that they had no intention of provoking any incidents, in spite of the provocation at Danzig, which was becoming "more and more intolerable" (No. 86, p. 142).

Exchange of correspondence between the British and German Governments with regard to the opening of direct German-Polish negotiations (August 30).

At 2.45 p.m. and again at 5.30 p.m. on the 30th August His Majesty's Government instructed Sir N. Henderson to inform the German Government of the representations which the British Government had made in Warsaw for the avoidance of all frontier incidents and urged the German Government to reciprocate (Nos. 83 and 87, pp. 140 and 142). They repeated at 6.50 p.m., in view of the German insistence on the point, that it was "wholly unreasonable" for the German Government to insist upon the arrival in Berlin of a Polish representative with full powers to receive German proposals, and that they could not advise the Polish Government in this sense. They suggested the normal procedure of giving the Polish Ambassador the German proposals for transmission to Warsaw (No. 88, p. 142).

At midnight on the 30th-31st August Sir N. Henderson handed to Herr von Ribbentrop the full British reply to the German letter of the 29th August (No. 78, pp. 136-138). The reply noted the German Government's acceptance of the British proposal for direct German-Polish discussions, and of the "position of His Majesty's Government as to Poland's vital interests and independence." The reply also noted that the German Government accepted "in principle the condition that any settlement should be made the subject of an international guarantee." His Majesty's Government stated that they were informing the Polish Government of the German Government's reply. "The method of contact and arrangements for discussions must obviously be agreed with all urgency between the German and Polish Governments, but in His Majesty's Government's view it would be impracticable to establish contact so early as to-day (*i.e.*, the 30th August) (No. 89, pp. 143-144).

The British reply was also telegraphed to the Polish Government, and Viscount Halifax hoped that "provided the method and general arrangement for discussions can be satisfactorily agreed," the Polish Government, which had authorised His Majesty's Government to say that they were prepared to enter into direct discussions, would be ready to do so without delay (No. 90, pp. 144-145).

In his interview at midnight the 30th-31st August with Herr von Ribbentrop, Sir N. Henderson suggested that the German Government should adopt the normal procedure of making contact with the Polish Government, *i.e.*, that when the German proposals were ready the Polish Ambassador should be invited to call and to receive these proposals "for transmission to his Government with a view to the immediate opening of negotiations."

"Herr von Ribbentrop's reply was to produce a lengthy document which he read out in German aloud at top-speed." When His Majesty's Ambassador asked for the text of the proposals in the document, he was told that it was "now too late," as a Polish representative had not arrived in Berlin by midnight (the 30-31st August). Sir N. Henderson described this procedure as an "ultimatum," in spite of the assurances previously given by the German Government. He asked why Herr von Ribbentrop could not adopt the normal procedure, give him a copy of the proposals, and ask the Polish Ambassador to call on him (Herr von Ribbentrop) to receive them. "In the most violent terms Herr von Ribbentrop said that he would never ask the Polish Ambassador to visit him," though he hinted that it might be different if the Polish Ambassador asked for an interview (No. 92, p. 146).

Exchange of correspondence between the British and Polish Governments on August 31 with regard to direct negotiations.

On hearing of the reply of His Majesty's Government to the German Government (No. 89, pp. 143-144) on the subject of direct German-Polish negotiations, M. Beck said that he would do "everything possible to facilitate the efforts of His Majesty's Government." He promised the "considered reply of his Government" by midday on the 31st August (No. 93, p. 147). Later on the 31st August Viscount Halifax advised the Polish Government immediately to instruct the Polish Ambassador in Berlin to say that he was ready to transmit to his Government any proposals made by the German Government so that they (the Polish Government) "may at once consider them and make suggestions for early discussions" (No. 95, p. 148).

At 6.30 p.m. on the 31st August Sir H. Kennard communicated to London the formal Polish confirmation of the readiness of the Polish Government to enter into direct discussions with the German Government on the basis proposed by Great Britain (No. 97, p. 149). M. Beck said that "he would now instruct M. Lipski [Polish Ambassador in Berlin] to seek an interview either with the (German) Minister for Foreign Affairs or the State Secretary" in order to establish contact for the initiation of direct discussions, but that the Polish Ambassador would not be authorised to receive a document containing the German proposals, since, "in view of past experience, it might be accompanied by some sort of ultimatum." In M. Beck's view "it was essential that contact should be made, in the first instance," for the discussion of details "as to where, with whom, and on what basis negotiations should be commenced" (No. 96, p. 148).

SUMMARY OF CONTENTS

German proposals for German-Polish settlement, presented to the British Ambassador in Berlin at 9.15 p.m. on August 31, and German invasion of Poland on September 1.

It was not until 9.15 p.m. on the 31st August that the German Government gave Sir N. Henderson a copy of their proposals, which had been read to him so rapidly by Herr von Ribbentrop on the previous night. The German Government stated that the note contained the sixteen points of their proposed settlement, but that, as the Polish plenipotentiary, with powers "not only to discuss but to conduct and conclude negotiations," had not arrived in Berlin, they regarded their proposals as "to all intents and purposes rejected" (No. 98, pp. 149-153). At 11 p.m. Viscount Halifax telephoned instructions to Sir N. Henderson to inform the German Government that the Polish Government were taking steps to establish contact with them through the Polish Ambassador in Berlin (No. 99, p. 153). At 9 p.m. British summer time the German Government had, however, broadcast their proposals together with the statement that they regarded them as having been rejected. They had, however, never been communicated to the Polish Government and all means of communication between the Polish Ambassador in Berlin and the Polish Government had been cut off.

As a final attempt to meet the German demands, Viscount Halifax telegraphed to Sir H. Kennard in the night of the 31st August-1st September his view that the Polish Ambassador in Berlin might receive a document for transmission to his Government and might say that "(a) if it contained anything like an ultimatum, the Polish Government would certainly be unable to discuss on such a basis; and (b) that, in any case, in the view of the Polish Government, questions as to the *venue* of the negotiations, the basis on which they should be held, and the persons to take part in them, must be discussed and decided between the two Governments" (No. 100, p. 154).

In answer to this telegram, Sir H. Kennard replied on the 1st September that M. Lipski "had already called on the German Foreign Minister at 6.30 p.m." on the 31st August. "In view of this fact, which was followed by the German invasion of Poland at dawn to-day (1st September), it was clearly useless for me to take the action suggested" (No. 101, p. 155).

These facts were announced to the House of Commons by the Prime Minister on the 1st September (No. 105, pp. 156-161). A further "explanatory note, upon the actual course of events," reprinted from White Paper (Misc. No. 8 (1939), Cmd. 6102) (No. 104, p. 156) should be read in connexion with Herr Hitler's version of events as given in his speech of the 1st September to the Reichstag (No. 106, pp. 161-165) and in his proclamation to the German army (No. 107, p. 166).

Reunion of Danzig with the Reich (September 1).

On the 1st September Herr Forster announced in a proclamation to the people of Danzig the reunion of Danzig with the Reich. He telegraphed an account of his action to Herr Hitler, who replied at once accepting the reunion and ratifying the so-called legal act by which it was brought about (No. 108, pp. 166-167).

Action taken by His Majesty's Government after the receipt of news of the German attack on Poland (September 1-3).

On the 1st September, after His Majesty's Government had received news of the German invasion of Poland, Viscount Halifax instructed Sir N. Henderson to inform the German Government that the Governments of the United Kingdom and France considered that the German action had "created conditions (viz., an aggressive act of force against Poland threatening the independence of Poland) which call for the implementation by the Governments of the United Kingdom and France of the undertaking to Poland to come to her assistance." Unless the German Government suspended all aggressive action against Poland, and promptly withdrew their forces from Polish territory, His Majesty's Government in the United Kingdom would "without hesitation fulfil their obligations to Poland." Sir N. Henderson was authorised to explain, if asked, that this communication was "in the nature of a warning," and was "not to be considered as an ultimatum," but Viscount Halifax added, for Sir N. Henderson's own information, that, "if the German reply is unsatisfactory, the next stage will be either an ultimatum with time-limit or an immediate declaration of war" (Nos. 109 and 110, pp. 167-168).

On the night of the 1st-2nd September Sir N. Henderson reported that he had made the necessary communication to Herr von Ribbentrop at 9.30 p.m. and had asked for an immediate answer. Herr von Ribbentrop replied that he would submit the communication to Herr Hitler (No. 111, p. 168). Meanwhile, on the 1st September, the Polish Government announced to His Majesty's Government that, although the Polish Ambassador in Berlin had seen Herr von Ribbentrop at 6.30 p.m. on the 31st August, and had expressed the readiness of the Polish Government to enter into direct negotiations, Polish territory had been invaded, and the Polish Government had therefore been compelled to break off relations with Germany (No. 112, pp. 169-170) (see also Nos. 113 and 115, pp. 170-171). At 10.50 a.m. on the 1st September Viscount Halifax sent for the German Chargé d'Affaires in London, drew his attention to the reports which had reached His Majesty's Government about German action against Poland and informed him that these reports "created a very serious situation" (No. 114, p. 170).

The Prime Minister on the 2nd September made a statement in the House of Commons, in the course of which he said that no answer had been received to the message sent to the German Government on the 1st September, requesting the cessation of German aggression and the withdrawal of German troops from Poland. The Prime Minister also informed the House of proposals put forward by the Italian Government for a cessation of hostilities, but made it clear that His Majesty's Government could not take part in any conference unless German aggression ceased and German troops were withdrawn from Poland (No. 116, pp. 172-173). At 5 a.m. on the 3rd September Sir N. Henderson was instructed to ask for an interview at 9 a.m. with Herr von Ribbentrop and to inform him that, although His Majesty's Government had warned the German Government of the results which would follow if Germany did not suspend all aggressive action against Poland, no answer had been received from the German Government. His Majesty's Government therefore stated that unless satisfactory assurances were received from the German Government not later than 11 a.m. a state of war would exist between the United Kingdom and Germany (No. 118, p. 174).

At 11.20 a.m. on the 3rd September the German Government replied with a statement of their case, concluding with the suggestion that His Majesty's Government desired the destruction of the German people, and with the words "we shall answer any aggressive action on the part of England with the same weapons and in the same form" (No. 119, pp. 175-177). Shortly afterwards the Prime Minister announced in the House of Commons that Great Britain was at war with Germany (No. 120, pp. 177-178). This section of the documents concludes with Herr Hitler's proclamations of the 3rd September to the German people and to the German army (No. 121, pp. 178-180).

Attempts at mediation by other States.

The full text is given of the exchange of messages between the President of the United States of America and His Majesty the King of Italy (Nos. 122 and 123, pp. 181-182); the President of the United States of America and the President of Poland; and the messages of the President of the United States of America to Herr Hitler (Nos. 124-127, pp. 182-185); the broadcast appeal of the 23rd August

SUMMARY OF CONTENTS

by His Majesty the King of the Belgians in the name of the Heads of States of the Oslo Group of Powers and the replies (Nos. 128-133, pp. 185-188); the joint offer of mediation by His Majesty the King of the Belgians, and Her Majesty the Queen of the Netherlands and the replies (Nos. 134-138, pp. 188-190); the broadcast appeal of the 24th August by His Holiness the Pope with the reply of His Majesty's Government and telegrams describing a last peace attempt by the Pope on the 31st August, together with His Majesty's Government's reaction, are also given in full (Nos. 139-142, pp. 190-193).

A communiqué issued by the official Italian Stefani news agency on the 4th September recording the efforts made by the Italian Government to maintain peace is published as the last document in this chapter (No. 143, pp. 193-194).

The final Document (No. 144, pp. 195-196) is the Prime Minister's broadcast of the 4th September, 1939, to the German People.

This new edition also contains as a supplement, the final report of the British Ambassador to Berlin, Sir Nevile Henderson, on his return to London. (No. 145, pp. 197-224.)

List of Principal Persons mentioned in the Documents, showing their Official Positions.

UNITED KINGDOM.

Prime Minister	Mr. Neville Chamberlain.
Secretary of State for Foreign Affairs	Viscount Halifax.
Secretary of State for Foreign Affairs in 1914	Sir Edward Grey.
Secretary of State for Foreign Affairs in 1935	Sir Samuel Hoare.
Leader of His Majesty's Opposition	Mr. C. R. Atlee.
Polish Ambassador	Count Edward Raczynski.
German Ambassador	Herr von Dirksen.
German Chargé d'Affaires	Dr. Kordt.

FRANCE.

President of the Council	M. Daladier.

POLAND.

Polish Statesman	(The late) Marshal Pilsudski.
Polish Statesman and Inspector-General of Polish Army	Marshal Smigly-Rydz.
Minister for Foreign Affairs	M. Josef Beck.
Vice-Minister for Foreign Affairs	M. Arciszewski.
British Ambassador	Sir H. Kennard.
British Chargé d'Affaires	Mr. Norton.

DANZIG.

League of Nations High Commissioner	M. Burckhardt.
Polish Commissioner-General	M. Chodacki.
Nazi Gauleiter	Herr Forster.
President of Senate	Herr Greiser.
State Counsellor dealing with Foreign Relations	Dr. Boettcher.
British Consul-General	Mr. G. Shepherd.
Acting British Consul-General (from 10th July)	Mr. F. M. Shepherd.

GERMANY.

Prime Minister of Prussia, &c.	Field-Marshal Göring.
Nazi leader and Deputy to the Führer	Herr Hess.
Minister for Propaganda	Dr. Goebbels.
Minister for Foreign Affairs	Herr von Ribbentrop.
State Secretary at Ministry for Foreign Affairs	Baron von Weizsäcker.
Under-Secretary at Ministry for Foreign Affairs	Dr. Keppler.
Official Interpreter at Ministry for Foreign Affairs	Dr. Schmidt.
Former Minister for Foreign Affairs	Freiherr von Neurath.
British Ambassador	Sir Nevile Henderson.
Polish Ambassador	M. Josef Lipski.

Soviet Union.

Leading Statesman.. M. Stalin.
Prime Minister and Minister for Foreign Affairs.. M. Molotov.

Czecho-Slovakia.

Former President.. Dr. Benes.
President (after the Munich Agreement).............. Dr. Hacha.

Italy.

Duce .... Signor Mussolini.
British Ambassador.. Sir P. Loraine.

Holy See.

British Minister.. Mr. Osborne.

Belgium.

British Ambassador.. Sir R. Clive.

Netherlands.

British Minister........... .... Sir N. Bland.

Lithuania.

British Chargé d'Affaires... Mr. Preston.

DOCUMENTS

CONCERNING
GERMAN-POLISH RELATIONS
AND THE
OUTBREAK OF HOSTILITIES BETWEEN
GREAT BRITAIN AND GERMANY
ON SEPTEMBER 3, 1939

German-Polish Agreement

1.

Text of German-Polish Agreement of January 26, 1934.

(Translation.)

The German Government and the Polish Government consider that the time has come to introduce a new phase in the political relations between Germany and Poland by a direct understanding between State and State. They have, herefore, decided to lay down the principles for the future development of these relations in the present declaration.

The two Governments base their action on the fact that the maintenance and guarantee of a lasting peace between their countries is an essential pre-condition for the general peace of Europe.

They have therefore decided to base their mutual relations on the principles laid down in the Pact of Paris of the 27th August, 1928, and propose to define more exactly the application of these principles in so far as the relations between Germany and Poland are concerned.

Each of the two Governments, therefore, lays it down that the international obligations undertaken by it towards a third party do not hinder the peaceful development of their mutual relations, do not conflict with the present declaration, and are not affected by this declaration. They establish, moreover, that this declaration does not extend to those questions which under international law are to be regarded exclusively as the internal concern of one of the two States.

Both Governments announce their intention to settle directly all questions of whatever sort which concern their mutual relations.

Should any disputes arise between them and agreement thereon not be reached by direct negotiation, they will in each particular case,

1

on the basis of mutual agreement, seek a solution by other peaceful means, without prejudice to the possibility of applying, if necessary, those methods of procedure in which provision is made for such cases in other agreements in force between them. In no circumstances, however, will they proceed to the application of force for the purpose of reaching a decision in such disputes.

The guarantee of peace created by these principles will facilitate the great task of both Governments of finding a solution for problems of political, economic and social kinds, based on a just and fair adjustment of the interests of both parties.

Both Governments are convinced that the relations between their countries will in this manner develop fruitfully, and will lead to the establishment of a neighbourly relationship which will contribute to the well-being not only of both their countries, but of the other peoples of Europe as well.

The present declaration shall be ratified, and the instruments of ratification shall be exchanged in Warsaw as soon as possible.

The declaration is valid for a period of ten years, reckoned from the day of the exchange of the instruments of ratification.

If the declaration is not denounced by one of the two Governments six months before the expiration of this period, it will continue in force, but can then be denounced by either Government at any time on notice of six months being given. Made in duplicate in the German and Polish languages.

Berlin, January 26, 1934.

For the German Government:
FREIHERR von NEURATH.

For the Polish Government:
JOSEF LIPSKI.

Statements made by Herr Hitler since the German-Polish Agreement recording his satisfaction at the improvement in German-Polish relations.

2.

Reichstag Speech, May 21, 1935.

(Translation.)

"We recognize, with the understanding and the heartfelt friendship of true Nationalists, the Polish State as the home of a great, nationally-conscious people."

"The German Reich and, in particular, the present German Government, have no other wish than to live on friendly and peaceable terms with all neighbouring States."

3.

Reichstag Speech, March 7, 1936.

(Translation.)

"I would like the German people to learn to see in other nations historical realities which a visionary may well like to wish away, but which cannot be wished away. I should like them to realise that it is unreasonable to try and bring these historical realities into opposition with the demands of their vital interests and to their understandable claims to live. I would therefore like the German people to understand the inner motives of National Socialist foreign policy, which finds it painful that the outlet to the sea of a people of 35 millions is situated on territory formerly belonging to the Reich, but which recognises that it is unreasonable and impossible to deny a State of such a size as this any outlet to the sea at all. . . . It is possible that politicians, particularly by invoking might, may carry out such violations of national interests; but the more frequently this happens, the greater becomes the pressure for an outlet of the excited and constrained powers and energies."

4.

Reichstag Speech, January 30, 1937.

(Translation.)

"By a series of agreements we have removed existing tensions and thereby contributed considerably to an improvement in the European atmosphere. I merely recall our agreement with Poland, which has worked out to the advantage of both sides. . . . And to my own fellow-citizens I would say that the Polish nation and the Polish State have also become a reality. . . . The peoples of these States (*i.e.*, Italy, Poland and the Balkan States) desire to live and they will live."

5.

Reichstag Speech, February 20, 1938.

(Translation.)

"It fills us, in the fifth year following the first great foreign political agreement of the Reich, with sincere gratification to be able to establish that in our relationship to the State with which we had perhaps the greatest differences, not only has there been a *détente,* but that in the course of these years a constant improvement in relations has taken place. I know perfectly well that this was above all attributable to the circumstance that at the time there was no Western parliamentarism in Warsaw, but a Polish field-marshal, who as an eminent personality felt the significance, so important to Europe, of such a Germano-Polish *détente*. This good work, which had been doubted by so many at the time, has meanwhile stood the test, and I may say that, since the League of Nations finally gave up its perpetual attempts to unsettle Danzig and appointed in the new commissioner a man of great personal attainments, this most dangerous spot from the point of view of European peace has entirely lost its menacing character. The Polish State respects the national conditions in this State, and both the city of Danzig and Germany respect Polish rights. And so the way to a friendly understanding has been successfully paved, an understanding which, starting from Danzig, has to-day succeeded in spite of the attempts of certain mischief-makers in finally taking the poison out of the relations between Germany and Poland and transforming them into a sincere, friendly co-operation."

6.

Speech at Nuremberg, September 14, 1938.

(Translation.)

"In Poland a great patriot and a great statesman was ready to make an accord with Germany; we immediately proceeded to action and completed an agreement which was of greater importance to the peace of Europe than all the chattering in the temple of the League of Nations at Geneva."

Speech in the Sportpalast, September 26, 1938.

(Translation.)

"The most difficult problem with which I was confronted was that of our relations with Poland. There was a danger that Poles and Germans would regard each other as hereditary enemies. I wanted to prevent this. I know well enough that I should not have been successful if Poland had had a democratic Constitution. For these democracies which indulge in phrases about peace are the most bloodthirsty war agitators. In Poland there ruled no democracy, but a man; and with him I succeeded, in precisely twelve months, in coming to an agreement which, for ten years in the first instance, entirely removed the danger of a conflict. We are all convinced that this agreement will bring lasting pacification. We realise that here are two peoples which must live together and neither of which can do away with the other. A people of 33 millions will always strive for an outlet to the sea. A way for understanding, then, had to be found; it has been found; and it will be ever further extended. Certainly things were hard in this area. The nationalities and small national groups frequently quarrelled among themselves. But the main fact is that the two Governments, and all reasonable and clear-sighted persons among the two peoples and in the two countries, possess the firm will and determination to improve their relations. It was a real work of peace, of more worth than all the chattering in the League of Nations Palace at Geneva."

8.

Reichstag Speech, January 30, 1939.

(Translation.)

"We have just celebrated the fifth anniversary of the conclusion of our non-aggression pact with Poland. There can scarcely be any difference of opinion to-day among the true friends of peace with regard to the value of this agreement. One only needs to ask oneself what might have happened to Europe if this agreement, which brought such relief, had not been entered into five years ago. In signing it, this great Polish marshal and patriot rendered his people just as great a service as the leaders of the National Socialist State rendered the German people. During the troubled months of the past year the friendship between Germany and Poland was one of the reassuring factors in the political life of Europe."

Deterioration in European situation resulting from German Action against Czecho-Slovakia on March 15, 1939.

9.

Speech by the Prime Minister at Birmingham on March 17, 1939.

I had intended to-night to talk to you upon a variety of subjects, upon trade and employment, upon social service, and upon finance. But the tremendous events which have been taking place this week in Europe have thrown everything else into the background, and I feel that what you, and those who are not in this hall but are listening to me, will want to hear is some indication of the views of His Majesty's Government as to the nature and the implications of those events.

One thing is certain. Public opinion in the world has received a sharper shock than has ever yet been administered to it, even by the present régime in Germany. What may be the ultimate effects of this profound disturbance on men's minds cannot yet be foretold, but I am sure that it must be far-reaching in its results upon the future. Last Wednesday we had a debate upon it in the House of Commons. That was the day on which the German troops entered Czecho-Slovakia, and all of us, but particularly the Government, were at a disadvantage, because the information that we had was only partial; much of it was unofficial. We had no time to digest it, much less to form a considered opinion upon it. And so it necessarily followed that I, speaking on behalf of the Government, with all the responsibility that attaches to that position, was obliged to confine myself to a very restrained and cautious exposition, on what at the time I felt I could make but little commentary. And, perhaps naturally, that somewhat cool and objective statement gave rise to a misapprehension, and some people thought that because I spoke quietly, because I gave little expression to feeling, therefore my colleagues and I did not feel strongly on the subject. I hope to correct that mistake to-night.

But I want to say something first about an argument which has developed out of these events and which was used in that debate, and has appeared since in various organs of the press. It has been suggested that this occupation of Czecho-Slovakia was the direct consequence of the visit which I paid to Germany last autumn, and that, since the result of these events has been to tear up the settlement that was arrived at at Munich, that proves that the whole circumstances of those visits were wrong. It is said that, as this was the personal policy of the Prime Minister, the blame for the fate of Czecho-Slovakia must rest upon his shoulders. That is an entirely unwarrantable conclusion. The facts as they are to-day cannot change the facts as they were last September. If I was right then, I am still right now. Then there are some people who say: "We considered you were wrong in September, and now we have been proved to be right."

Let me examine that. When I decided to go to Germany I never expected that I was going to escape criticism. Indeed, I did not go there to get popularity. I went there first and foremost because, in what appeared to be an almost desperate situation, that seemed to me to offer the only chance of averting a European war. And I might remind you that, when it was first announced that I was going, not a voice was raised in criticism. Everyone applauded that effort. It was only later, when it appeared that the results of the final settlement fell short of the expectations of some who did not fully appreciate the facts —it was only then that the attack began, and even then it was not the visit, it was the terms of settlement that were disapproved.

Well, I have never denied that the terms which I was able to secure at Munich were not those that I myself would have desired. But, as I explained then, I had to deal with no new problem. This was something that had existed ever since the Treaty of Versailles—a problem that ought to have been solved long ago if only the statesmen of the last twenty years had taken broader and more enlightened views of their duty. It had become like a disease which had been long neglected, and a surgical operation was necessary to save the life of the patient.

After all, the first and the most immediate object of my visit was achieved. The peace of Europe was saved; and, if it had not been for those visits, hundreds of thousands of families would to-day have been in mourning for the flower of Europe's best manhood. I would like once again to express my grateful thanks to all those correspondents who have written me from all over the world to express their gratitude and their appreciation of what I did then and of what I have been trying to do since.

Really I have no need to defend my visits to Germany last autumn, for what was the alternative? Nothing that we could have done, nothing that France could have done, or Russia could have done could possibly have saved Czecho-Slovakia from invasion and destruction. Even if we had subsequently gone to war to punish Germany for her actions, and if after the frightful losses which would have been inflicted upon all partakers in the war we had been victorious in the end, never could we have reconstructed Czecho-Slovakia as she was framed by the Treaty of Versailles.

But I had another purpose, too, in going to Munich. That was to further the policy which I have been pursuing ever since I have been in my present position—a policy which is sometimes called European appeasement, although I do not think myself that that is a

7

very happy term or one which accurately describes its purpose. If that policy were to succeed, it was essential that no Power should seek to obtain a general domination of Europe; but that each one should be contented to obtain reasonable facilities for developing its own resources, securing its own share of international trade, and improving the conditions of its own people. I felt that, although that might well mean a clash of interests between different States, nevertheless, by the exercise of mutual goodwill and understanding of what were the limits of the desires of others, it should be possible to resolve all differences by discussion and without armed conflict. I hoped in going to Munich to find out by personal contact what was in Herr Hitler's mind, and whether it was likely that he would be willing to co-operate in a programme of that kind. Well, the atmosphere in which our discussions were conducted was not a very favourable one, because we were in the middle of an acute crisis; but, nevertheless, in the intervals between more official conversations I had some opportunities of talking with him and of hearing his views, and I thought that results were not altogether unsatisfactory.

When I came back after my second visit I told the House of Commons of a conversation I had had with Herr Hitler, of which I said that, speaking with great earnestness, he repeated what he had already said at Berchtesgaden—namely, that this was the last of his territorial ambitions in Europe, and that he had no wish to include in the Reich people of other races than German. Herr Hitler himself confirmed this account of the conversation in the speech which he made at the Sportpalast in Berlin, when he said: "This is the last territorial claim which I have to make in Europe." And a little later in the same speech he said: "I have assured Mr. Chamberlain, and I emphasise it now, that when this problem is solved Germany has no more territorial problems in Europe." And he added: "I shall not be interested in the Czech State any more, and I can guarantee it. We don't want any Czechs any more."

And then in the Munich Agreement itself, which bears Herr Hitler's signature, there is this clause: "The final determination of the frontiers will be carried out by the international commission"— the *final* determination. And, lastly, in that declaration which he and I signed together at Munich, we declared that any other question which might concern our two countries should be dealt with by the method of consultation.

Well, in view of those repeated assurances, given voluntarily to me, I considered myself justified in founding a hope upon them that once this Czecho-Slovakian question was settled, as it seemed at Munich it would be, it would be possible to carry farther that policy of appeasement which I have described. But, notwithstanding, at the same time I was not prepared to relax precautions until I was satisfied that the policy had been established and had been accepted by others, and therefore, after Munich, our defence programme was actually accelerated, and it was expanded so as to remedy certain weaknesses which had become apparent during the crisis. I am convinced that after Munich the great majority of British people shared my hope, and ardently desired that that policy should be carried further. But to-day I share their disappointment, their indignation, that those hopes have been so wantonly shattered.

How can these events this week be reconciled with those assurances which I have read out to you? Surely, as a joint signatory of the Munich Agreement, I was entitled, if Herr Hitler thought it ought to be undone, to that consultation which is provided for in the Munich declaration. Instead of that he has taken the law into his own hands. Before even the Czech President was received, and confronted with demands which he had no power to resist, the German troops were on the move, and within a few hours they were in the Czech capital.

According to the proclamation which was read out in Prague yesterday, Bohemia and Moravia have been annexed to the German Reich. Non-German inhabitants, who, of course, include the Czechs, are placed under the German Protector in the German Protectorate. They are to be subject to the political, military and economic needs of the Reich. They are called self-governing States, but the Reich is to take charge of their foreign policy, their customs and their excise, their bank reserves, and the equipment of the disarmed Czech forces. Perhaps most sinister of all, we hear again of the appearance of the Gestapo, the secret police, followed by the usual tale of wholesale arrests of prominent individuals, with consequences with which we are all familiar.

Every man and woman in this country who remembers the fate of the Jews and the political prisoners in Austria must be filled to-day with distress and foreboding. Who can fail to feel his heart go out in sympathy to the proud and brave people who have so suddenly been subjected to this invasion, whose liberties are curtailed, whose national independence has gone? What has become of this declaration of "No further territorial ambition"? What has become of the assurance "We don't want Czechs in the Reich"? What regard had been paid here to that principle of self-determination on which Herr Hitler argued so vehemently with me at Berchtesgaden when he was asking for the severance of Sudetenland from Czecho-Slovakia and its inclusion in the German Reich?

Now we are told that this seizure of territory has been necessitated by disturbances in Czecho-Slovakia. We are told that the proclamation of this new German Protectorate against the will of its inhabitants has been rendered inevitable by disorders which threatened the peace and security of her mighty neighbour. If there were disorders, were they not fomented from without? And can anybody outside Germany take seriously the idea that they could be a danger to that great country, that they could provide any justification for what has happened?

Does not the question inevitably arise in our minds, if it is so easy to discover good reasons for ignoring assurances so solemnly and so

9

repeatedly given, what reliance can be placed upon any other assurances that come from the same source?

There is another set of questions which almost inevitably must occur in our minds and to the minds of others, perhaps even in Germany herself. Germany, under her present régime, has sprung a series of unpleasant surprises upon the world. The Rhineland, the Austrian Anschluss, the severance of Sudetenland—all these things shocked and affronted public opinion throughout the world. Yet, however much we might take exception to the methods which were adopted in each of those cases, there was something to be said, whether on account of racial affinity or of just claims too long resisted—there was something to be said for the necessity of a change in the existing situation.

But the events which have taken place this week in complete disregard of the principles laid down by the German Government itself seem to fall into a different category, and they must cause us all to be asking ourselves: "Is this the end of an old adventure, or is it the beginning of a new?"

"Is this the last attack upon a small State, or is it to be followed by others? Is this, in fact, a step in the direction of an attempt to dominate the world by force?"

Those are grave and serious questions. I am not going to answer them to-night. But I am sure they will require the grave and serious consideration not only of Germany's neighbours, but of others, perhaps even beyond the confines of Europe. Already there are indications that the process has begun, and it is obvious that it is likely now to be speeded up.

We ourselves will naturally turn first to our partners in the British Commonwealth of Nations and to France, to whom we are so closely bound, and I have no doubt that others, too, knowing that we are not disinterested in what goes on in South-Eastern Europe, will wish to have our counsel and advice.

In our own country we must all review the position with that sense of responsibility which its gravity demands. Nothing must be excluded from that review which bears upon the national safety. Every aspect of our national life must be looked at again from that angle. The Government, as always, must bear the main responsibility, but I know that all individuals will wish to review their own position, too, and to consider again if they have done all they can to offer their service to the State.

I do not believe there is anyone who will question my sincerity when I say there is hardly anything I would not sacrifice for peace. But there is one thing that I must except, and that is the liberty that we have enjoyed for hundreds of years, and which we will never surrender. That I, of all men, should feel called upon to make such a declaration—that is the measure of the extent to which these events have shattered the confidence which was just beginning to show its head and which, if it had been allowed to grow, might have made this year memorable for the return of all Europe to sanity and stability.

It is only six weeks ago that I was speaking in this city, and that I alluded to rumours and suspicions which I said ought to be swept away. I pointed out that any demand to dominate the world by force was one which the democracies must resist, and I added that I could not believe that such a challenge was intended, because no Government with the interests of its own people at heart could expose them for such a claim to the horrors of world war.

And, indeed, with the lessons of history for all to read, it seems incredible that we should see such a challenge. I feel bound to repeat that, while I am not prepared to engage this country by new unspecified commitments operating under conditions which cannot now be foreseen, yet no greater mistake could be made than to suppose that, because it believes war to be a senseless and cruel thing, this nation has so lost its fibre that it will not take part to the utmost of its power in resisting such a challenge if it ever were made. For that declaration I am convinced that I have not merely the support, the sympathy, the confidence of my fellow-countrymen and countrywomen, but I shall have also the approval of the whole British Empire and of all other nations who value peace, indeed, but who value freedom even more.

10.

Speech by the Secretary of State for Foreign Affairs in the House of Lords on March 20, 1939.

It is quite true, as both the noble Lord who spoke first and the noble Marquess have said, that recent events have been a profound shock to all thinking people in this country and very far outside it. It may perhaps be of use if with all brevity I give the House a short narrative in order to make sure we have the setting correct of what has actually passed during the last few days. The German military occupation of Bohemia and Moravia began on the morning of the 15th March, and was completed, as we know, without serious incident. It is to be observed—and the fact is surely not without significance—that the towns of Mährisch-Ostrau and Vitkovice were actually occupied by German S.S. detachments on the evening of the 14th March, while the President and the Foreign Minister of Czecho-Slovakia were still on their way to Berlin and before any discussion had taken place. On the 16th March Herr Hitler issued the decree, to which the noble Marquess has just referred, proclaiming that the former Czecho-Slovak territory occupied by German troops belonged henceforth to the German Reich and came under its protection under the title of "The Protectorate of Bohemia and Moravia".

It is not necessary to recapitulate the terms of that decree—it has been published — but it should be noted that, while the head of the

Administration now to be set up is said to hold the rank of Head of State, and while the protectorate is said to be autonomous and self-administering, a Reich protector is resident in Prague with full powers of veto on legislation. Foreign affairs and the protection of nationals abroad devolve on the German Government, which will also maintain military garrisons and establishments in the protectorate. The protectorate is, further, in the German Customs Union, and, finally, the German Government can issue decrees valid in the protectorate and take any measures for the preservation of security and order. Perhaps I might quote one short article which seems to me to sum up the situation. It says:—

"The Protectorate of Bohemia and Moravia shall exercise its sovereign rights in consonance with the political, military and economic importance of the Reich."

As to Slovakia, the independence of Slovakia was proclaimed on the 14th March, but at the request of Dr. Tiso, the head of the Slovak State, Herr Hitler has undertaken to place Slovakia under German protection and the military occupation of the territory by German troops is now proceeding. As regards Ruthenia, the occupation of Ruthenia by Hungary, which began on the 14th March, has also proceeded. By the 16th March the Hungarian troops had reached the Polish frontier and had virtually completed the occupation of the province. Therefore, as a result of these several actions, the dismemberment of Czecho-Slovakia may be said now to be complete.

Before I come to some one or two of the things that fell from the noble Lord who moved, I would like to say something as to the grounds on which the German Government seek to justify the action that they have taken. The immediate cause of the present crisis in Central Europe originated in Slovakia, and it is claimed that the German Government was entitled to intervene on receiving the request for assistance from the dismissed Slovak Prime Minister. As your Lordships are well aware, there has always been a party in Slovakia which advocated autonomy. That autonomy was, in face, achieved after Munich in agreement between the various Slovak parties and the Central Government in Prague. The extremist elements in Slovakia, however, were not satisfied with these arrangements, but on all the evidence that is available to me I find it impossible to believe that the sudden decision of certain Slovak leaders to break off from Prague, which was followed so closely by their appeal for protection to the German Reich, was reached independently of outside influence.

It is said that German intervention in Czecho-Slovakia was justified owing to the oppression of the German minority by the Czechs. But, as a matter of fact again, it was only very shortly before Herr Hitler's ultimatum to the Czech President that the German press began to renew its campaign of last summer about the alleged Czech brutalities against German citizens. Actually the position of the German minority, which is about 250,000, would appear, since the Munich Agreement,

12

to have been one of what might be termed exceptional privilege. Notwithstanding the right of option which had been accorded by article 7 of that agreement, the members of the German minority were encouraged to remain in Czecho-Slovakia in order that they might form useful centres of German activity and propaganda; and advice to that effect was given to the minority by its leader.

It was as a result of the German-Czecho-Slovak Agreement for the mutual protection of minorities that the German Government obtained the legal right to take a direct interest in the treatment of their minority in Czecho-Slovakia. That minority at once obtained the right to set up separate organisations, and the Czecho-Slovak Government subsequently agreed that the German National Socialist Party in Czecho-Slovakia should be given full liberty to pursue its activities in Bohemia and Moravia. It is difficult to avoid the conclusion that the bulk of the incidents which occurred before the German invasion were deliberately provoked and that the effects were greatly magnified. It must be added in fairness that the Czecho-Slovak authorities received orders to act, and did act, with great restraint in the face of that provocation. It is not necessary, I think, to say much upon the assertion that the Czecho-Slovak President really assented to the subjugation of his people. In view of the circumstances in which he came to Berlin, and of the occupation of Czech territory which had already taken place, I think most sensible people must conclude that there was little pretence of negotiation, and that it is more probable that the Czech representatives were presented with an ultimatum under the threat of violence, and that they capitulated in order to save their people from the horrors of a swift and destructive aerial bombardment.

Finally, it is said that Germany was in some danger from Czecho-Slovakia. But surely the German Government itself can hardly have expected that that contention could be seriously entertained in any quarter. Indeed, if I may sum up my own thought on these various explorations, I could wish that, instead of the communications and explanations which have been issued and which carry scant conviction, German superior force had been frankly acknowledged as the supreme arbiter that in fact it was.

In these circumstances, as you are aware, His Majesty's Government thought fit at once to take certain action. Here I touch a point which was touched both by the noble Lord who moved and by the noble Marquess who followed him. His Majesty's Government immediately suspended the visit of the President of the Board of Trade and the Secretary of the Department of Overseas Trade to Berlin, by means of which it had been hoped that His Majesty's Government could directly intervene in those unofficial contacts of industrial representatives which were at that very moment taking place. We felt, and feel, as I think I said in my statement a few days ago, that in the circumstances which have arisen any development of our efforts in that direction was, as the noble Marquess said, frankly out of the

13

question, and that that and many other things had to be and must remain indefinitely postponed. His Majesty's Government, as your Lordships also know, have recalled to report His Majesty's Ambassador in Berlin, and he reached this country yesterday.

Further than those two practical steps, we have lodged a formal protest with the German Government in the sense of informing them that we cannot but regard the events of the last few days as a complete repudiation of the Munich Agreement and a denial of the spirit in which the negotiators of that agreement bound themselves to co-operate for a peaceful settlement. We have also taken occasion to protest against the change effected in Czecho-Slovakia by German military action, and have said that, in our view those changes are devoid of any basis of legality. I think, therefore, that we may claim to have left the German Government in no doubt of the attitude of His Majesty's Government, and although I do not cherish any exaggerated hopes of what may be the effect of protests, I think your Lordships will feel it abundantly right that such protests should be registered.

I have from time to time seen efforts made by German apologists to justify the action of their Government by some reference to the past history of the British Empire. It is not necessary to remind you that the principle on which the British Empire is conducted is education in self-government. Wherever we have been in the world, we have left a trail of freedom and of self-government, and our record has nothing in common with the suppression of liberty and independence of people whose political developments had already brought them to the point of enjoyment of those opportunities for self-expression. It has also been objected that what has happened in Czecho-Slovakia is of no interest or concern to this country. It is quite true that we have always recognised that, for reasons of geography, if for no other, Germany must from some points of view be more interested in Czecho-Slovakia or South-Eastern Europe than we are ourselves. It was the natural field for the expansion of German trade. But apart from the fact that changes in any part of Europe produce profound effects elsewhere, the position is entirely changed when we are confronted with the arbitrary suppression of an independent sovereign State by force, and by the violation of what I must regard as the elementary rules of international conduct.

It is natural enough that in the light of these events His Majesty's Government should be told, as the noble Lord told them this afternoon, that the policy of Munich was a tragic mistake. I cannot, of course, claim to correct the noble Lord upon an expression of opinion which he sincerely holds, but I can correct him, I think, on one limited observation that fell from him. He referred to the policy pursued by the Prime Minister as a personal policy. If by that he means that it was a policy to which the Prime Minister had given every ounce of energy, imagination and resolution that he possessed, I should not disagree with him, but if he suggests that it was a policy that was pursued without the fullest co-operation of myself as Foreign Secretary, and of every member of His Majesty's Government, then I must take leave to oppose to what he said the most emphatic contradiction.

My Lords, the Munich Settlement, which was approved by this House and in another place, was accepted by His Majesty's Government for two purposes, quite distinct. The first purpose was to effect a settlement, as fair as might be in all the extremely difficult circumstances of that time, of a problem which was a real one, and of which the treatment was an urgent necessity if the peace of Europe was to be preserved. As to that, I would say, as I have said before in this House, that I have no doubt whatever that His Majesty's Government were right, in the light of all the information available to them, to take the course they did. The second purpose of Munich was to build a Europe more secure, upon the basis of freely accepted consultation as the means by which all future differences might be adjusted; and that long-term purpose, my Lords, has been, as we have come to observe, disastrously belied by events. We are charged with having too readily believed the assurances which were given by Herr Hitler—that after Munich he had no further territorial ambitions, and no desire to incorporate non-German elements in the Reich. The noble Lord referred to the Prime Minister as the "too-simple Prime Minister". I can assure your Lordships that neither the Prime Minister nor I, myself, nor any member of His Majesty's Government, has failed at any moment to be acutely conscious of the difference between beliefs and hope. It was surely legitimate and right to have hopes. But we have always acted—and I challenge any noble Lord to produce any evidence to the contrary—in the knowledge that only with time can hope be converted into sure beliefs.

It is no doubt the case that previous assurances had been broken, whatever justification might have been advanced by Herr Hitler, on the grounds of his mission, as he conceives it, to incorporate ex-German territory and predominantly German areas in the Reich. But in his actions until after Munich a case could be made that Herr Hitler had been true to his own principles, the union of Germans in, and the exclusion of non-Germans from, the Reich. Those principles he has now overthrown, and in including 8 million Czechs under German rule he has surely been untrue to his own philosophy. The world will not forget that in September last Herr Hitler appealed to the principle of self-determination in the interests of 2 million Sudeten Germans. That principle is one on which the British Empire itself has been erected, and one to which accordingly, as your Lordships will recollect, we felt obliged to give weight in considering Herr Hitler's claim. That principle has now been rudely contradicted by a sequence of acts which denies the very right on which the German attitude of six months ago was based, and whatever may have been the truth about the treatment of 250,000 Germans, it is impossible for me to believe that it could only be remedied by the subjugation of 8 million Czechs.

What conclusions, as asked the noble Marquess, are we to draw from this conquest of Czecho-Slovakia? Are we to believe that

15

German policy has thus entered upon a new phase? Is German policy any longer to be limited to the consolidation of territory predominantly inhabited by persons of German race? Or is German policy now to be directed towards domination over non-German peoples? These are very grave questions which are being asked in all parts of the world to-day. The German action in Czecho-Slovakia has been furthered by new methods, and the world has lately seen more than one new departure in the field of international technique. Wars without declarations of war. Pressure exercised under threat of immediate employment of force. Intervention in the internal struggles of other States. Countries are now faced with the encouragement of separatism, not in the interest of separatist or minority elements but in the imperial interests of Germany. The alleged ill-treatment of German minorities in foreign countries which, it is true, may sometimes, perhaps often, arise from natural causes, but which may also be the subject and result of provocation from outside, is used as a pretext for intervention.

These methods are simple and, with growing experience, quite unmistakable. Have we any assurance that they will not be employed elsewhere? Every country which is Germany's neighbour is now uncertain of the morrow, and every country which values its national identity and sovereignty stands warned against the danger from within, inspired from without. During the last few days there have been rumours that the German Government were adopting a harsh attitude in their negotiations with the Roumanian Government on economic matters. I am glad to say that the Roumanian Government have themselves denied a report that went so far as to speak of an "ultimatum"; but even if there is no menace to Roumania to-day, or even if that menace has not to-day developed, and even though it may not develop on these lines, it is not surprising if the Government of Bucharest, like other Governments, should view with the gravest misgivings the happenings of these last few days.

For years past the British people have steadily desired to be on friendly terms with the German people. There is no stronger national instinct among our people than the instinct that leads them, when they have a fight, to shake hands and try to make it up. Our people were not backward in recognising some of the mistakes of the Versailles Treaty that required remedying, but each time during these last years that there has seemed a chance of making progress in understanding, the German Government has taken action which has made that progress impossible. More especially has that been the case in recent months. Very shortly after Munich certain measures were taken by the German Government that gave a profound shock to world opinion. Quite recently it was to be hoped, although there were many clouds still over and below the horizon, that we could look forward to closer economic collaboration, and it was in the hope of developing that economic collaboration into something wider that, as your Lordships know, we had decided on those visits to which I referred a moment ago. All that initiative has been frustrated by the action of the German Government last week, and it is difficult to see when it can be easily resumed.

These affairs, as I said a moment or two ago, have raised wide issues, and the events in Czecho-Slovakia require His Majesty's Government and require every free people to rethink their attitude towards them. Broadly speaking, there have been, at all events since the war, two conflicting theses as to the best method of avoiding conflicts and creating security for the nations of the world. The first thesis is that which upholds the creation of and supports machinery for consultation, conciliation and arbitration with, if possible, the sanction of collective force, and involves an invitation to all States, willing to accept a wide degree of obligation to one another, to agree that an attack on one should be treated as an attack on all. That, your Lordships know well enough, has been the thesis expressed in the Covenant of the League of Nations. Perhaps it is true to say that more precise effect was sought to be given to it in the Geneva Protocol, and it has itself given rise to a number of regional agreements for mutual assistance between the several Powers concerned. That is the first thesis.

The second, which has been in conflict, has been upheld by those who consider that systems seeking to provide collective security, as it has been termed, involved dangerously indefinite commitments quite disproportionate to the real security that these commitments gave. Those who took that view were persuaded that States, conscious of their own pacific purposes, would be wise to refrain from such commitments which might draw them into a war in which their own vital interests were not threatened, and that, therefore, States should not bind themselves to intervene in conflicts unless they themselves were directly attacked.

That is the conflict of philosophy of which your Lordships are very well aware, because in one form or another it has constantly been debated in this House. I have no doubt that in considering these two theses the judgment of many has been influenced by the estimate that they place, rightly or wrongly, upon the probability of direct attack. If it were possible, in their judgment, to rate that probability low, then that low probability of direct attack had to be weighed against what might seem to them the greater risk of States being involved in conflicts that were not necessarily arising out of their own concerns. But if and when it becomes plain to States that there is no apparent guarantee against successive attacks directed in turn on all who might seem to stand in the way of ambitious schemes of domination, then at once the scale tips the other way, and in all quarters there is likely immediately to be found a very much greater readiness to consider whether the acceptance of wider mutual obligations, in the cause of mutual support, is not dictated, if for no other reason than the necessity of self-defence. His Majesty's Government have not failed to draw the moral from these events, and have lost no time in placing themselves

17

in close and practical consultation, not only with the Dominions, but with other Governments concerned upon the issues that have suddenly been made so plain.

It is not possible, as yet fully to appraise the consequences of German action. History, to which the noble Marquess always refers us with great profit and enjoyment, records many attempts to impose a domination on Europe, but all these attempts have, sooner or later, terminated in disaster for those who made them. It has never in the long run proved possible to stamp out the spirit of free peoples. If history is any guide, the German people may yet regret the action that has been taken in their name against the people of Czecho-Slovakia. Twenty years ago that people of Czecho-Slovakia recovered their liberties with the support and encouragement of the greater part of the world. They have now been deprived of them by violence. In the course of their long history this will not be the first time that this tenacious, valiant and industrious people have lost their independence, but they have never lost that which is the foundation of independence —the love of liberty. Meanwhile, just as after the last war the world watched the emergence of the Czech nation, so it will watch today their efforts to preserve intact their cultural identity and, more important, their spiritual freedom under the last and most cruel blow of which they have been the victims.

11

Question and the Prime Minister's Answer in the House of Commons on March 23, 1939.

Mr. Attlee (by Private Notice) asked the Prime Minister whether he has any further statement to make on the European situation?

Answer.

The Prime Minister: His Majesty's Government have already made clear that the recent actions of the German Government have raised the question whether that Government is not seeking by successive steps to dominate Europe, and perhaps even to go further than that. Were this interpretation of the intentions of the German Government to prove correct, His Majesty's Government feel bound to say that this would rouse the successful resistance of this and other countries who prize their freedom, as similar attempts have done in the past.

I am not yet in a position to make a statement on the consultations which have been held with other Governments as a result of recent developments. I wish to make it clear, however, that there is no desire on the part of His Majesty's Government to stand in the way of any reasonable efforts on the part of Germany to expand her export trade. On the contrary, we were on the point of discussing in the most friendly way the possibility of trade arrangements which would have benefited both countries when the events took place which, for the time being at any rate, put a stop to those discussions. Nor is this Government anxious to set up in Europe opposing blocks of countries with different ideas about the forms of their internal administration. We are solely concerned here with the proposition that we cannot submit to a procedure under which independent States are subjected to such pressure under threat of force as to be obliged to yield up their independence, and we are resolved by all means in our power to oppose attempts, if they should be made, to put such a procedure into operation.

12.

Sir N. Henderson to Viscount Halifax.

My Lord,   Berlin, May 28, 1939.

I paid a short visit to Field-Marshal Göring at Karinhall yesterday.

2. Field-Marshal Göring, who had obviously just been talking to someone else on the subject, began by inveighing against the attitude which was being adopted in England towards everything German and particularly in respect of the gold held there on behalf of the National Bank of Czecho-Slovakia. Before, however, I had had time to reply, he was called to the telephone and on his return did not revert to this specific question. He complained, instead, of British hostility in general, of our political and economic encirclement of Germany and the activities of what he described as the war party in England, &c.

3. I told the Field-Marshal that, before speaking of British hostility, he must understand why the undoubted change of feeling towards Germany in England had taken place. As he knew quite well the basis of all the discussions between Mr. Chamberlain and Herr Hitler last year had been to the effect that, once the Sudeten were allowed to enter the Reich, Germany would leave the Czechs alone and would do nothing to interfere with their independence. Herr Hitler had given a definite assurance to that effect in his letter to the Prime Minister of the 27th September. By yielding to the advice of his "wild men" and deliberately annexing Bohemia and Moravia, Herr Hitler had not only broken his word to Mr. Chamberlain but had infringed the whole principle of self-determination on which the Munich Agreement rested.

4. At this point the Field-Marshal interrupted me with a description of President Hacha's visit to Berlin. I told Field-Marshal Göring that it was not possible to talk of free will when I understood that he himself had threatened to bombard Prague with his aeroplanes, if Dr. Hacha refused to sign. The Field-Marshal did not deny the fact but explained how the point had arisen. According to him Dr. Hacha had from the first been prepared to sign everything but had said that constitutionally he could not do so without reference first to Prague. After considerable difficulty telephonic communication with Prague was obtained and the Czech Government had agreed, while adding that they could not guarantee that one Czech battalion at least would

not fire on the German troops. It was, he said, only at that stage that he had warned Dr. Hacha that, if German lives were lost, he would bombard Prague. The field-marshal also repeated, in reply to some comment of mine, the story that the advance occupation of Witkowitz had been effected solely in order to forestall the Poles who, he said, were known to have the intention of seizing this valuable area at the first opportunity.

5. I thereupon reminded Field-Marshal Göring that, while I had always appreciated the necessity for the Czechs, in view of their geographical position, to live in the friendliest political and economic relations with Great Germany, he had personally assured me last October that this was all that his Government desired. The precipitate action of Germany on the 15th March, which I again ascribed to the wild men of the party, had consequently, apart from everything and everybody else, been a great shock to me personally and had undone all that I had sought to achieve during my two years at Berlin. Moreover, however indifferent this might seem to him, I could not but regard the destruction of the independence of the Czechs as a major political error, even in Germany's own interests.

6. The Field-Marshal appeared a little confused at this personal attack on his own good faith, and assured me that he himself had known nothing of the decision before it had been taken. He would not, he said, have gone to San Remo if he had; nor had his stay there profited him, as he had hoped, owing to the unexpected amount of work which had in consequence been thrust upon him. He then proceeded to give a somewhat unconvincing explanation, though similar to that which Baron von Weizsäcker had furnished me with last March, of the German attempt to come to a satisfactory arrangement with the Czechs and of its failure owing to Czech obstinacy and the revival of what he called the Benes spirit as the result of American encouragement.

7. As my time was limited, I told Field-Marshal Göring that I was well aware of the reasons adduced by his Government to justify its action, but I thought it more important that he himself should understand the British point of view in consequence of it. As the result of the Prague *coup* His Majesty's Government and the British people were determined to resist by force any new aggression. No one desired an amiable arrangement between Germany and Poland in respect of Danzig and the Corridor more than ourselves. But, if Germany endeavoured to settle these questions by unilateral action such as would compel the Poles to resort to arms to safeguard their independence, we and the French as well as other countries would be involved, with all the disastrous consequences which a prolonged world war would entail, especially for Germany, &c. Field-Marshal Göring did not appear to question our readiness to fight and restricted his reply to an attempt to prove that circumstances in 1939 were different to those in 1914, that no Power could overcome Germany in Europe, that a blockade this time would prove unavailing, that France would

not stand a long war, that Germany could do more harm to Great Britain than the latter to her, that the history of Germany was one of ups and downs, and that this was one of the "up" periods, that the Poles had no military experience and that their only officers of any value were those who had acquired their training in the German army, that they were not and never had been a really united nation and that, since France and ourselves could not, and Russia out of self-interest would not, give them any effective military assistance, they would be taught a terrible lesson, &c. The Field-Marshal used, in fact, all the language which might be expected in reply to a statement that Germany was bound to be defeated. While I was perturbed at his reference to the unreality of Polish unity, which resembled the German arguments last year in regard to Czecho-Slovakia, he gave me the impression, by somewhat overstating his case, of considerably less confidence than he expressed.

8. At the end of this tirade, moreover, he asked me whether England, "out of envy of a strong Germany," was really bent on war with her and, if not, what was to be done to prevent it. I said that nobody in their senses could contemplate modern war without horror, but that we should not shrink from it if Germany resorted to another act of aggression. If, therefore, war was to be avoided, patience was necessary and the wild men in Germany must be restrained. Admittedly present-day Germany was in a dynamic condition, whereas England was by tradition the land of compromise. But compromise had its limits, and I did not see how the situation could be saved unless his Government were prepared to wait in order to allow excited spirits to calm down again and negotiations to be resumed in a better atmosphere.

9. At this point Field-Marshal Göring remarked that if the Poles tried to seize Danzig nothing would stop the Germans from acting at once. As my time was short, I made no comment on this but continued that neither the Prime Minister nor yourself had yet abandoned hope of a peaceful solution either as between Germany and Poland or between Germany and Great Britain, but that everything now entirely depended on Germany's behaviour and actions.

10. As I had already got up to go, the conversation then took a more amicable turn. Though I was in a hurry, he insisted on showing me with much pride the great structural alterations which he is making to the house at Karinhall and which include a new dining-room to hold an incredible number of guests and to be all of marble and hung with tapestries. He mentioned incidentally that the rebuilding would not be completed before November. He also produced with pride drawings of the tapestries, mostly representing naked ladies labelled with the names of various virtues, such as Goodness, Mercy, Purity, &c. I told him that they looked at least pacific, but that I failed to see Patience among them.

I have, &c.

NEVILE HENDERSON.

German-Polish Discussions.

Explanatory Note.

Certain discussions took place between the German and Polish Governments at the end of 1938 and in the early part of 1939. The German and Polish statements regarding these negotiations are to be found in the annexed documents.

13.

Extract from Herr Hitler's speech to the Reichstag on April 28, 1939.

(Translation.)

There is little to be said as regards German-Polish relations. Here, too, the Peace Treaty of Versailles—of course intentionally—inflicted a most severe wound on Germany. The strange way in which the Corridor giving Poland access to the sea was marked out was meant, above all, to prevent for all time the establishment of an understanding between Poland and Germany. This problem is—as I have already stressed—perhaps the most painful of all problems for Germany. Nevertheless, I have never ceased to uphold the view that the necessity of a free access to the sea for the Polish State cannot be ignored, and that as a general principle, valid for this case, too, nations which Providence has destined or, if you like, condemned to live side by side would be well advised not to make life still harder for each other artificially and unnecessarily. The late Marshal Pilsudski, who was of the same opinion, was therefore prepared to go into the question of clarifying the atmosphere of German-Polish relations, and, finally, to conclude an agreement whereby Germany and Poland expressed their intention of renouncing war altogether as a means of settling the questions which concerned them both. This agreement contained one single exception which was in practice conceded to Poland. It was laid down that the pacts of mutual assistance already entered into by Poland—this applied to the past with France—should not be affected by the agreement. But it was obvious that this could apply only to the pact of mutual assistance already concluded beforehand, and not to whatever new pacts might be concluded in the future. It is a fact that the German-Polish Agreement resulted in a remarkable lessening of the European tension. Nevertheless, there remained one open question between Germany and Poland, which sooner or later quite naturally had to be solved—the question of the German city of Danzig. Danzig is a German city and wishes to belong to Germany On the other hand, this city has contracts with Poland, which were admittedly forced upon it by the dictators of the Peace of Versailles. But since, moreover, the League of Nations, formerly the greatest stirrer-up of trouble, is now represented by a High Commissioner—incidentally a man of extraordinary tact—the problem of Danzig must in any case come up for discussion, at the latest with the gradual extinction of this calamitous institution. I regarded the peaceful settlement of this problem as a further contribution to a final loosening of the European tension. For this loosening of the tension is assuredly not to be achieved through the agitations of insane warmongers, but through the removal of the real elements of danger. After the problem of Danzig had already been discussed several times some months ago, I made a concrete offer to the Polish Government. I now make this offer known to you, Gentlemen, and you yourselves will judge whether this offer did not represent the greatest imaginable concession in the interests of European peace. As I have already pointed out, I have always seen the necessity of an access to the sea for this country, and have consequently taken this necessity into consideration. I am no democratic statesman, but a National Socialist and a realist.

I considered it, however, necessary to make it clear to the Government in Warsaw that just as they desire access to the sea, so Germany needs access to her province in the east. Now these are all difficult problems. It is not Germany who is responsible for them, however, but rather the jugglers of Versailles, who either in their maliciousness or their thoughtlessness placed 100 powder barrels round about in Europe, all equipped with hardly extinguishable lighted fuses. These problems cannot be solved according to old-fashioned ideas; I think, rather, that we should adopt new methods. Poland's access to the sea by way of the Corridor, and, on the other hand, a German route through the Corridor have, for example, no kind of military importance whatsoever. Their importance is exclusively psychological and economic. To accord military importance to a traffic route of this kind, would be to show oneself completely ignorant of military affairs. Consequently, I have had the following proposal submitted to the Polish Government: —

(1) Danzig returns as a Free State into the framework of the German Reich.
(2) Germany receives a route through the Corridor and a railway line at her own disposal possessing the same extraterritorial status for Germany as the Corridor itself has for Poland.

In return, Germany is prepared: —

(1) To recognise all Polish economic rights in Danzig.
(2) To ensure for Poland a free harbour in Danzig of any size desired which would have completely free access to the sea.
(3) To accept at the same time the present boundaries between Germany and Poland and to regard them as ultimate.
(4) To conclude a twenty-five-year non-aggression treaty with Poland, a treaty therefore which would extend far beyond the duration of my own life.
(5) To guarantee the independence of the Slovak State by Germany, Poland and Hungary jointly — which means in practice the renunciation of any unilateral German hegemony in this territory.

The Polish Government have rejected my offer and have only

declared that they are prepared (1) to negotiate concerning the question of a substitute for the Commissioner of the League of Nations and (2) to consider facilities for the transit traffic through the Corridor.

I have regretted greatly this incomprehensible attitude of the Polish Government, but that alone is not the decisive fact; the worst is that now Poland, like Czecho-Slovakia a year ago, believes, under the pressure of a lying international campaign, that it must call up troops, although Germany on her part has not called up a single man and had not thought of proceeding in any way against Poland. As I have said, this is in itself very regrettable and posterity will one day decide whether it was really right to refuse this suggestion made this once by me. This—as I have said—was an endeavour on my part to solve a question which intimately affects the German people by a truly unique compromise, and to solve it to the advantage of both countries. According to my conviction Poland was not a giving party in this solution at all but only a receiving party, because it should be beyond all doubt that Danzig will never become Polish. The intention to attack on the part of Germany, which was merely invented by the international press, led as you know to the so-called guarantee offer and to an obligation on the part of the Polish Government for mutual assistance, which would also, under certain circumstances, compel Poland to take military action against Germany in the event of a conflict between Germany and any other Power and in which England, in her turn, would be involved. This obligation is contradictory to the agreement which I made with Marshal Pilsudski some time ago, seeing that in this agreement reference is made exclusively to existing obligations, that is at that time, namely, to the obligations of Poland towards France of which we were aware. To exceed these obligations subsequently is contrary to the terms of the German-Polish non-aggression pact. Under these circumstances I should not have entered into this pact at that time, because what sense can non-aggression pacts have if one partner in practice leaves open an enormous number of exceptions.

There is either collective security, that is collective insecurity and continuous danger of war, or clear agreements which, however, exclude fundamentally any use of arms between the contracting parties. I therefore look upon the agreement which Marshal Pilsudski and I at one time concluded as having been unilaterally infringed by Poland and thereby no longer in existence!

I have sent a communication to this effect to the Polish Government. However, I can only repeat at this point that my decision does not constitute a modification of my attitude in principle with regard to the problems mentioned above. Should the Polish Government wish to come to fresh contractual arrangements governing its relations with Germany, I can but welcome such an idea, provided, of course, that these arrangements are based on an absolutely clear obligation binding both parties in equal measure. Germany is perfectly willing at any time to undertake such obligations and also to fulfil them.

14.

*German Government Memorandum handed to the Polish Government
on April 28, 1939.*

(Translation.)

The German Government have taken note of the Polish-British
declaration regarding the progress and aims of the negotiations recently
conducted between Poland and Great Britain. According to this
declaration there has been concluded between the Polish Government
and the British Government a temporary understanding, to be replaced
shortly by a permanent agreement which will provide for the giving
of mutual assistance by Poland and Great Britain in the event of the
independence of one of the two States being directly or indirectly
threatened.

2. The German Government consider themselves obliged to communicate the following to the Polish Government:—

3. When in 1933 the National Socialist Government set about the
reshaping of German policy, after Germany's departure from the
League of Nations, their first object was to stabilise German-Polish
relations on a new plane. The Chancellor of the German Reich and
the late Marshal Pilsudski concurred in the decision to break with
the political methods of the past and to enter, as regards the settlement
of all questions affecting both States, on the path of direct understanding between them.

4. By means of the unconditional renunciation of the use of force,
guarantees of peace were instituted in order to assist the two States
in the difficult task of solving all political, economic and cultural
problems by means of the just and equitable adjustment of mutual
interests. These principles, contained in a binding form in the German-
Polish Peace Declaration of the 26th January, 1934, had this aim in
view [*sic*] and by their practical success were intended to introduce
an entirely new phase of German-Polish relations. The political history
of the last five years shows that they proved efficacious in practice for
both nations. As recently as the 26th January of this year, on the fifth
anniversary of the signature of the declaration, both sides publicly
confirmed this fact, while emphasising their united will to maintain in
the future their adhesion to the principles established in 1934.

5. The agreement which has now been concluded by the Polish
Government with the British Government is in such obvious contradiction to these solemn declarations of a few months ago that the
German Government can take note only with surprise and astonish-
ment of such a violent reversal of Polish policy. Irrespective of the
manner in which its final formulation may be determined by both
parties, the new Polish-British Agreement is intended as a regular
pact of alliance, which by reason of its general sense and of the present
state of political relations is directed exclusively against Germany.

From the obligation now accepted by the Polish Government it appears that Poland intends in certain circumstances to take an active part in any possible German-British conflict in the event of aggression against Germany, even should this conflict not affect Poland and her interests. This is a direct and open blow against the renunciation of all use of force contained in the 1934 declaration.

6. The contradiction between the German-Polish Declaration and the Polish-British Agreement is, however, even more far-reaching in its importance than that. The 1934 declaration was to constitute a basis for the regulation of all differences arising between the two countries, independently of international complications and combinations, by means of direct discussion between Berlin and Warsaw, to the exclusion of external influences. Naturally, such a basis must rest on the mutual confidence of both parties and on the political loyalty of the intentions of one party with regard to the other.

7. The Polish Government, however, by their recent decision to accede to an alliance directed against Germany, have given it to be understood that they prefer a promise of help by a third Power to the direct guarantee of peace by the German Government. In view of this the German Government are obliged to conclude that the Polish Government do not at present attach any importance to seeking a solution of German-Polish problems by means of direct friendly discussions with the German Government. The Polish Government have thus abandoned the path traced out in 1934 for the shaping of German-Polish relations.

8. The Polish Government cannot in this connexion appeal to the fact that the 1934 declaration was not to affect the obligations previously accepted by Poland and Germany in relation to third parties, and that the Treaty of Alliance between Poland and France maintained its value side by side with that declaration. The Polish-French Alliance already existed in 1934 when Poland and Germany proceeded to reorganise their relations. The German Government were able to accept this fact, since they were entitled to expect that the possible dangers of the Polish-French Alliance, dating from the period of the acutest German-Polish differences, would automatically lose more and more of their significance through the establishment of friendly relations between Germany and Poland. However, the entry of Poland into relations of alliance with Great Britain, which was effected five years after the publication of the declaration of 1934, can for this reason in no way be compared politically with the still valid Polish-French Alliance. By this new alliance the Polish Government have subordinated themselves to a policy inaugurated from another quarter aiming at the encirclement of Germany.

9. The German Government for their part have not given the least cause for such a change in Polish policy. Whenever opportunity offered, they have furnished the Polish Government, both publicly and in confidential conversations, with the most binding assurances that the friendly development of German-Polish relations is a funda-

mental aim of their foreign policy, and that, in their political decisions, they will always respect Poland's proper interests. Thus the action taken by Germany in March of this year with a view to the pacification of Central Europe did not, in the opinion of the Government of the Reich, disturb Polish interests in any way. This action led to the creation of a common Polish-Hungarian frontier, which had constantly been described on Poland's side as an important political objective. Moreover, the German Government gave unequivocal expression to their readiness to discuss with the Polish Government in a friendly manner all problems which, in the Polish Government's opinion, might arise out of the changed conditions in Central Europe.

10. In an equally friendly spirit the German Government tried to regulate yet another question outstanding between Germany and Poland, namely, that of Danzig. The fact that this question required settlement had long been emphasised on the German side, and was not denied on the Polish side. For a long time past the German Government have endeavoured to convince the Polish Government that a solution was certainly possible which would be equitable to the interests of both parties and that the removal of this last obstacle would open a path for a political collaboration of Germany and Poland with the most favourable prospects. In this connexion the German Government did not confine themselves to allusions of a general nature, but in March of this year proposed to the Polish Government in a friendly form a settlement of this question on the following basis: —

11. The return of Danzig to the Reich. An extra-territorial railway line and *autostrada* between East Prussia and the Reich. In exchange, the recognition by the Reich of the whole Polish Corridor and the whole of Poland's western frontier; the conclusion of a non-aggression pact for twenty-five years; the maintenance of Poland's economic interests in Danzig and the settlement of the remaining economic and communications problems arising for Poland out of the union of Danzig with the Reich. At the same time, the German Government expressed their readiness to respect Polish interests in ensuring the independence of Slovakia.

12. Nobody knowing conditions in Danzig and the Corridor and the problems connected therewith can deny, in judging the matter objectively, that this proposal constitutes the very minimum which must be demanded from the point of view of German interests, which cannot be renounced. The Polish Government, however, gave a reply which, although couched in the form of counter-proposals, showed in its essence an entire lack of comprehension for the German point of view and was equivalent merely to a rejection of the German proposals. The Polish Government proved that they did not consider their reply suitable for the initiation of friendly discussions by proceeding at the same time, in a manner as unexpected as it was drastic, to effect a partial mobilisation of the Polish army on a large scale. By these entirely unjustified measures, the Polish Government demonstrated the meaning and object of the negotiations which they immediately

27

afterwards entered upon with the British Government. The German Government do not consider it necessary to reply to the partial Polish mobilisation by counter-measures of a military character. They cannot, however, disregard without a word the decisions recently taken by the Polish Government, and are forced, to their own regret, to declare as follows: —

(1) The Polish Government did not avail themselves of the opportunity offered to them by the German Government for a just settlement of the Danzig question, for the final safeguarding of Poland's frontiers with the Reich, and thereby for a permanent strengthening of the friendly neighbourly relations between the two countries. The Polish Government even rejected German proposals made with this object.

(2) At the same time the Polish Government accepted, with regard to another State, political obligations which are not compatible either with the spirit, the meaning or the text of the German-Polish Declaration of the 26th January, 1934. Thereby the Polish Government arbitrarily and unilaterally rendered this declaration null and void.

13. In spite of this necessary statement of fact, the Government of the Reich do not intend to alter their fundamental attitude towards the question of the future of German-Polish relations. Should the Polish Government attach importance to a new settlement of these relations by means of a treaty, the German Government are ready to do this, but on one condition, namely, that such a settlement would have to consist of a clear obligation binding on both parties.

15.

Speech made by M. Beck, the Polish Minister for Foreign Affairs in Parliament on May 5, 1939.

(Translation.)

The session of the Parliament provides me with an opportunity of filling in some gaps which have occurred in my work of recent months. The course of international events might perhaps justify more statements by a Foreign Minister than my single *exposé* in the Senate Commission for Foreign Affairs.

2. On the other hand it was precisely that swift development of events that prompted me to postpone a public declaration until such time as the principal problems of our foreign policy had taken on a more definite form.

3. The consequences of the weakening of collective international institutions and of a complete change in the method of intercourse between nations, which I have reported on several occasions in the Houses, caused many new problems to arise in different parts of the world. That process and its results have in recent months reached the borders of Poland.

4. A very general definition of these phenomena may be given by saying that relations between individual Powers have taken on a more individual character, with their own specific features. The general rules have been weakened. One nation simply speaks more and more directly to another.

5. As far as we are concerned, very serious events have taken place. Our contact with some Powers has become easier and more profound, while in some cases serious difficulties have arisen. Looking at things chronologically, I refer, in the first place, to our agreement with the United Kingdom, with Great Britain. After repeated diplomatic contacts, designed to define the scope and object of our future relations, we reached on the occasion of my visit to London a direct agreement based on the principle of mutual assistance in the event of a direct or indirect threat to the independence of one of our countries. The formula of the agreement is known to you from the declaration of Mr. Neville Chamberlain of the 6th April, the text of which was drafted by mutual agreement and should be regarded as a pact concluded between the two Governments. I consider it my duty to add that the form and character of the comprehensive conversations held in London give a particular value to the agreement. I should like Polish public opinion to be aware that I found on the part of British statesmen not only a profound knowledge of the general political problems of Europe, but also such an attitude towards our country as permitted me to discuss all vital problems with frankness and confidence without any reservations or doubts.

6. It was possible to establish rapidly the principles of Polish-British collaboration, first of all because we made it clear to each other that the intentions of both Governments coincide as regards fundamental European problems; certainly, neither Great Britain nor Poland have any aggressive intentions whatever, but they stand equally firmly in defence of certain basic principles of conduct in international life.

7. The parallel declarations of French political leaders confirm that it is agreed between Paris and Warsaw that the efficacy of our defence pact not only cannot be adversely affected by changes in the international situation, but, on the contrary, that this agreement should constitute one of the most essential elements in the political structure of Europe. The Polish-British Agreement has been employed by the Chancellor of the German Reich as the pretext for unilaterally declaring non-existent the agreement which the Chancellor of the Reich concluded with us in 1934.

8. Before passing to the present stage of this matter, allow me to sketch a brief historical outline.

9. The fact that I had the honour actively to participate in the conclusion and execution of that pact imposes on me the duty of analysing it. The pact of 1934 was a great event in 1934. It was an attempt to improve the course of history as between two great nations, an attempt to escape from the unwholesome atmosphere of daily discord and wider hostile intentions, to rise above the animosity which had

accumulated for centuries, and to create deep foundations of mutual respect. An endeavour to oppose evil is always the best form of political activity.

10. The policy of Poland proved our respect for that principle in the most critical moments of recent times.

11. From this point of view, Gentlemen, the breaking off of that pact is not an insignificant matter. However, every treaty is worth as much as the consequences which follow it. And if the policy and conduct of the other party diverges from the principles of the pact, we have no reason for mourning its slackening or dissolution. The Polish-German Pact of 1934 was a treaty of mutual respect and good neighbourly relations, and as such it contributed a positive value to the life of our country, of Germany and of the whole of Europe. But since there has appeared a tendency to interpret it as limiting the freedom of our policy, or as a ground for demanding from us unilateral concessions contrary to our vital interests, it has lost its real character.

12. Let us now pass to the present situation. The German Reich has taken the mere fact of the Polish-British understanding as a motive for the breaking off of the pact of 1934. Various legal objections were raised on the German side. I will take the liberty of referring jurists to the text of our reply to the German memorandum, which will be handed to-day to the German Government. I will not detain you any longer on the diplomatic form of this event, but one of its aspects has a special significance. The Reich Government, as appears from the text of the German memorandum, made its decision on the strength of press reports, without consulting the views of either the British or the Polish Government as to the character of the agreement concluded. It would not have been difficult to do so, for immediately on my return from London I expressed my readiness to receive the German Ambassador, who has hitherto not availed himself of the opportunity.

13. Why is this circumstance important? Even for the simplest understanding it is clear that neither the character nor the purpose and scope of the agreement influenced this decision, but merely the fact that such an agreement had been concluded. And this in turn is important for an appreciation of the objects of German policy, since if, contrary to previous declarations, the Government of the Reich interpreted the Polish-German declaration of non-aggression of 1934 as intended to isolate Poland and to prevent the normal friendly collaboration of our country with Western Powers, we ourselves should always have rejected such an interpretation.

14. To make a proper estimate of the situation, we should first of all ask the question, what is the real object of all this? Without that question and our reply, we cannot properly appreciate the character of German statements with regard to matters of concern to Poland. I have already referred to our attitude towards the West. There remains the question of the German proposals as to the future of the Free City of Danzig, the communication of the Reich with East

Prussia through our province of Pomorze, and the further subjects raised as of common interest to Poland and Germany.

15. Let us, therefore, investigate these problems in turn.

16. As to Danzig, first some general remarks. The Free City of Danzig was not invented by the Treaty of Versailles. It has existed for many centuries as the result—to speak accurately, and rejecting the emotional factor—of the positive interplay of Polish and German interests. The German merchants of Danzig ensured the development and prosperity of that city, thanks to the overseas trade of Poland. Not only the development, but the very *raison d'être* of the city has been due to the formerly decisive fact of its situation at the mouth of our only great river, and to-day to its position on the main waterway and railway line connecting us with the Baltic. This is a truth which no new formulæ can obliterate. The population of Danzig is to-day predominantly German, but its livelihood and prosperity depend on the economic potential of Poland.

17. What conclusions have we drawn from this fact? We have stood and stand firmly on the ground of the rights and interests of our sea-borne trade and our maritime policy in Danzig. While seeking reasonable and conciliatory solutions, we have purposely not endeavoured to exert any pressure on the free national, ideological and cultural development of the German majority in the Free City.

18. I shall not prolong this speech by quoting examples. They are sufficiently well-known to all who have been in any way concerned with the question. But when, after repeated statements by German statesmen, who had respected our standpoint and expressed the view that "this provincial town will not be the object of a conflict between Poland and Germany," I hear a demand for the annexation of Danzig to the Reich, when I receive no reply to our proposal of the 26th March for a joint guarantee of the existence and rights of the Free City, and subsequently I learn that this has been regarded as a rejection of negotiations—I have to ask myself, what is the real object of all this?

19. Is it the freedom of the German population of Danzig, which is not threatened, or a matter of prestige—or it is a matter of barring Poland from the Baltic, from which Poland will not allow herself to be barred?

20. The same considerations apply to communication across our province of Pomorze. I insist on the term "province of Pomorze." The word "corridor" is an artificial invention, for this is an ancient Polish territory with an insignificant percentage of German colonists.

21. We have given the German Reich all railway facilities, we have allowed its citizens to travel without customs or passport formalities from the Reich to East Prussia. We have suggested the extension of similar facilities to road traffic.

22. And here again the question arises—what is the real object of it all?

23. We have no interest in obstructing German citizens in their communication with their eastern province. But we have, on the

31

other hand, no reason whatever to restrict our sovereignty on our own territory.

24. On the first and second points, *i.e.*, the question of the future of Danzig and of communication across Pomorze, it is still a matter of unilateral concessions which the Government of the Reich appear to be demanding from us. A self-respecting nation does not make unilateral concessions. Where, then, is the reciprocity? It appears somewhat vague in the German proposals. The Chancellor of the Reich mentioned in his speech a triple condominium in Slovakia. I am obliged to state that I heard the proposal for the first time in the Chancellor's speech of the 28th April. In certain previous conversations allusions were merely made to the effect that in the event of a general agreement the question of Slovakia could be discussed. We did not attempt to go further with such conversations, since it is not our custom to bargain with the interests of others. Similarly, the proposal for a prolongation of the pact of non-aggression for twenty-five years was also not advanced in any concrete form in any of the recent conversations. Here also unofficial hints were made, emanating, it is true, from prominent representatives of the Reich Government. But in such conversations various other hints were made which extended much further than the subjects under discussion. I reserve the right to return to this matter if necessary.

25. In his speech the Chancellor of the Reich proposes, as a concession on his part, the recognition and definite acceptance of the present frontier between Poland and Germany. I must point out that this would have been a question of recognising what is *de jure* and *de facto* our indisputable property. Consequently, this proposal likewise cannot affect my contention that the German desiderata regarding Danzig and a motor road constitute unilateral demands.

26. In the light of these explanations, the House will rightly expect from me an answer to the last passage of the German memorandum, which says: "Should the Polish Government attach importance to a new settlement of Polish-German relations by means of a treaty, the German Government are prepared to do this." It appears to me that I have already made clear our attitude, but for the sake of order I will make a résumé.

27. The motive for concluding such an agreement would be the word "peace," which the Chancellor emphasised in his speech.

28. Peace is certainly the object of the difficult and intensive work of Polish diplomacy. Two conditions are necessary for this word to be of real value: (1) peaceful intentions, (2) peaceful methods of procedure. If the Government of the Reich is really guided by those two pre-conditions in relation to this country, then all conversations, provided, of course, that they respect the principles I have already enumerated, are possible.

29. If such conversations took place, the Polish Government will, according to their custom, approach the problem objectively, having

regard to the experience of recent times, but without withholding their utmost goodwill.

30. Peace is a valuable and desirable thing. Our generation, which has shed its blood in several wars, surely deserves a period of peace. But peace, like almost everything in this world, has its price, high but definable. We in Poland do not recognise the conception of "peace at any price". There is only one thing in the life of men, nations and States which is without price, and that is honour.

16.

*Memorandum communicated to the German Government by the Polish Government on May 5, 1939, in reply to the German Government memorandum of April 28, 1939.**

(Translation.)

As appears from the text of the Polish-German Declaration of the 26th January, 1934,† and from the course of the negotiations which preceded its conclusion, this declaration had as its object to lay the foundations for a new framing of mutual relations based on the following two principles: —

(a) The renunciation of the use of force as between Poland and Germany, and

(b) The friendly settlement by means of free negotiations of any contentious questions which might arise in the relations between the two countries.

The Polish Government have always understood in this manner their obligations under the declaration, and it is in this spirit that they have always been prepared to conduct neighbourly relations with the German Reich.

2. The Polish Government had foreseen for several years that the difficulties encountered by the League of Nations in carrying out its functions at Danzig would create a confused situation which it was in Poland's and Germany's interest to unravel. For several years the Polish Government had given the German Government to understand that frank conversations should be held on this subject. The German Government, however, avoided these and confined themselves to stating that Polish-German relations should not be exposed to difficulties by questions relating to Danzig. Moreover, the German Government more than once gave assurances to the Polish Government regarding the Free City of Danzig. It is sufficient here to quote the declaration made by the Chancellor of the Reich on the 20th February, 1938.

The Chancellor made publicly in the Reichstag the following declaration regarding Danzig: —

"The Polish State respects the national conditions in this State and the Free City and Germany respect Polish rights. It has thus

* No. 14. † No. 1.

33

been possible to clear the way for an understanding which, while arising out of the question of Danzig, has to-day in spite of the efforts of certain disturbers of the peace succeeded in effectively purifying relations between Germany and Poland and has transformed them into sincere and friendly collaboration."

It was only after the events of September, 1938, that the German Government suggested the opening of Polish-German conversations regarding the alteration in the situation in Danzig and regarding the transit routes between the Reich and East Prussia. In this connexion the German memorandum of the 28th April, 1939, refers to the suggestion put forward by the Reich Minister for Foreign Affairs in his conversation of the 21st March, 1939, with the Polish Ambassador in Berlin. In this conversation emphasis was laid on the German side on the necessity for a rapid settlement of these questions which was a condition of the Reich maintaining its proposals in force in their entirety. The Polish Government, animated by the desire to maintain good relations with the Reich, although surprised at the pressing form in which these proposals were put forward, and by the circumstances in which they were advanced, did not refuse conversations although they considered the German demands thus couched to be unacceptable.

In order to facilitate endeavours to reach an amicable solution of the question, the Polish Government on the 26th March, 1939, formulated their point of view in writing to the German Government, stating that they attached full importance to the maintenance of good neighbourly relations with the German Reich. The Polish point of view was summarised in the following points:—

(a) The Polish Government propose a joint guarantee by Poland and Germany of the separate character of the Free City of Danzig, the existence of which was to be based on complete freedom of the local population in internal affairs and on the assurance of respect for Polish rights and interests.

(b) The Polish Government were prepared to examine together with the German Government any further simplifications for persons in transit as well as the technical facilitating of railway and motor transit between the German Reich and East Prussia. The Polish Government were inspired by the idea of giving every possible facility which would permit the citizens of the Reich to travel in transit across Polish territory, if possible without any hindrances. The Polish Government emphasised that their intention was to secure the most liberal treatment possible of the German desiderata in this respect with the sole reservation that Poland could not give up her sovereignty over the belt of territory through which the transit routes would run. Finally, the Polish Government indicated that their attitude in the question of facilitating communications across Pomerania depended on the attitude of the Reich regarding the Free City of Danzig.

In formulating the above proposals the Polish Government acted in the spirit of the Polish-German Declaration of 1934 which, by providing the direct exchanges of views on questions of interest to both countries, authorised each State to formulate its point of view in the course of negotiations.

The Polish Government received no formal reply to their counter-proposals for a month, and it was only on the 28th April, 1939, that they learnt from the Chancellor's speech and from the German Government's memorandum that the mere fact of the formulation of counter-proposals instead of the acceptance of the verbal German suggestions without alteration or reservation had been regarded by the Reich as a refusal of discussions.

It is clear that negotiations in which one State formulates demands and the other is to be obliged to accept those demands unaltered are not negotiations in the spirit of the declaration of 1934 and are incompatible with the vital interests and dignity of Poland.

In this connexion it should be pointed out that the Polish Government were unable at that time to express an opinion regarding the Polish-German-Hungarian guarantee of the independence of Slovakia which was alluded to in a general way in the German memorandum and more precisely stated in the Chancellor's speech of the 28th April, 1939, since a proposal of this description and in this form had never been made to them before. It is, moreover, difficult to imagine how such guarantee could be reconciled with the political and military protectorate of the Reich over Slovakia which had been announced a few days previously before the German Reich formulated its proposals towards Poland.

3. The Polish Government cannot accept such an interpretation of the declaration of 1934 as would be equivalent to a renunciation of the right to conclude political agreements with third States and, consequently, almost a renunciation of independence in foreign policy. The policy of the German Reich in recent years has clearly indicated that the German Government have not drawn conclusions of this sort from the declaration as far as they themselves were concerned. The obligations publicly accepted by the Reich towards Italy and the German-Slovak Agreement of March, 1939, are clear indications of such an interpretation by the German Government of the declaration of 1934. The Polish Government must here recall that in their relations with other States they give and require full reciprocity as being the only possible foundation of normal relations between States.

The Polish Government reject as completely without foundation all accusations regarding the alleged incompatibility of the Anglo-Polish Mutual Guarantee of April, 1939, with the Polish-German Declaration of 1934. This guarantee has a purely defensive character and in no way threatens the German Reich, in the same way as the Polish-French Alliance, whose compatability with the Declaration of 1934 has been recognised by the German Reich. The declaration of 1934 in its introductory paragraphs clearly stated that both Governments have "decided to base their mutual relations on the principles laid down in the Pact of Paris of the 27th August, 1928." Now the Pact of Paris, which constituted a general renunciation of war as an instrument of national policy, just as the declaration of 1934 constituted such renunciation in bilateral Polish-German relations, contained the explicit reservation that "any signatory Power which shall hereafter seek to promote its national interests by resort to war should be denied the benefits furnished by this treaty." Germany accepted this principle in signing the Pact of Paris and re-affirmed it in the declaration of 1934, together with other principles of the Pact of Paris. It appears from this that the declaration of 1934 would cease to be binding on Poland should Germany have recourse to war in violation of the Pact of Paris. Poland's obligations arising out of the Polish-British understanding would come into operation in the event of German action threatening the independence of Great Britain, and, consequently, in the very circumstances in which the declaration of 1934 and the Pact of Paris had ceased to be binding on Poland as regards Germany.

The German Government in making a complaint against the Polish Government for undertaking obligations to guarantee the independence of Great Britain and in regarding this as a violation by Poland of the declaration of 1934, ignore their own obligations towards Italy of which the Chancellor spoke on the 30th January, 1939, and in particular their obligations towards Slovakia contained in the agreement of the 18th and 23rd March, 1939. The German guarantees of Slovakia did not exclude Poland [sic], and, indeed, as appears from the provisions of the above agreement regarding the distribution of garrisons and military fortifications in Western Slovakia, were directed primarily against Poland.

4. It appears from the above that the Government of the German Reich had no justification for their unilateral decision to regard the declaration of 1934 as not binding. The pact was, indeed, concluded for ten years without any possibility of denunciation during that time. It should be pointed out that the decision to regard the 1934 Declaration as not binding took place after the previous refusal of the German State to accept explanations as to the compatibility of the Anglo-Polish guarantee with the 1934 Declaration, which it was the intention of the Polish Government to furnish to the representative of the Reich in Warsaw.

5. Although the Polish Government do not share the view of the German Government that the treaty of 1934 has been violated by Poland, nevertheless, should the German Government attach importance to the fresh regulation, by means of a treaty, of Polish-German relations on a good neighbourly basis, the Polish Government would be prepared to entertain suggestions of this kind with the reservation of their fundamental observations contained above in the present memorandum.

Anglo-Polish Agreement.

17.

Statement by the Prime Minister in the House of Commons on March 31, 1939.

The Prime Minister (Mr. Chamberlain): The right hon. gentleman the leader of the Opposition asked me this morning whether I could make a statement as to the European situation. As I said this morning, His Majesty's Government have no official confirmation of the rumours of any projected attack on Poland and they must not, therefore, be taken as accepting them as true.

I am glad to take this opportunity of stating again the general policy of His Majesty's Government. They have constantly advocated the adjustment, by way of free negotiation between the parties concerned, of any differences that may arise between the parties concerned, of any differences that may arise between them. They consider that this is the natural and proper course where differences exist. In their opinion there should be no question incapable of solution by peaceful means, and they would see no justification for the substitution of force or threats of force for the method of negotiation.

As the House is aware, certain consultations are now proceeding with other Governments. In order to make perfectly clear the position of His Majesty's Government in the meantime before those consultations are concluded, I now have to inform the House that during that period, in the event of any action which clearly threatened Polish independence, and which the Polish Government accordingly considered it vital to resist with their national forces, His Majesty's Government would feel themselves bound at once to lend the Polish Government all support in their power. They have given the Polish Government an assurance to this effect.

I may add that the French Government have authorised me to make it plain that they stand in the same position in this matter as do His Majesty's Government.

37

18.

Anglo-Polish communiqué issued on April 6, 1939.

The conversations with M. Beck have covered a wide field and shown that the two Governments are in complete agreement upon certain general principles.

It was agreed that the two countries were prepared to enter into an agreement of a permanent and reciprocal character to replace the present temporary and unilateral assurance given by His Majesty's Government to the Polish Government. Pending the completion of the permanent agreement, M. Beck gave His Majesty's Government an assurance that the Polish Government would consider themselves under an obligation to render assistance to His Majesty's Government under the same conditions as those contained in the temporary assurance already given by His Majesty's Government to Poland.

Like the temporary assurance, the permanent agreement would not be directed against any other country but would be designed to assure Great Britain and Poland of mutual assistance in the event of any threat, direct or indirect, to the independence of either. It was recognised that certain matters, including a more precise definition of the various ways in which the necessity for such assistance might arise, would require further examination before the permanent agreement could be completed.

It was understood that the arrangements above mentioned should not preclude either Government from making agreements with other countries in the general interest of the consolidation of peace.

19.

Agreement of Mutual Assistance between the United Kingdom and Poland.—London, August 25, 1939.

The Government of the United Kingdom of Great Britain and Northern Ireland and the Polish Government:

Desiring to place on a permanent basis the collaboration between their respective countries resulting from the assurances of mutual assistance of a defensive character which they have already exchanged;

Have resolved to conclude an Agreement for that purpose and have appointed as their Plenipotentiaries:

The Government of the United Kingdom of Great Britain and Northern Ireland:

The Rt. Hon. Viscount Halifax, K.G., G.C.S.I., G.C.I.E., Principal Secretary of State for Foreign Affairs;

The Polish Government:

His Excellency Count Edward Raczynski, Ambassador Extraordinary and Plenipotentiary of the Polish Republic in London;

Who, having exchanged their Full Powers, found in good and due form, have agreed on the following provisions: —

ARTICLE 1.

Should one of the Contracting Parties become engaged in hostilities with a European Power in consequence of aggression by the latter against that Contracting Party, the other Contracting Party will at once give the Contracting Party engaged in hostilities all the support and assistance in its power.

ARTICLE 2.

(1) The provisions of Article 1 will also apply in the event of any action by a European Power which clearly threatened, directly or indirectly, the independence of one of the Contracting Parties, and was of such a nature that the Party in question considered it vital to resist it with its armed forces.

(2) Should one of the Contracting Parties become engaged in hostilities with a European Power in consequence of action by that Power which threatened the independence or neutrality of another European State in such a way as to constitute a clear menace to the security of that Contracting Party, the provisions of Article 1 will apply, without prejudice, however, to the rights of the other European State concerned.

ARTICLE 3

Should a European Power attempt to undermine the independence of one of the Contracting Parties by processes of economic penetration or in any other way, the Contracting Parties will support each other in resistance to such attempts. Should the European Power concerned thereupon embark on hostilities against one of the Contracting Parties, the provisions of Article 1 will apply.

ARTICLE 4

The methods of applying the undertakings of mutual assistance provided for by the present Agreement are established between the competent naval, military and air authorities of the Contracting Parties.

ARTICLE 5

Without prejudice to the foregoing undertakings of the Contracting Parties to give each other mutual support and assistance immediately on the outbreak of hostilities, they will exchange complete and speedy information concerning any development which might threaten their independence and, in particular, concerning any development which threatened to call the said undertakings into operation.

ARTICLE 6

(1) The Contracting Parties will communicate to each other the terms of any undertakings of assistance against aggression which they have already given or may in future give to other States.

(2) Should either of the Contracting Parties intend to give such an undertaking after the coming into force of the present Agreement, the other Contracting Party shall, in order to ensure the proper functioning of the Agreement, be informed thereof.

(3) Any new undertaking which the Contracting Parties may enter into in future shall neither limit their obligations under the present Agreement nor indirectly create new obligations between the Contracting Party not participating in these undertakings and the third State concerned.

ARTICLE 7

Should the Contracting Parties be engaged in hostilities in consequence of the application of the present Agreement, they will not conclude an armistice or treaty of peace except by mutual agreement.

ARTICLE 8

(1) The present Agreement shall remain in force for a period of five years.

(2) Unless denounced six months before the expiry of this period it shall continue in force, each Contracting Party having, thereafter the right to denounce it at any time by giving six months' notice to that effect.

(3) The present Agreement shall come into force on signature.

In faith whereof the above-named Plenipotentiaries have signed the present Agreement and have affixed thereto their seals.

Done in English in duplicate, at London, the 25th August, 1939. A Polish text shall subsequently be agreed upon between the Contracting Parties and both texts will then be authentic.

(L.S.)   HALIFAX.

(L.S.)   EDWARD RACZYNSKI.

Developments in Anglo-German Relations.

20.

Speech by Herr Hitler at Wilhelmshaven on April 1, 1939

(Translation.)

Germans! Volksgenossen und Volksgenossinnen!

Whoever wishes to estimate the decline and regeneration of Germany must look at the development of a city like Wilhelmshaven. A short time ago it was a dead spot almost without any title to existence, without any prospect of a future; to-day it is filled again with the hum of work and production. It is good if one recalls again to memory this past.

When the city experienced its first rise to prosperity, this coincided with the regeneration of the German Reich after its battle for unification. This Germany was a Germany of peace. At the same time as the so-called peace-loving virtuous nations were carrying on quite a number of wars, the Germany of that time had only one aim, namely, to preserve peace, to work in peace, to increase the prosperity of her inhabitants and thereby to contribute to human culture and civilization.

This peace-time Germany tried with unceasing industry, with genius and with perseverance to set up its inner life and to assure for itself a proper place in the sun through participation in peaceful rivalry with other nations.

In spite of the fact that this Germany was for decades the surest guarantor of peace and devoted herself only to her own peaceful business, other nations, and particularly their statesmen, could not refrain from persecuting this regeneration with envy and hate and finally answering it with a war.

We know to-day from historical records how the encirclement policy of that time had been systematically pursued by England. We know from numerous established facts and publications that in that land one was imbued with the conception that it was necessary to crush Germany militarily because its annihilation would assure to every British citizen a larger measure of this world's goods.

Certainly Germany at that time committed errors. Its worst error was to see this encirclement and to take no steps in time to avoid it. The only reproach which we can level at the régime of that day is the fact that it had full knowledge of the devilish plan for a surprise

41

attack on the Reich, and even so was unable to make up its mind to avoid in time such an attack, but allowed this encirclement to mature right up to the outbreak of the catastrophe.

The result was the World War.

In this war the German people, although they were in no way armed the best, fought heroically. No nation can claim for itself the glory of having beaten us to our knees, least of all those whose statesmen to-day are boasting.

Germany at that time remained unbeaten and unvanquished on land, sea and in the air. And yet we lost the war. We know the power which at that time vanquished Germany. It was the power of falsehood, the poison of a propaganda which did not shrink from distortion and untruthfulness and which caught the German Reich because it was unprepared and defenceless.

When the Fourteen Points of President Wilson were announced, many German *"Volksgenossen,"* particularly the leading men of the time, saw in those Fourteen Points not only the possibility for ending the World War but for a final pacification of all nations of this world. There would come a peace of reconciliation and understanding, a peace which would recognise neither victors nor vanquished, a peace without war indemnities, a peace of equal rights for all, a peace of equal distribution of colonial territory and of equal consideration for colonial desiderata. A peace which would finally be crowned with a league of free nations. A peace which, by guaranteeing equal rights would make it appear superfluous for nations in future still to endure the burden of armament which, as is known, previously weighed down so heavily on them.

Disarmament, therefore, and in fact disarmament of all nations. Germany was to give a good example by taking the lead and all undertook to follow her disarmament.

The era of so-called secret diplomacy was to come to an end as well. All problems were to be discussed and negotiated openly and freely.

The right of self-determination for nations was to be finally established and be regarded as the most important factor.

Germany believed these assurances. Relying on these declarations Germany laid down her weapons. And then a breach of faith began such as world history has never seen.

At the moment when our people had laid down their arms a period of blackmail, oppression, pillage and slavery began.

No longer any word of peace without victors and vanquished, but a sentence of condemnation for the vanquished for time without end.

No longer any word of equal rights, but rights for one side and absence of rights and injustice for the other. One robbery after another, one blackmail after another were the results.

No man in this democratic world bothered about the suffering of our people. Hundreds of thousands fell in the war, not through enemy action, but through the hunger blockade. And when the war came to

42

an end this blockade was continued still for months in order to bring still further pressure on our nation. Even the German prisoners of war had to remain in captivity for indefinite periods. The German colonies were stolen from us, German foreign securities were simply confiscated, and our mercantile marine was taken away.

Then came financial pillage such as the world has never up to this day seen. Payments were imposed on the German people which reached astronomical figures, and about which English statesmen said that they could only be effected if the whole German nation reduced its standard of living to the utmost and worked fourteen hours a day.

What German spirit and German diligence had created and saved in decades was now lost in a few years. Millions of Germans were torn away from the Reich, others were prevented from returning into the Reich. The League of Nations was made not an instrument of a just policy of understanding, but a guarantor of the meanest dictate that human beings had ever thought out.

A great people was thus raped and led towards the misery that all of you know. A great people was deprived of its rights by breach of promise and its existence in practice was made impossible. A French statesman gave sober expression to this by declaring: "There are 20 million Germans too many in the world!"

There were Germans who, in despair, committed suicide, others who lethargically submitted to their inevitable fate, and others again who were of the opinion that there was nothing left to do but to destroy everything; others again ground their teeth and clenched their fists in impotent rage, others again believed that the past must be restored as it had been.

Every individual had adopted some sort of attitude. And I at that time, as the unknown soldier of the World War, took up my position.

It was a short and simple programme; it ran: removal of the domestic enemies of the nation, termination of the internal division of Germany, co-ordination of the entire national force of our people in a new community, and the smashing of the Peace Treaty in one way or another ("so oder so!") For as long as this dictate of Versailles weighed upon the German people, it was actually doomed to go under.

When other statesmen talk about the necessity of justice reigning in this world, then I may tell them that their crime is not justice, that their dictate was neither rightful nor legal, and that the permanent vital rights of peoples come before this dictate.

The German people was created by Providence, not in order to obey a law which suits Englishmen or Frenchmen, but to stand up for its vital right. That is what we are there for!

I was determined to take up this struggle for standing up for German vital rights. I took it up first of all within the nation. The place of a number of parties, classes and associations has now been

43

taken by one single community, the community of the German people!

It is the duty of us all to realise this community and to continue to intensify it. In the course of this time I have had to hurt many an individual. But I believe that the happiness shared to-day by the entire nation must more than compensate every individual for the things which were dear to him and which he individually had to give up.

You have all sacrificed your parties, your clubs, your associations, but you have instead received a great and strong Reich!

And this Reich is to-day, thank God, sufficiently strong to take under its protection your rights. We are now no longer dependent upon the favour or disfavour of other States or their statesmen.

When over six years ago I came into power, I took over a pitiful heritage. The Reich appeared to possess no possibilities for existence for its citizens. At that time I began work with the only capital which I possessed. It was the capital of your power to work! It was your power to work, my "Volksgenossen," that I began to put into use. I had not foreign exchange and no gold; I only had one thing: my faith and your work! We have now founded a new economic system, a system which is called: capital is power to work, and money is covered by our production. We have founded a system based upon the most noble principle in existence, namely, form your life yourself! Work for your existence! Help yourself, then God will also help you!

We thus began a gigantic work of reconstruction, supported by the confidence of the nation, filled with faith and confidence in its permanent values. In a few years we tore Germany from its despair. The world did not help us in doing so!

If an English statesman to-day believes that all problems can and must be solved by frank discussion and negotiations, then I would like to say to this statesman: an opportunity to do so existed for fifteen years before our time! If the world to-day says that one must divide the nations into virtuous and non-virtuous categories—and that the English and French belong in the first place to the virtuous nations and the Germans and Italians to the non-virtuous—then we can only answer: the decision as to whether a nation is virtuous or not virtuous can hardly be made by a mortal human being, and should be left to God!

Perhaps this same British statesman will reply: God has already delivered judgment, for he has given to the virtuous nations one-quarter of the globe and has taken away everything from the non-virtuous! In answer to that, one may be permitted to ask: by what means have the virtuous nations acquired this quarter of the globe? And the answer must be, they have not been virtuous methods!

For 300 years this England has acted only as an unvirtuous nation, and now in old age she is beginning to talk about virtue. It was thus possible that during the British non-virtuous period 46 million Englishmen have conquered almost a quarter of the world, while 80 million Germans, on account of their virtue, have to exist at the rate of 140 to the square kilometre.

Yes, twenty years ago the question of virtue was not yet quite clear in the minds of British statesmen, in so far as it touched conceptions of property. At that time it was still thought to be compatible with virtue simply to take away from another people the colonies which it had acquired by contract or by purchase because one had the power to do so.

A power which now it is true is to count as something disgusting and contemptible. In this respect, I can only say one thing to these gentlemen: we do not know whether they believe that sort of thing themselves or not. We assume, however, that they do not believe it. For if we were to assume that they really believed it themselves, then we would lose every feeling of respect for them.

For fifteen years Germany had borne this fate patiently. I also tried at the beginning to solve every problem by discussion. At every problem I made offers, and they were every time refused! There can be no doubt that every people possess sacred interests, simply because they are identical with its life and its vital right.

If a British statesman to-day demands that every problem concerning vital German interests should first be discussed with England, then I could make precisely the same claim and demand that every British problem must first be discussed with us. Admittedly, this Englishman would answer: Palestine is none of your business! But, just as Germany has no business in Palestine, so has England no business in the German *Lebensraum!* And if the problem is claimed to be a question of general rights, then I can only agree to this opinion if it were regarded as universal and obligatory. One says we had no right to do this or that. I would like to ask a counter-question: what right—just to quote only one example—has England to shoot down Arabs in Palestine, only because they are standing up for their home? Who gives England the right to do so?

We at any rate have not slaughtered thousands in Central Europe, but have solved our problems in a peaceful and orderly manner! There is one thing, however, that I must say: the German people of to-day, the German Reich of the present time, are not willing to sacrifice vital interests, and they are also not willing to stand up to rising dangers without taking action! When the allies at one time changed the map of Europe with no consideration for expediency, justice, tradition or even common-sense, we did not have the power to prevent them from doing so. But if they expect the Germany of the present day patiently to allow vassal States, whose only duty consists in their being set to work against Germany, to carry on as they like until the day comes when their services are to be actively employed, then they are confounding present-day Germany with the Germany of pre-war days. Those who declare that they are prepared to pull chestnuts out of the fire for these Great Powers must also expect to burn their fingers in the course of the process.

We have really no feelings of hatred for the Czech people, we have lived together for years. English statesmen do not know that. They have no idea that the Hradschin was built not by Englishmen but by Germans, and that the St. Veit's Cathedral was also not built by Englishmen but by Germans. Frenchmen also were not active there. They do not know that already, at a time when England was still very small, homage was done to a German Emperor on this hill, and that, a thousand years before I did so myself, the first German King stood there and received the homage of this people. This the English do not know, they cannot know it and they need not know it.

It is sufficient that we know it, and that it is true that for a thousand years this area belonged to the *Lebensraum* of the German people. We would, nevertheless, have had nothing against an independent Czech State if this State had not, firstly, oppressed Germans, and, secondly, if it had not been an instrument for a future attack on Germany.

But when a former French Air Minister writes in a newspaper that it is the task of this Czechia, because of her splendid geographical position, to strike at Germany's industry by air attacks in a war, then one will understand that it is not without interest to us, and that we drew certain conclusions therefrom.

It would have been a matter for England and France to defend this air base. It was our affair, at any rate, to prevent the possibility of such an attack taking place. I believed that I could achieve this end in a natural and simple way. It was not until I saw that such an attempt was doomed to fail, and that the anti-German elements would once more gain the upper hand, and it was not until I also saw that this State had for a long time lost its inner capacity to live and that it had already collapsed, that I re-enforced ancient German right and reunited what had to be united by history, geographical position and all rules of common-sense.

Not for the purpose of suppressing the Czech people! It will have more freedom than the oppressed peoples of the virtuous nations!

I have, so I believe, thereby rendered a great service to peace, for I have in good time made valueless an instrument that was designed to become effective in time of war against Germany.

If people now say that this is the signal for Germany's desire to attack the whole world, then I do not believe they mean it seriously; such a statement could only be the expression of the very worst of consciences. Perhaps it is anger at the failure of a far-reaching plan; perhaps it is belief that the premises can thereby be created for a new policy of encirclement? Whatever the case may be, I am convinced that I have thereby rendered a great service to peace.

And it is from this conviction that I determined three weeks ago to give the coming Party Rally the name of "Party Rally of Peace." For Germany does not dream of attacking other nations.

What we do not, however, desire to renounce is the extension of our economic relations. To this we have a right, and I do not accept orders in this respect from any statesman inside or outside Europe!

The German Reich is not only a great producer, but also a tremendous consumer. In the same way as we become an unreplaceable commercial partner as consumer, so are we suited as a producer honestly to pay what we consume.

We do not dream of waging war on other nations, subject, of course, to their leaving us in peace also. The German Reich is, however, in no case prepared permanently to tolerate intimidation, or even a policy of encirclement.

I once concluded an agreement with England—the Naval Agreement. It is based on the ardent desire, shared by us all, never to be forced to fight a war against England. This desire can, however, only be a reciprocal one. If it no longer exists in England, then the practical premises for the agreement have been removed. Germany would accept even a situation of this kind with calm composure! We are so sure of ourselves because we are strong, and we are strong because we are united, and also because we keep our eyes open! And in this town more than elsewhere I can only urge you to look at the world and all happenings therein around us with open eyes. Do not deceive yourselves regarding the most important prerequisite which exists in life, namely, the necessary power at one's own disposal. He who does not possess power loses the right to live! We have had fifteen years' experience of such a condition. That is why I have made Germany strong again and why I have created a defence force on land, on the waters and in the air.

But when there is talk in other countries of present rearmament and of continued and still greater rearmament, then I can only say to these statesmen: it will not be me whom they will tire out!

I am determined to continue to march along this road, and I am convinced that we shall advance faster than the others. No Power in the world will ever wheedle our arms from us by mere words. But should anyone at any time show any desire to measure his strength against ours by force, then the German people will always be in a position and ready and determined to do the same!

And our friends think just as we do, especially the State with which we are closely bound and with which we march, now, and in all circumstances, and for all time. When hostile journalists do not know what else to write about, then they write of cracks in the Axis. They can be at ease.

This Axis is the most natural political instrument in the world. It is a political combination of ideas which owes its existence not only to reason and the desire for justice, but also to strength inspired by idealism.

This structure will hold out better than the present alliances of non-homogeneous bodies on the other side. For if anybody tells me to-day that there are no differences in world outlook or ideologies between England and Soviet Russia, I can only say: I congratulate you, Gentlemen.

47

I believe we shall not have long to wait before we see that the unity in world outlook between Fascist Italy and National Socialist Germany is, after all, different from that between democratic Great Britain and the Bolshevik Russia of Stalin.

But if there should really be no ideological difference between them, then I can only say: how right is, after all, my attitude towards Marxism, communism and to democracy! Why two apparitions, when after all they are made of the same substance?

We are experiencing in these days a very great triumph and a feeling of deep inner satisfaction. A country that was also devastated by bolshevism, in which hundreds and thousands of human beings, women, men, children and old people, were slaughtered, has liberated itself, and liberated itself in spite of ideological friends of bolshevism who sit in Great Britain, France and other countries.

We can only too well understand this Spain in her struggle, and we greet her and congratulate her on her victory. We Germans can say so with special pride, for many young German men have done their duty there.

They have helped as volunteers to break a tyrannical régime and to recover for a nation its right to self-determination. We are glad to see how quickly, yes, how extremely quickly, here also a change in the world outlook of the suppliers of war material to the Red side has come about, how extensively one now suddenly understands National Spain and how ready one is to do business with this National Spain, perhaps not ideological business, but at least economic business!

This also is an indication of the direction developments are taking. For I believe that all States will have to face the same problems that we once had to face. State after State will either succumb to the Jewish Bolshevik pest or will ward it off. We have done so, and we have now erected a national German People's State.

This People's State desires to live in peace and friendship with every other State, it will, however, never again permit itself to be forced to its knees by any other State.

I do not know whether the world will become Fascist! I do not believe that the world will become National Socialist! But that the world will in the end ward off this worst form of bolshevistic threat in existence, of that I am absolutely convinced.

And, therefore, I believe in a conclusive understanding among peoples which will come sooner or later. There is no point in bringing about co-operation among nations, based upon permanent understanding, until this Jewish fission-fungus of peoples has been removed.

To-day we must depend upon our own power! And we can be satisfied with results of this confidence in ourselves! At home and abroad!

When I came into power, Germany was torn and impotent at home, and abroad a toy of foreign will. To-day we have order at home and our economy is flourishing. Abroad we are perhaps not popular, but we are respected. That is the decisive factor. Above all, we have given millions of our *"Volksgenossen"* the greatest happiness they could have wished for: their home-coming into our Great German Reich. And, secondly, we have given great happiness to Central Europe, namely, peace, peace protected by German power. And this power shall not be broken again by any force in the world. That shall be our oath.

We thus realise that the *"Volksgenossen,"* more than 2 million in number, who died in the Great War, did not die in vain. From their sacrifice a new Great German Reich has arisen. From their sacrifice this strong young German Reich of the *"Volk"* has been called to life and has now stood its test in life.

And in the face of this sacrifice, we would not fear any sacrifice if it should ever become necessary. This the world should take note of!

They can conclude agreements, make declarations, as many as they like: I put my trust not in scraps of paper, but I put my trust in you, my *"Volksgenossen."*

Germans have been the victims of the greatest breach of promise of all time. Let us see to it that our people at home may never again become easy to break up, then no one in the world will ever be able to threaten us. Then peace will be maintained for our people or, if necessary, it will be enforced. And then our people will flourish and prosper.

It will be able to place its genius, its capability, its diligence, and its perseverance at the disposal of the work of peace and home culture. That is our desire; it is that which we hope and in which we believe.

Twenty years ago the party was founded, at that time a very small structure. Recall the distance covered from that time until to-day. Recall the extent of the miracle that has been worked upon us. And have faith, therefore, by the very reason of our miraculous progress, in the further road of the German people in the coming great future!

Germany: Sieg-Heil! Sieg-Heil! Sieg-Heil!

21.

Extract from speech by Herr Hitler to the Reischstag on April 28, 1939.

(Translation.)

I believe that it is a good thing for millions and millions of people that I, thanks to the last-minute insight of responsible men on the other side, succeeded in averting such an explosion, and found a solution which I am convinced has finally abolished this problem of a source of danger in Central Europe.

The contention that this solution is contrary to the Munich Agreement can neither be supported nor confirmed. This agreement could, under no circumstances, be regarded as final, because it admitted that other problems required and remained to be solved. We cannot really be reproached for the fact that the parties concerned—and this is the deciding factor—did not turn to the four Powers, but only to Italy and Germany; nor yet for the fact that the State as such finally split up of its own accord, and there was, consequently, no longer any Czecho-Slovakia. It was, however, understandable that, long after the ethnographic principle had been made invalid, Germany should take under her protection her interests dating back a thousand years, which are not only of a political but also of an economic nature.

The future will show whether the solution which Germany has found is right or wrong. However, it is certain that the solution is not subject to English supervision or criticism. For Bohemia and Moravia, as the remnants of former Czecho-Slovakia, have nothing more whatever to do with the Munich Agreement. Just as English measures in, say, Northern Ireland, whether they be right or wrong, are not subject to German supervision or criticism, this is also the case with these old German electorates.

However, I entirely fail to understand how the agreement reached between Mr. Chamberlain and myself at Munich can refer to this case, for the case of Czecho-Slovakia was settled in the Munich protocol of the four Powers as far as it could be settled at all at that time. Apart from this, provision was merely made that if the interested parties should fail to come to an agreement they should be entitled to appeal to the four Powers, who had agreed in such a case to meet for further consultation after the expiration of three months. However, these interested parties did not appeal to the four Powers at all, but only to Germany and Italy. That this was fully justified, moreover, is proved by the fact that neither England nor France have raised any objections thereto, but have themselves accepted the decision given by Germany and Italy. No, the agreement reached between Mr. Chamberlain and myself did not relate to this problem but exclusively to questions which refer to the mutual relationship between England and Germany. This is clearly shown by the fact that such questions are to be treated in future in the spirit of the Munich Agreement and of the Anglo-German Naval Agreement, that is, in a friendly spirit by way of consultation. If, however, this agreement were to be applied to every future German activity of a political nature, England too should not take any step, whether in Palestine or elsewhere, without first consulting Germany. It is obvious that we do not expect this; likewise we refuse to gratify any similar expectation of us. Now, if Mr. Chamberlain concludes from this, that the Munich Agreement is for this reason annulled, as if we had broken it, then I shall take cognisance of the fact and proceed accordingly.

During the whole of my political activity I have always expounded the idea of a close friendship and collaboration between Germany and England. In my movement I found innumerable others of like mind. Perhaps they joined me because of my attitude in this matter. This desire for Anglo-German friendship and co-operation conforms not merely to sentiments which result from the racial origins of our two peoples, but also to my realisation of the importance for the whole of mankind of the existence of the British Empire. I have never left room for any doubt of my belief that the existence of this empire is an inestimable factor of value for the whole of human cultural and economic life. By whatever means Great Britain has acquired her colonial territories—and I know that they were those of force and often brutality—nevertheless, I know full well that no other empire has ever come into being in any other way, and that in the final resort it is not so much the methods that are taken into account in history as success, and not the success of the methods as such, but rather the general good which the methods yield. Now there is no doubt that the Anglo-Saxon people have accomplished immeasurable colonising work in the world. For this work I have a sincere admiration. The thought of destroying this labour appeared and still appears to me, seen from a higher human point of view, as nothing but the effluence of human wanton destructiveness. However, this sincere respect of mine for this achievement does not mean forgoing the securing of the life of my own people. I regard it as impossible to achieve a lasting friendship between the German and Anglo-Saxon peoples if the other side does not recognise that there are German as well as British interests, that not only is the preservation of the British Empire the meaning and purpose of the lives of Britishers, but also that for Germans the freedom and preservation of the German Reich is their life purpose. A genuine, lasting friendship between these two nations is only conceivable on the basis of mutual regards. The English people rules a great empire. It built up this empire at a time when the German people was internally weak. Previously Germany had been a great empire. At one time she ruled the Occident. In bloody struggles and religious dissensions, and as a result of internal political disintegration, this empire declined in power and greatness, and finally fell into a deep sleep. But as this old empire appeared to have reached its end, the seeds of its rebirth were springing up. From Brandenburg and Prussia there arose a new Germany, the second Reich, and out of it has grown at last the German People's Reich. And I hope that all English people understand that we do not possess the slightest feeling of inferiority to Britishers. Our historical past is far too tremendous for that!

England has given the world many great men and Germany no fewer. The severe struggle for the maintenance of the life of our people has in the course of three centuries cost a sacrifice in lives which far exceeds that which other peoples have had to make in asserting their existence.

If Germany, a country that was for ever being attacked, was not able to retain her possessions, but was compelled to sacrifice many of her provinces, this was due only to her political misdevelopment and her impotence as a result thereof! That condition has now been overcome. Therefore, we Germans do not feel in the least inferior to the British nation. Our self-esteem is just as great as that of an Englishman for England. In the history of our people, now of approximately two thousand years' standing, there are occasions and actions enough to fill us with sincere pride.

Now, if England cannot understand our point of view, thinking perchance she may look upon Germany as a vassal State, then our love and friendly feelings have, indeed, been wasted on England. We shall not despair or lose heart on that account, but—relying on the consciousness of our own strength and on the strength of our friends —we shall then find ways and means to secure our independence without impairing our dignity.

I have heard the statement of the British Prime Minister to the effect that he is not able to put any trust in German assurances. Under the circumstances I consider it a matter of course that we no longer wish to expect him or the British people to bear the burden of a situation which is only conceivable in an atmosphere of mutual confidence. When Germany became National Socialist and thus paved the way for her national resurrection, in pursuance of my unswerving policy of friendship with England, of my own accord I made the proposal for a voluntary restriction of German naval armaments. That restriction was, however, based on one condition, namely, the will and the conviction that a war between England and Germany would never again be possible. This wish and this conviction is alive in me to-day.

I am, however, now compelled to state that the policy of England is both unofficially and officially leaving no doubt about the fact that such a conviction is no longer shared in London, and that, on the contrary, the opinion prevails there that no matter in what conflict Germany should some day be entangled, Great Britain would always have to take her stand against Germany. Thus a war against Germany is taken for granted in that country. I most profoundly regret such a development, for the only claim I have ever made, and shall continue to make, on England is that for a return of our colonies. But I always made it very clear that this would never become the cause of a military conflict. I have always held that the English, to whom those colonies are of no value, would one day understand the German situation and would then value German friendship higher than the possession of territories, which, while yielding no real profit whatever to them, are of vital importance to Germany.

Apart from this, however, I have never advanced a claim which might in any way have interfered with British interests or have become a danger to the Empire and thus have meant any kind of damage to England. I have always kept within the limit of such demands as are intimately connected with Germany's living space and thus the eternal property of the German nation. Since England to-day, both by the press and officially, upholds the view that Germany should be opposed under all circumstances, and confirms this by the policy of encirclement known to us, the basis for the Naval Treaty has been removed. I have therefore resolved to send to-day a communication to this effect to the British Government. This is to us not a matter of practical material importance—for I still hope that we shall be able to avoid an armaments race with England—but an action of self-respect. Should the British Government, however, wish to enter once more into negotiations with Germany on this problem, no one would be happier than I at the prospect of still being able to come to a clear and straightforward understanding.

22.

Memorandum from the German Government denouncing the Anglo-German Naval Agreement.

(Translation.)

When in the year 1935 the German Government made the British Government the offer to bring the strength of the German fleet to a fixed proportion of the strength of the naval forces of the British Empire by means of a treaty, it did so on the basis of the firm conviction that for all time the recurrence of a warlike conflict between Germany and Great Britain was excluded. In voluntarily recognizing the priority of British interests at sea through the offer of the ratio 100: 35 it believed that, by means of this decision, unique in the history of the Great Powers, it was taking a step which would lead to the establishment of a friendly relationship for all time between the two nations. This step on the part of the German Government was naturally conditional on the British Government for their part also being determined to adopt a political attitude which would assure a friendly development of Anglo-German relations.

On this basis and under these conditions was the Anglo-German Naval Agreement of the 18th June, 1935, brought into being. This was expressed in agreement by both parties on the conclusion of the agreement. Moreover, last autumn after the Munich Conference the German Chancellor and the British Prime Minister solemnly confirmed in the declaration, which they signed, that they regarded the agreement as symbolical of the desire for both peoples never again to wage war on one another.

The German Government has always adhered to this wish and is still to-day inspired by it. It is conscious of having acted accordingly in its policy and of having in no case intervened in the sphere of English interests or of having in any way encroached on these interests. On the other hand, it must to its regret take note of the fact that the British Government of late is departing more and more from the course of an analogous policy towards Germany. As is clearly shown by the political decisions made known by the British Government in the last weeks as well as by the inspired anti-German attitude of the English press, the British Government is now governed by the opinion that England, in whatever part of Europe Germany might be involved in warlike conflict, must always take up an attitude hostile to Germany, even in a case where English interests are not touched in any way by such a conflict. The British Government thus regards war by England against Germany no longer as an impossibility, but on the contrary as a capital problem of English foreign policy.

By means of this encirclement policy the British Government has unilaterally deprived the Naval Agreement of the 18th June, 1935, of its basis, and has thus put out of force this agreement as well as the complementary declaration of the 17th July, 1937.

The same applies to Part III of the Anglo-German Naval Agreement of the 17th July, 1937, in which the obligation is laid down to make a mutual Anglo-German exchange of information. The execution of this obligation rests naturally on the condition that a relationship of open confidence should exist between two partners. Since the German Government to its regret can no longer regard this relationship as existing, it must also regard the provisions of Part III referred to above as having lapsed.

The qualitative provisions of the Anglo-German Agreement of the 17th July, 1937, remain unaffected by these observations which have been forced upon the German Government against its will. The German Government will abide by these provisions also in the future and so make its contribution to the avoidance of a general unlimited race in the naval armaments of the nations.

Moreover, the German Government, should the British Government desire to enter into negotiations with Germany, in regard to the future problems here arising, is gladly ready to do so. It would welcome it if it then proved possible to reach a clear and categorical understanding on a sure basis.

Berlin, April 27, 1939.

23.

Viscount Halifax to Sir N. Henderson (Berlin).

Foreign Office, June 16, 1939.

Sir,

The German Ambassador called at the Foreign Office this morning to sign a technical agreement of no great importance between the two Governments, and I had a few moments' conversation with him afterwards. In part this followed the familiar line of assertion on his part of the effect that was being produced in Germany by encirclement. The Ambassador expressed the view that, just as the old phrase "The Fleet in being" suggested pressure even without overt action, so now the regrouping of Powers that we were organising was, in fact, designed to operate as coercive pressure on Germany, and it was this which was resented. His Excellency said, and made the same observation at a later stage in our conversation, that much of the feeling at the present time was due to all the discussion about our anti-aggression negotiations with Russia. In his view the situation would be easier when these negotiations were settled one way or the other. I thought this observation perhaps not without significance.

2. I replied by saying that, if anybody was encircling Germany, it was herself by the policy that she persisted in pursuing. Whatever might be thought about the policy now being pursued by this country, it seemed to us quite plain that the German Chancellor had broken the china in Europe and it was only he who could put it together again. We repeatedly made efforts from this side to open the way to a diminution of tension and improvement of relations, but this had so far elicited nothing in the nature of response from Herr Hitler.

3. I told Herr von Dirksen that I hoped he would let me know if at any time he had anything that he might wish to communicate to me that he thought of value, and he replied by expressing a similar wish that I would not hesitate at any time to send for him.

I am,&c.
HALIFAX.

24.

Memorandum from His Majesty's Government of June 23, 1939, replying to the German memorandum* denouncing the Anglo-German Naval Agreement.

General Considerations.

In their memorandum of the 27th April last the German Government state that, in making their offer in 1935 to limit themselves to a percentage of the British naval forces, they did so "on a basis of the firm conviction that for all time the recurrence of a warlike conflict between Germany and Great Britain was excluded."

2. The German Government justify their action in terminating the Anglo-German Naval Agreement of 1935, the Supplementary Declaration of 1937, and Part III of the Naval Agreement of 1937, on the ground that the attitude of His Majesty's Government in the United Kingdom showed that they now held the view that, in whatever part of Europe Germany might be involved in warlike conflict, Great Britain must always be hostile to Germany even in cases where English interests were not touched by such a conflict.

3. The question whether the attitude of His Majesty's Government can in any case justify the German Government in terminating these instruments without, at least, previous consultation between the two Governments is dealt with hereafter. It is not the case that in whatever part of Europe Germany might be involved in warlike conflict Great Britain must always take up an attitude hostile to Germany. Great Britain could only be hostile to Germany if Germany were to

* No. 22.

commit an act of aggression against another country; and the political decisions, to which it is understood the German Government refer in their memorandum, involving guarantees by Great Britain to certain countries, could only operate if the countries concerned were to be attacked by Germany.

4. In the memorandum from the German Government the claim is made to describe British policy as a policy of encirclement. This description is without any justification, and indicates a misunderstanding and misreading of British purposes which must be corrected.

5. The action recently taken by the German Government to incorporate certain territories in the Reich, whatever may have been held by them to be the justifying reasons, has undoubtedly resulted in a great increase of anxiety in many quarters. The actions subsequently taken by the United Kingdom Government have no other purpose than to contribute to the removal of this anxiety, by assisting smaller nations to feel secure in the enjoyment of their independence, to which they have the same right as Great Britain or Germany herself. The commitments which Great Britain has recently undertaken in pursuance of this purpose are limited, and as stated above could only become effective if the countries concerned were the victims of aggression.

6. Nor have His Majesty's Government either the intention or the desire to restrict the development of German trade. On the contrary, under the Anglo-German Payments Agreement a considerable supply of free exchange has been made available to Germany for the acquisition of raw materials. This agreement is as favourable to Germany as any which has been concluded, and His Majesty's Government would look forward to further discussion of measures for the improvement of Germany's economic position, if only the essential pre-condition could be secured, namely, the establishment of mutual confidence and goodwill which is the necessary preliminary to calm and unprejudiced negotiation.

7. The consistent desire of His Majesty's Government, far from being the promotion of a war with Germany, has been and is to establish Anglo-German relations on the basis of the mutual recognition of the needs of both countries, consistently with due regard for the rights of other nations.

8. But, while for these reasons His Majesty's Government cannot agree that there has been any change in their policy or attitude which would justify the recent action of the German Government, they must add that in their view the main object of the Anglo-German Naval Agreement was to introduce an element of stability into the naval situation and to avoid unnecessary competition in armaments.

The Anglo-German Naval Agreement of 1935.

9. For this reason the Agreements contained no provision for unilateral denunciation at the instance of one of the parties alone, but

56

clearly contemplated termination or modification only by mutual consultation — a procedure which His Majesty's Government regret that the German Government have not seen their way to adopt in the present case. The Agreement of 1935, indeed, was expressly stated to be permanent in character, and His Majesty's Government would draw the attention of the German Government to the actual terms of the Exchange of Notes of the 18th June, 1935, which constituted the Anglo-German Naval Agreement of that year, from which both the character of the Agreement and the circumstances in which its modification was contemplated are made absolutely clear.

10. In the opening Note, Sir Samuel Hoare referred to the conversations which had taken place "the primary purpose of which has been to prepare the way for the holding of a general conference on the subject of the limitation of naval armaments." He then referred to the German proposal for a ratio of 100:35 between the fleets of the British Commonwealth and Germany and said that "His Majesty's Government regard this proposal as a contribution of the greatest importance to future naval limitation." He expressed the belief that the Agreement would "facilitate the conclusion of a general agreement on the subject of naval limitation between all the naval Powers of the world."

11. In his reply of the same date, Herr von Ribbentrop recapitulated the terms of Sir Samuel Hoare's Note and confirmed that it correctly set forth the proposal of the German Government. He expressed the opinion that the Agreement "will facilitate the conclusion of a general agreement on this question between all the naval Powers of the world."

12. The wording of the notes thus shows clearly that the Agreement was regarded as a contribution to the solution of the problem of naval limitation. If the German Government now allege that the Agreement has a different meaning, His Majesty's Government must observe that such an allegation finds no warrant in the terms of the Agreement itself, comprehensive and detailed though they were.

13. The Agreement was equally clear on the subject of its duration. In Sir Samuel Hoare's Note it is stated to be "a permanent and definite Agreement as from to-day." Herr von Ribbentrop in his reply stated that the German Government also regarded it "as a permanent and definite agreement with effect from to-day."

14. In paragraph 2 (a) of the Notes it is stated that "the ratio of 35:100 is to be a permanent relationship, i.e., the total tonnage of the German Fleet shall never exceed a percentage of 35 of the aggregate tonnage of the naval forces of the members of the British Commonwealth.

15. In paragraph 2 (c) of the Notes it is stated that "Germany will adhere to the ratio 35:100 in all circumstances, e.g., the ratio will not be affected by the construction of other Powers. If the general equilibrium of naval armaments, as normally maintained in the past, should

be violently upset by any abnormal and exceptional construction by other Powers, the German Government reserve the right to invite His Majesty's Government in the United Kingdom to examine the new situation thus created." This was the only provision which contemplated any general modification (*i.e.*, apart from the special case of submarines) of the terms of the Agreement; and it will be observed that the only condition foreseen that might entail modification was a violent disturbance of the general equilibrium of naval armaments. Moreover, under the terms of the Agreement modification could even then only take place after the situation had been examined in consultation with His Majesty's Government.

16. The German Government, however, do not maintain that such a condition in fact exists. Still less have they invited His Majesty's Government to examine the situation before taking their action. That such consultation was essential is further clear from paragraph 3 of the Notes, which states that His Majesty's Government recognised Germany's right to depart from the 35 per cent. ratio in the circumstances contemplated by paragraph 2 (*c*) "on the understanding that the 35:100 ratio will be maintained in default of agreement to the contrary between the two Governments."

17. Even if the memorandum which the German Government have now addressed to his Majesty's Government is intended to be read, not as a denunciation, but as a statement of the opinion of the German Government that His Majesty's Government have so acted as to cause the Agreement to lose its force, His Majesty's Government cannot admit that such a plea could properly be advanced without any prior consultation between the two Governments as a reason for non-compliance with the express terms of the Agreement.

The Anglo-German Naval Agreement of 1937.

18. Considerations of a similar character apply to the German action regarding Part III of the Anglo-German Naval Agreement of the 17th July, 1937. This Agreement also makes no provision for unilateral denunciation or modification apart from the special cases contemplated by the so-called "escalator clauses" which are not here relevant. Apart from these, the Agreement is expressed to "remain in force until the 31st December, 1942."

19. This Agreement is, moreover, complementary to the London Naval Treaty of 1936, to which France, Italy and the United States are also parties, and to similar agreements between His Majesty's Government and other naval Powers. All these instruments have as their object the avoidance of a useless and expensive competition in naval armaments. This may arise by one country producing special types of ships to which others feel they must reply; or by uncertainty as to the actions and intentions of others and the suspicion that large numbers of ships are being built which must then be matched by competitive

building on the part of those affected. The qualitative limits of these agreements are therefore designed to prevent useless competition in types, and the provisions for exchange of information are designed to destroy unfounded suspicions of excessive building. Even if the relations between two countries were not good, this would not appear to His Majesty's Government to afford ground for terminating an agreement which eliminates unprofitable competition, and prevents a wasteful race in armaments which can benefit neither party.

Qualitative limitation.

20. It is in the light of these considerations, presumably, that the German Government desire the "qualitative provisions of the Anglo-German Agreement of the 17th July, 1937, to remain unaffected." In principle, His Majesty's Government would share this desire: but they are bound to point out that the retention of the qualitative provisions alone will not suffice to create that feeling of mutual security, to which it was the purpose of the Anglo-German Agreement to contribute, and of which the provisions for the exchange of information were the expression. His Majesty's Government would, however, at all times be ready to consider with the German Government the possibility in the words of their Note of reaching "a clear and categorical understanding" on a sure basis.

21. From the terms in which the German Government announced their decision to retain the qualitative limits of the 1937 Agreement, it is not clear what are the exact limitations by which they consider themselves to be bound in the matter of cruisers. The qualitative limits of cruisers are fixed by Article 6 (1) of the Anglo-German Agreement of 1937 as 8,000 tons displacement with guns not exceeding 6.1-inch calibre, and it is by this limit that all signatory Powers of the London Naval Treaty of 1936 are also bound. Although Article 6 (2) of the Anglo-German Agreement of 1937 permitted Germany under certain circumstances to increase her 8-inch gun cruiser tonnage, she was in practice precluded from building more than five such cruisers by the limits of her quota under the 1935 Agreement. Now that the German Government have terminated the latter Agreement, the position with regard to cruiser limits is no longer clear, but it is presumed that the limit to which the German Government intend to adhere is that of 8,000 tons and 6.1-inch guns. The German Government are requested to confirm this assumption.

22. The past forecasts of strength at the end of 1942 and 1943 that His Majesty's Government have made to the German Government have been given solely for the purpose of implementing the provisions of the 1935 Agreement. It is clear that no further forecasts will be necessary since they were designed merely to allow Germany to make full use of her 1935 quota. But if Germany is to be no longer bound to the limit of 35 per cent. specified in the Agreement, it should be clearly understood that His Majesty's Government can no longer be

bound by their past forecasts of strength, which must therefore be considered to be cancelled.

23. In the last paragraph of their memorandum the German Government declare that they are ready to enter into negotiations in regard to future problems, if His Majesty's Government desire to do so. As indicated above, there results from the recent German action a situation which is in some respects uncertain, and an exchange of views would help to clarify it. For instance, besides the question of tonnage and gun limits for cruisers, it is desirable to know whether the German Government intend to regard themselves as bound by all the articles of the Agreement of 1937 other than those in Part III.

24. If, however, what the German Government contemplate is the negotiation of another Agreement to replace those provisions which they have now terminated, His Majesty's Government would be glad to receive some indication of the scope and purpose which the German Government would consider appropriate to such an Agreement.

25. In particular His Majesty's Government desire to know, first, when, in the German view, discussion for the conclusion of such an Agreement should take place. Secondly, His Majesty's Government desire to know how the German Government would propose to ensure that any action in the shape of denunciation or modification of the new Agreement during the terms of its validity should carry the consent of both parties.

25.

Speech by the Secretary of State for Foreign Affairs at Chatham House on June 29, 1939.

When I look back to the speech which I delivered at the Chatham House Dinner in June a year ago, I am conscious, as we all are, of the great changes that have taken place. A year ago we had undertaken no specific commitments on the Continent of Europe, beyond those which had then existed for some considerable time and are familiar to you all. To-day we are bound by new agreements for mutual defence with Poland and Turkey: we have guaranteed assistance to Greece and Roumania against aggression, and we are now engaged with the Soviet Government in a negotiation, to which I hope there may very shortly be a successful issue, with a view to associating them with us for the defence of States in Europe whose independence and neutrality may be threatened. We have assumed obligations, and are preparing to assume more, with full understanding of their causes and with full understanding of their consequences. We know that, if the security and independence of other countries are to disappear, our own security and our own independence will be gravely threatened. We know that, if international law and order is to be preserved, we must be prepared to fight in its defence.

60

In the past we have always stood out against the attempt by any single Power to dominate Europe at the expense of the liberties of other nations, and British policy is, therefore, only following the inevitable line of its own history, if such an attempt were to be made again. But it is not enough to state a policy. What matters is, firstly, to convince the nation that the policy is right, and secondly, to take the steps necessary for that policy to succeed. I believe that at no time since the War has there been such national unity on the main essentials of our foreign policy, and that with this spirit of unity goes a deep and widespread determination to make that policy effective. But I believe, too, that among all classes of our people who, in virtue of their common citizenship, are being called upon to defend their country, and the causes for which it stands, there is an increasing desire to look beyond the immediate present, and to see before them some goal for which they would willingly sacrifice their leisure and, if need be, their lives.

We are already asking for great sacrifices from all ages and classes in the call for national service. In one way and another, every man and woman has a part to play, and I know is prepared to do so. The immense effort that the country is making in equipping itself for defence at sea, in the air and on land is without parallel in peace time. We have an unchallengeable Navy. Our Air Force, still undergoing an expansion which has outstripped all expectations of a few months ago, has now nothing to fear from any other. I have little doubt that its personnel, in spirit and in skill, is superior to all others. Our army, once derided, but which survived to prove its worth so that it made a boast of that derision, is, no doubt, small in comparison with that of some other countries. But, as happened once before, we are creating here also a powerful weapon for the defence of our own liberty and that of other peoples. With every week that passes, that effort gains momentum, and on every side of life, political, administrative, industrial, we have abundant evidence of how firmly this national effort is driven and supported by the people's will. Behind all our military effort stand the British people, more united than ever before, and at their service their wealth and industrial resources. These, again are the object of contemptuous reference, but they have been earned by the labour, skill and courage of our people. None of this formidable array of strength will be called into play except in defence against aggression. No blow will be struck, no shot fired. Of the truth of that, everyone in this country is convinced. I believe, myself, that most people in other countries really accept it in spite of the propaganda that dins into their ears the contrary. What is also now fully and universally accepted in this country, but what may not even yet be as well understood elsewhere, is that, in the event of further aggression, we are resolved to use at once the whole of our strength in fulfilment of our pledges to resist it.

These great changes in our national life could not, indeed, be brought about, were they not backed by deep conviction, which is

61

immensely strengthened by what we hear and read almost daily from other parts of the world. We are often told that, though once we were a great nation, our ways are now old-fashioned, and that our democracy has no life in it. We read the mischievous misrepresentations of our actions and of our motives, which some people in countries holding a different international philosophy from our own think fit to make. We read them with resentment, knowing that they are false and knowing that those who make them know it, too. These things do not pass unnoticed here, nor, I may say, do provocative insults offered to our fellow-countrymen further afield. I can say at once that Great Britain is not prepared to yield either to calumnies or force. It may afford some satisfaction to those who have pronounced our nation to be decadent to learn that they themselves have found the cure—and one most effective. Every insult that is offered to our people, every rude challenge that is made to what we value and are determined to defend, only unites us, increases our determination and strengthens our loyalty to those others who share our feelings and aspirations. Over a large part of the world the old standards of conduct and of ordinary human decency, which man had laboriously built up, are being set aside. Things are being done to-day which we can hardly read without amazement; so alien are they to our conception of how men should deal with their fellow-men. Rules of conduct between nations are overridden with the same callous indifference as rules of conduct between man and man.

The first thing, therefore, which we have to do is to see that our own standards of conduct do not deteriorate. On that point there must be—and I know there is—complete national unity. We respect our fellow-men. We know that without that there can be no real self-respect either for individuals, or, in the long run, for nations. The day that we lose our respect for our fellow-men, our democracy would have lost something on which its vitality depends, and would justly become what our critics like to think it, moribund and dead, for it would, indeed, have lost the right to live. If, then, we hold fast to these principles, what is the application of them to our foreign policy? At a time when our aims are being constantly misrepresented, it is perhaps well to restate them boldly and with such plainness of speech as I can command. And I would try to deal briefly both with our aims in the immediate present, and our aims in the future; what we are doing now and what we should like to see done as soon as circumstances make it possible.

Our first resolve is to stop aggression. I need not recapitulate the acts of aggression which have taken place, or the effect they have had upon the general trust that European nations feel able to place in words and undertakings. For that reason, and for that reason alone, we have joined with other nations to meet a common danger. These arrangements we all know, and the world knows, have no purpose other than defence. They mean what they say—no more and no less. But they have been denounced as aiming at the isolation—or, as it is called, the encirclement—of Germany and Italy, and as designed to prevent them from acquiring the living space necessary for their national existence. I shall deal with these charges to-night, and I propose to do so with complete frankness.

We are told that our motives are to isolate Germany within a ring of hostile States, to stifle her natural outlets, to cramp and throttle the very existence of a great nation. What are the facts? They are very simple and everybody knows them. Germany is isolating herself, and doing it most successfully and completely. She is isolating herself from other countries economically by her policy of autarky, politically by a policy that causes constant anxiety to other nations, and culturally by her policy of racialism. If you deliberately isolate yourself from others by your own actions you can blame nobody but yourself, and so long as this isolation continues, the inevitable consequences of it are bound to become stronger and more marked. The last thing we desire is to see the individual German man, or woman, or child suffering privations; but if they do so, the fault does not lie with us, and it depends on Germany and Germany alone whether this process of isolation continues or not, for any day it can be ended by a policy of co-operation. It is well that this should be stated plainly so that there may be no misunderstanding here or elsewhere.

I come next to *Lebensraum*. This word, of which we have not heard the last, needs to be fairly and carefully examined. Every developed community is, of course, faced with the vital problem of living space. But the problem is not solved simply by acquiring more territory. That may indeed only make the problem more acute. It can only be solved by wise ordering of the affairs of a country at home, and by adjusting and improving its relations with other countries abroad. Nations expand their wealth, and raise the standard of living of their people by gaining the confidence of their neighbours, and thus facilitating the flow of goods between them. The very opposite is likely to be the consequence of action by one nation in suppression of the independent existence of her smaller and weaker neighbours. And if *Lebensraum* is to be applied in that sense, we reject it and must resist its application. It is noteworthy that this claim to "living space" is being put forward at a moment when Germany has become an immigration country, importing workers in large numbers from Czecho-Slovakia, Holland and Italy to meet the needs of her industry and agriculture. How then can Germany claim to be over-populated? Belgium and Holland, and to a less extent our own islands, have already proved that what is called over-population can be prevented by productive work. The wide spaces and the natural resources of the British Empire and the United States of America were not able to save them from widespread distress during the great slump of 1929 to 1932. Economically the world is far too closely knit together for any one country to hope to profit itself at the expense of its neighbours, and no more than any other country can Germany hope to solve her economic problems in isolation. It is no doubt impossible

63

at present for us to foresee the day when all trade everywhere will be completely free. But it is possible to make arrangements, given the opportunities, which would greatly enlarge the area of freedom. Through co-operation—and we, for our part, are ready to co-operate—there is ample scope for extending to all nations the opportunity of a larger economic life with all that this means, which is implied in the term "*Lebensraum.*"

If the world were organised on such lines, neither Germany nor Italy need fear for her own safety, and no nation could fail to profit from the immense material benefits which the general application of science has brought within universal reach. But no such society of nations can be built upon force, in a world which lives in fear of violence, and has to spend its substance in preparing to resist it. It is idle to cry peace where there is no peace, or to pretend to reach a settlement unless it can be guaranteed by the reduction of warlike preparations, and by the assured recognition of every nation's right to the free enjoyment of its independence. At this moment the doctrine of force bars the way to settlement, and fills the world with envy, hatred, malice and all uncharitableness. But if the doctrine of force were once abandoned, so that the fear of war that stalks the world was lifted, all outstanding questions would become easier to solve. If all the effort which is now devoted to the senseless multiplication of armaments, with the consequent increase of insecurity and distrust, were to be applied to the common peaceful development of resources, the peoples of the world would soon find an incentive to work together for the common good; they would realise that their true interests do not conflict, and that progress and well-being depend upon community of aim and effort. The nations would then be in a position to discuss with real promise of success both political grievances and economic difficulties, whether in the international or colonial field.

This brings me to say something about the principles of our colonial administration. There was a time when in the British Empire, as elsewhere, colonies were regarded merely as a source of wealth and a place of settlement for Europeans. You have only to read any of the colonial literature of those days to see for how little counted the rights and welfare of the natives. But during the last half century a very different view has gained ground, a view which has been finely expressed in Article 22 of the Covenant, namely, that the well-being and development of "people not yet able to stand by themselves under the strenuous conditions of the modern world" is "a sacred trust of civilisation."

That trust has been steadily fulfilled since the War in the case of the Mandated Territories, on which the operation of the provisions of Article 22 of the Covenant has conferred immense benefits. The British Commonwealth is fully aware of the heavy responsibility resting upon it to see that, through respect for these principles, continuity and development is assured to the native populations. The mandatory system, in fact, derives from exactly the same inspiration as

64

that which governs British colonial administrative policy. We have applied the same principles to India and Burma, where they are now steadily at work on a scale that twenty or thirty years ago would have seemed far beyond the bounds of reasonable expectation. Within the last few years we have seen the transformation of Eire into a separate and independent member of the British Commonwealth, enjoying with our other partners of the Empire full Dominion status. For many years we tried, as the phrase went, to hold Ireland, under the mistaken belief, which is to-day invoked to justify the subjection of Czecho-Slovakia, that it was indispensable to our national security. But we have now realised that our safety is not diminished, but immeasurably increased, by a free and friendly Ireland. And so both here and in every country for which we have been responsible we have steadily moved in one direction. The whole picture is a significant and faithful reflection of British thought, projected into political form, and expressing itself, through history and now, in the development of institutions. We recognise, as the United States have recognised, that self-government should be the ultimate goal of colonial policy, a goal which is near or distant, according to the capacity of the peoples concerned to manage their own affairs. In one of your own studies, "The Colonial Problem," the type of research which enhances the name and reputation of Chatham House, you have considered the question whether colonies pay. You drew attention to the benefits of cheap imports which the consumers of a country possessing colonies obtain as the result of the relatively low cost of production of certain commodities in colonial territories. But under an international system, under which the present trade barriers were to a great extent abolished, those benefits, already shared as they are to a considerable extent by many countries not possessing colonies, would be shared still more widely. On all sides there could be more free and ready access to markets and raw materials of the world; wider channels of trade down which would flow the goods which nations require to buy and sell. Such are some of the possibilities within everybody's reach.

How does all this affect our wider problems? One of the most significant facts in world history is the extent to which the principle of trusteeship has come to be adopted in the British Commonwealth during the last thirty years, and there is surely something here that can be used for the great benefit of mankind. Can we not look forward to a time when there may be agreement on common methods and aims of colonial development, which may ensure not only that the universally acknowledged purpose of colonial administration will be to help their inhabitants steadily to raise their level of life, but also that colonial territories may make a growing contribution to the world's resources? On such an agreed foundation of purpose we hope that others might be prepared with us to make their contribution to a better world. If so, I have no doubt that in the conduct of our colonial administration we should be ready to go far upon the economic side, as we have already done on the political side, in making wider applica-

65

tion of the principles which now obtain in the mandated territories, including, on terms of reciprocity, that of the open door. Whatever may be the difficulties of the colonial problem, or of any other, I would not despair of finding ways of settlement, once everybody has got the will to settle. But, unless all countries do, in fact, desire a settlement, discussions would only do more harm than good. It is, moreover, impossible to negotiate with a Government whose responsible spokesmen brand a friendly country as thieves and blackmailers and indulge in daily monstrous slanders on British policy in all parts of the world. But if that spirit, which is clearly incompatible with any desire for a peaceful settlement, gave way to something different, His Majesty's Government would be ready to pool their best thought with others in order to end the present state of political and economic insecurity. If we could get so far, what an immense stride the world would have made! We should have exorcised the anxiety which is cramping and arresting business expansion and we should have brought back an atmosphere of confidence among nations and assurance for the future among the youth of this and every other European country. Our next task would be the reconstruction of the international order on a broader and firmer foundation. That is too large a topic for me to embark upon this evening, but I should like to commend it to your thinking.

We must ask ourselves how far the failure of the League was due to shortcomings in the Covenant itself, or how far it was the absence of some of the greatest countries at every stage of its history that has crippled both its moral authority and strength. Is it beyond the political genius of mankind to reconcile national individuality with international collaboration? Can human purpose rise high enough to solve the riddle? An examination of the history of the Covenant may perhaps disclose that some of its obligations were too loose and others too rigid. It has been suggested, for instance, that some system of specific regional guarantees for the preservation of the peace would be more effective than the indefinite but universal obligations of Articles 10 and 16, and it is not impossible that the grouping of the Powers as it exists to-day, instead of dividing Europe, might be so moulded as to become the embryo of a better European system.

That is one side of the problem. But it is not enough to devise measures for preventing the use of force to change the *status quo*, unless there is also machinery for bringing about peaceful change. For a living and changing world can never be held in iron clamps, and any such attempt is the high road to disaster. Changes in the relations, needs, and outlook of nations are going on all the time. And there is no more urgent need, if we are ever to find a workable system of international organisation, than to invent peaceful means by which such changes can be handled. To-day when the European nations, forgetful of their common civilisation, are arming to the teeth, it is more important than ever that we should remind ourselves of the essential unity of European civilisation. European minds meet across

66

political frontiers. With the same background of knowledge, with the same heritage of culture, they study the same problems; the work of the great masters of science, and literature or art is the common property of all peoples; and thinkers in every land exchange knowledge on equal and friendly terms. Truly is a divided Europe a house divided against itself. Our foreign policy must, therefore, constantly bear in mind the immediate present and the more distant future, the steps we are now taking and the goal to which they are meant to lead.

I have strained your patience, but if you will allow me a few moments more I will endeavour to pick up the threads of my thought and perhaps make a few points more explicit. British policy rests on twin foundations of purpose. One is determination to resist force. The other is our recognition of the world's desire to get on with the constructive work of building peace. If we could once be satisfied that the intentions of others were the same as our own, and that we all really wanted peaceful solutions—then, I say here definitely, we could discuss the problems that are to-day causing the world anxiety. In such a new atmosphere we could examine the colonial problem, the questions of raw materials, trade barriers, the issue of *Lebensraum,* the limitation of armaments, and any other issue that affects the lives of all European citizens.

But that is not the position which we face to-day. The threat of military force is holding the world to ransom, and our immediate task is — and here I end as I began — resist aggression. I would emphasize that to-night with all the strength at my command, so that nobody may misunderstand it. And if we are ever to succeed in removing misunderstanding and reaching a settlement which the world can trust, it must be upon some basis more substantial than verbal undertakings. It has been said that deeds, not words, are necessary. That also is our view. There must be give and take in practical form on both sides, for there can be no firm bargains on the basis of giving something concrete in return for mere assurances. None of us can in these days see very far ahead in the world in which we live, but we can and must always be sure of the general direction in which we wish to travel. Let us, therefore, be very sure that, whether or not we are to preserve for ourselves and for others the things that we hold dear, depends in the last resort upon ourselves, upon the strength of the personal faith of each one of us, and upon our resolution to maintain it.

Deterioration in the local situation at Danzig

26.

Note from the President of the Danzig Senate to the Polish Commissioner-General of June 3, 1939, about the question of Polish Customs Inspectors.

(Translation.)

Mr. Minister,

Several months ago I had the honour to draw your attention to the fact that the ever-increasing number of Polish Customs Inspectors was not compatible with the execution of their prescribed duties. Since the latest additions there are now well over 100 Polish Customs Inspectors in Danzig territory. Their behaviour, both in their official and their private life, has given rise to increasing complaint. The Danzig population, like the German population, in their local frontier intercourse feel themselves constantly offended by the way in which the Polish Customs officials perform their duty and by their behaviour in private life.

I have no fear that incidents on the part of the population might arise on that account. Still less is the safety of the Polish officials in any way endangered. I have therefore taken steps to ensure that they may, as hitherto, perform their duties absolutely safely and without hindrance. I believe, however, that ways and means must be found to eliminate the constant friction and tension.

For all these reasons I consider it necessary forthwith to restrict the activity of the Polish Customs Inspectors to a general supervision in conformity with the agreement. In particular, I must urge that their official activities be confined to the offices, and not performed outside of them. I can also no longer permit the Danzig Customs officials to take instructions, even in the form of suggestions, from the Polish Customs officials. I will, however, see that questions addressed to officials will be answered officially.

I have directed the President of the Customs Administration of the Free City to instruct his officials accordingly. I have the honour, Mr. Minister, to request you to inform your Government accordingly and to exert your influence towards meeting the wishes of the Danzig Government.

I avail myself of this opportunity to revert to our conversation of the 8th February last. At that time I explained to you, Mr. Minister, that I would give instructions to abstain for the present from swearing in the customs officials, and that, should the occasion arise, I would communicate with you before administering the oath.

I have the honour to inform you, with reference to the contents of my letter of the 3rd January last (pages 2 and 3), that I have now left it to the discretion of the Finance Department of the Senate to administer the oath to the customs officials if they regard it as desirable.

I have, &c.
GREISER.

27.

Sir H. Kennard to Viscount Halifax.

(Telegraphic.) *Warsaw, June 11, 1939.*

Following is full summary of note, as published here, addressed on 10th June by Polish Commissioner-General to President of Danzig Senate in reply to latter's note of 3rd June*:—

2. President of Senate's complaint of behaviour of Polish Customs Inspectors on and off duty is not supported by any proofs and must be regarded as unfounded. On the other hand, behaviour of certain Danzig elements, including Customs officials, has been highly provocative, as Commissioner-General has frequently pointed out orally and in writing. Polish Inspectors have reacted with dignity and moderation and refused to be provoked. The Polish Government still expect Senate to take measures to secure personal safety of Polish Customs Inspectors to allow free execution of their duty, with reference to Point 3 of Polish-Danzig Agreement of 1922, which lays down that Polish officials in Danzig should receive the same treatment as corresponding Danzig officials.

3. As regards alleged excessive number of Polish Customs officials, Polish Government, on the contrary, consider it at present rather insufficient. This can be shown by present state of affairs as regards handling of goods in Danzig harbour and passenger traffic between Danzig and Poland, and is partly due to obstruction encountered by officials in execution of their duty.

4. Polish Government, moreover, cannot agree to any restriction of activity of Polish Inspectors as forecast in note of Danzig Senate. Present treaty arrangements would not permit of Inspectors merely exercising general supervision within customs offices, a restriction which would be contrary to Sections 1 and 4 of Article 204 of the Warsaw Treaty of the 24th October, 1921. In this connexion Polish note also quotes Article 10 of Polish-Danzig Customs Agreement of the 6th August, 1934, which lays down that Danzig officials shall conform to instructions of Polish Customs Inspectors in connexion with manifest cases of smuggling.

5. Polish Government must regard Senate as fully responsible for any disputes which may arise in this last connexion, and must

* No. 26.

69

regard as illegal and contrary to treaty obligations any attempts by Danzig Customs authorities arbitrarily to restrict Polish rights of control. Instructions given to Danzig Customs officials as described in Senate's note must be regarded as a violation of the principle of collaboration between Danzig Customs Administration and Polish Inspectors. Latter have been instructed to continue exercising their functioning within the same limits — which are in conformity with treaty situation — as in the past twenty years, and hope is expressed that they will not meet with obstruction from Danzig authorities.

6. As regards question of swearing-in Customs officials, Polish note refers to written communications of Senate on this subject and to Commissioner-General's interviews with President. Should Senate not take account of fully justified demands of Polish Government, and should they proceed to swearing-in of officials in spite of assurance by President of Senate that this would not take place except after consultation with Commissioner-General, Polish Government will have to consider question of strengthening customs control, since Danzig Customs officials will in future be giving a less binding guarantee of their respect for, and proper execution of, Polish Customs regulations.

7. Essence of whole question is that territory of Free City is part of Polish Customs Territory, both legally and in virtue of treaty obligations. Authorities must therefore be assured of thorough-going execution of their Polish customs policy and regulations on external frontier of their Customs territory. Hence any measures by Danzig authorities which threaten to obstruct, if only in part, the functioning of the Polish Customs system can only provoke reaction by Polish Government in the form of measures designed fully to protect Poland's rightful interest.

8. Polish Government desire, as before, to regulate all vital questions concerning Free City of Danzig in agreement with Danzig Senate. In the situation recently created, however, they consider it their duty to warn the Senate that any shortcomings or obstructions in functioning of Polish Customs system and administration must react unfavourably on the economic interests of Danzig and its population, a consequence which Polish Government desire to avoid.

28.

Sir H. Kennard to Viscount Halifax.

(Telegraphic.) *Warsaw, June 27, 1939.*

I asked the Vice-Minister for Foreign Affairs this morning what information he had regarding the constitution of the Freicorps at Danzig. He told me that according to Polish information a corps of 4,000 was being formed of whom 2,000 would be quartered at barracks in Danzig itself and 2,000 in new buildings which were being constructed at Praust.

2. As regards the general situation in Danzig it was perhaps a little better. There had been some fifty cases of Danzig officials refusing to carry out the instructions of the Polish Customs Inspectors during the past fortnight, but during the past few days there had been no cases of this kind. This may be due to the fact that the arms for the Freicorps were being surreptitiously introduced into the Free City from East Prussia during the past fortnight and that presumably now that the arms were in Danzig there is less occasion for contravention of the Polish Customs regulations.

3. M. Arciszewski did not think that Germany would go to the length of risking a general war in connexion with Danzig, but felt that she would gradually strengthen her position there, weaken any authority that Poland might still have there and hope that Poland would finally be reduced to such a state of economic exhaustion that she would have to accept some solution as regards Danzig which would be favourable to Germany. Further, Germany would in the meantime, no doubt, assiduously propagate the idea that Great Britain and France would not implement their guarantee as regards Danzig and thereby endeavour still further to undermine Polish morale.

29.

Mr. G. Shepherd to Viscount Halifax.

(Telegraphic.)   *Danzig, June 28, 1939.*

In contrast to calm in Warsaw, the last week has been increasingly eventful here.

2. For the past fortnight the S.A. men have been nightly preparing defences around the Free City, and on the night of 26th-27th June were ordered to stand by for a possible emergency, perhaps in connexion with celebration in Gdynia of Polish Feast of the Seas or because Polish frontier on Danzig-Gydnia road was closed to traffic from midnight on 26th-27th June until 4 p.m. on 27th June, presumably in connexion with completion of anti-tank defences.

3. The approaches for a pontoon bridge are in active construction on both sides of the Vistula.

4. On 23rd June Danzig members of German Automobile Club received an urgent request to complete and return a *questionnaire* regarding their cars.

5. All Danzig owners of motor lorries, trucks, &c., were recently ordered to leave them over-night at military police barracks for inspection after which each vehicle was numbered and returned to its owner.

6. To-day several hundred draught and saddle horses have been similarly ordered to barracks nominally for inspection, but as some of them have come from distant parts of the Free City, it seems possible

that they may be retained, especially as car-loads of saddles have also been delivered there.

7. Formation of Freicorps is proceeding rapidly.

8. In addition to unusually heavily advertised programme of week-end events, nearly 1,000 S.S. men from East Prussia and a number of high S.S. officers from Germany arrived here almost unannounced on 25th June ostensibly for sporting contests with local S.S.

9. Dr. Boettcher was absent from Danzig and presumably in Berlin on 26th June and 27th June.

10. In a speech on 25th June Herr Forster said: "Before us lies a new era and for Germany a great epoch. During recent weeks our Danzig has become the centre of political events. We are all aware that we are in the final throes of our fight for freedom. The Free State of Danzig has taken the longest time. To-day everyone knows that the Free State will soon come to an end and we also know how it will end."

11. A considerable number of visiting S.S. men remained here when others left last Sunday night. Those remaining are reputed to have performed their military service in Germany and to be members of Adolf Hitler's Verfüqungstruppen. They are readily distinguishable by their deportment and slightly different uniforms from local S.S. men. About 300 of them are in military police barracks which are now very full, and others are in other former local barracks which are capable of accommodating from 1,000 to 1,500 men, and have hitherto been occupied by Danzig social welfare organisation which is being transferred to an hotel that has been requisitioned for the purpose. According to sub-editor of *Dantziger Vorposten,* the largest youth hostel in the world, which is approaching completion here, is to be used as a barracks.

12. A number of workmen's dwellings at Praust are said to have been requisitioned for storage of ammunition, and my Argentine colleague informs me that he saw a number of military police equipped with gas masks.

13. All Danzig civil servants and students are required to remain within the Free City during their vacations, and the latter must devote their holidays to harvesting. All categories of military police have been kept in barracks yesterday and to-day, and to-night members of various National Socialist organisations are apparently again standing by, as remarkably few of them are visible about the City.

30.

Viscount Halifax to Sir H. Kennard (Warsaw).

(Telegraphic.) *Foreign Office, June 30, 1939.*

You should at once seek interview with Minister for Foreign Affairs and ask him how the Polish Government propose to deal with the situation which appears to be impending. It would seem that Hitler is laying his plans very astutely so as to present the Polish

Government with a *fait accompli* in Danzig, to which it would be difficult for them to react without appearing in the rôle of aggressors. I feel that the moment has come where consultation between the Polish, British and French Governments is necessary in order that the plans of the three Governments may be co-ordinated in time. It is in the view of His Majesty's Government essential that these plans shall be so devised as to ensure that Hitler shall not be able so to manage matters as to manoeuvre the Polish Government into the position of aggressors.

31.

Mr. G. Shepherd to Viscount Halifax.

(Telegraphic.)   *Danzig, June 30, 1939.*

Horses continued to arrive yesterday, and about 600 of them are being kept in barracks at which large quantities of hay have also been delivered.

2. For the last few nights the two great shipyards here which normally work all night were closed under strict guard and all workmen evacuated from them.

3. As from to-night Danzig and suburbs were to be blacked out until further notice and, in case of air raid alarm, all inhabitants were ordered to take refuge in their cellars or public shelters. This order was cancelled this afternoon.

4. Former local barracks are now occupied by large number of young men with obvious military training who wear uniforms similar to Danzig S.S. but with deathshead emblem on the right collar and "Heimwehr Danzig" on sleeves. Courtyard is occupied by about fifteen military motor lorries (some with trailers) with East Prussia licences and covered with tarpaulins, also by about forty field kitchens.

5. Two thousand men are working twenty-four hours a day in three shifts on construction of barracks at Matzkshuter to accommodate 10,000 men. Work is stated to be well advanced.

6. All dressmakers here are said to be working on bedding, clothing, &c., for barracks and their occupants.

7. It has just been announced that Tiegenmorse-Einlage section of Danzig-Elbing road is closed for major repairs until 1st August, and it seems unlikely that pontoon bridge will be ready before that date.

8. My personal impression is that extensive military preparations which are being pressed forward so feverishly are part of large-scale operations but not intended for use before August, unless unexpected developments precipitate matters and that emergency defensive measures, referred to in paragraphs 1, 2 and 3 of this telegram, may be due to fear lest those preparations should cause the Poles to substitute a sudden offensive for defensive measures which they have hitherto adopted.

32.

Mr. Norton to Viscount Halifax.

(Telegraphic.)   Warsaw, July 1, 1939.

Your telegram of 30th June.*

I read M. Beck the gist of your telegram. M. Beck said that he would first give me a piece of information. German Government yesterday notified the Polish Government in proper legal manner that the *Königsberg* would visit Danzig for three days on 25th August. Polish Government were at once passing this on to the Danzig Senate with all courtesy adding that they had no objection.

2. Passing to the substance of your Lordship's message, M. Beck asked me to assure you that he entirely shared your view as to the necessity of foreseeing a situation in which Poland might be manœuvred into a dilemma of either accepting a *fait accompli* or appearing to be aggressive.

3. He therefore was fully in favour of an exchange of views. He was, however, leaving Warsaw this evening for forty-eight hours and would prefer to go into the matter more thoroughly with me on Tuesday when he had thought things over especially as he had only returned yesterday from a week's leave.

4. He said that reading between the lines of your message he felt you might be thinking of a joint *démarche* in Berlin. He did not at first sight think the time had come for this. It might put us all into a position where we had to proceed more vigorously than seemed wise to either of our two countries.

5. I asked whether he thought Great Britain's action would be better taken with the Danzig Senate. He was inclined to think so but preferred not to commit himself at the moment.

6. He asked me to assure you that despite some people's ideas of Polish rashness, the Polish Government were determined not to be scared by any psychological terrorism into imprudent action. Only last night there had been a rumour (the forty-ninth of its kind) that the Germans were going to march into Danzig at once. He had seen the Polish Chief of Staff and it had been decided that not one Polish soldier was to be moved. He had gone to bed and slept peacefully.

7. I asked if it was not the case that recent Nazi activities in Danzig were creating a worse military position for Poland. M. Beck replied that it was in a sense true, but a war was not won by a few thousand "tourists". The Germans knew that quite well and were mainly hoping to provoke and intimidate Poland. They would not succeed, and it must be clear to them now that any actual aggression would be met by the solid block of Great Britain, France and Poland.

8. He had not changed his attitude one jot since he spoke with you and the Prime Minister in London. He still desired peaceful and normal relations with Germany.

* No. 30.

74

Mr. G. Shepherd to Viscount Halifax.

(Telegraphic.) *Danzig, July 1, 1939.*

Yesterday morning four German army officers in mufti arrived here by night express from Berlin to organize Danzig Heimwehr.

2. All approaches to hills and dismantled fort, which constitute a popular public promenade on western fringe of the city have been closed with barbed wire and "Verboten" notices.

3. The walls surrounding the shipyards bear placards "Comrades, keep your mouths shut lest you regret consequences."

4. Master of a British steamship whilst he was roving Königsberg from 28th June to 30th June observed considerable military activity, including extensive shipment of camouflaged covered lorries and similar material by small coasting vessels. On 28th June four medium-sized steamers loaded with troops, lorries, field kitchens, &c., left Königsberg ostensibly returning to Hamburg after manoeuvres but actually proceeding to Stettin. Names of steamers were *Hohenhorn,* with heavy derricks each capable of lifting about 50 tons, *Sharhorn, Tilsit* and *Utlandhorn,* all modern well-equipped vessels, each about 5,000 tons gross.

34.

Mr. Norton to Viscount Halifax.

(Telegraphic.) *Warsaw, July 3, 1939.*

From the austere calm which continues to prevail in Polish official circles and generally throughout Poland, it would appear that gradual remilitarisation of Free City of Danzig has not yet attained dimensions sufficiently serious to alarm Polish Government.

2. They are, of course, aware that the process is intended to facilitate a *coup* by Herr Hitler should he decide on one.

3. Their attitude to this latter possibility seems to be as follows:—

(a) They are strengthening their powers of defence ceaselessly and to the extent of their financial ability;

(b) They have no intention of provoking a quarrel or of showing weakness;

(c) If their rights in Danzig and the Corridor are seriously threatened they will reply by counter-measures proportionate to the circumstances;

(d) That Herr Hitler will think twice before challenging the anti-aggression front openly;

(e) If he does so, Poland will put up the best show she can.

4. This attitude may seem over-simplified, but at least it is comprehensible, restrained, and well-calculated to counteract German technique of "psychological terrorism".

5. It is unfortunately inevitable that the initiative should rest with the would-be aggressor.

British Attitude towards developments in Danzig.

35.

*Statement by the Prime Minister in the House of Commons on
July 10, 1939.*

Mr. Harold Macmillan asked the Prime Minister whether His
Majesty's Government will issue a declaration to the effect that any
change in the present status of Danzig, other than by an agreement
to which the Polish Government is a party, whether brought about
externally by military action on the part of Germany or internally by
a movement initiated or supported by the German Government, will
be regarded as an act of aggression on the part of Germany and,
therefore, covered by the terms of our pledge to Poland?

Lieut.-Commander Fletcher asked the Prime Minister whether any
attempt to alter the existing régime at Danzig by aggression from
outside or penetration from within will be regarded as within the
terms of our pledge to maintain the independence of Poland; and has
a communication been made to the Polish Government in these terms?

Mr. A. Henderson asked the Prime Minister whether he has any
statement to make on the present situation in Danzig?

Mr. V. Adams asked the Prime Minister whether he has any
further statement to make on the attitude of His Majesty's Government
towards the position of Danzig?

Mr. Thurtle asked the Prime Minister whether he is now satisfied
that the head of the German Government no longer has any doubt of
the intention of this country to discharge to the full the undertaking
it has given to Poland; or has he under consideration any further action
with a view to removing any possible doubt or misunderstanding which
may still exist?

The Prime Minister: I would ask hon. Members to be good enough
to await the statement which I propose to make at the end of questions.

Later—

The Prime Minister: I have previously stated that His Majesty's
Government are maintaining close contact with the Polish and French
Governments on the question of Danzig. I have nothing at present to
add to the information which has already been given to the House
about the local situation. But I may, perhaps, usefully review the
elements of this question as they appear to His Majesty's Government.

76

Racially Danzig is, almost wholly, a German city; but the prosperity of its inhabitants depends to a very large extent upon Polish trade. The Vistula is Poland's only waterway to the Baltic, and the port at its mouth is therefore of vital strategic and economic importance to her. Another Power established in Danzig could, if it so desired, block Poland's access to the sea and so exert an economic and military stranglehold upon her. Those who were responsible for framing the present statute of the Free City were fully conscious of these facts, and did their best to make provision accordingly. Moreover, there is no question of any oppression of the German population in Danzig. On the contrary, the administration of the Free City is in German hands, and the only restrictions imposed upon it are not of a kind to curtail the liberties of its citizens. The present settlement, though it may be capable of improvement, cannot in itself be regarded as basically unjust or illogical. The maintenance of the *status quo* had in fact been guaranteed by the German Chancellor himself up to 1944 by the ten-year Treaty which he had concluded with Marshal Pilsudski.

Up till last March Germany seems to have felt that, while the position of Danzig might ultimately require revision, the question was neither urgent nor likely to lead to a serious dispute. But in March, when the German Government put forward an offer in the form of certain desiderata accompanied by a press campaign, the Polish Government realised that they might presently be faced with a unilateral solution, which they would have to resist with all their forces. They had before them the events which had taken place in Austria, Czecho-Slovakia and the Memelland. Accordingly, they refused to accept the German point of view, and themselves made suggestions for a possible solution of the problems in which Germany was interested. Certain defensive measures were taken by Poland on the 23rd March and the reply was sent to Berlin on the 26th March. I ask the House to note carefully these dates. It has been freely stated in Germany that it was His Majesty's Government's guarantee which encouraged the Polish Government to take the action which I have described. But it will be observed that our guarantee was not given until the 31st March. By the 26th March no mention of it, even, had been made to the Polish Government.

Recent occurrences in Danzig have inevitably given rise to fears that it is intended to settle her future status by unilateral action, organized by surreptitious methods, thus presenting Poland and other Powers with a *fait accompli*. In such circumstances any action taken by Poland to restore the situation would, it is suggested, be represented as an act of aggression on her part, and if her action were supported by other Powers they would be accused of aiding and abetting her in the use of force.

If the sequence of events should, in fact, be such as is contemplated on this hypothesis, hon. Members will realise, from what I have said earlier, that the issue could not be considered as a purely local matter involving the rights and liberties of the Danzigers, which incidentally

77

are in no way threatened, but would at once raise graver issues affecting Polish national existence and independence. We have guaranteed to give our assistance to Poland in the case of a clear threat to her independence, which she considers it vital to resist with her national forces, and we are firmly resolved to carry out this undertaking.

I have said that while the present settlement is neither basically unjust nor illogical, it may be capable of improvement. It may be that in a clearer atmosphere possible improvements could be discussed. Indeed, Colonel Beck has himself said in his speech on the 5th May that if the Government of the Reich is guided by two conditions, namely, peaceful intentions and peaceful methods of procedure, all conversations are possible. In his speech before the Reichstag on the 28th April the German Chancellor said that if the Polish Government wished to come to fresh contractual arrangements governing its relations with Germany he could but welcome such an idea. He added that any such future arrangements would have to be based on an absolutely clear obligation equally binding on both parties.

His Majesty's Government realise that recent developments in the Free City have disturbed confidence and rendered it difficult at present to find an atmosphere in which reasonable counsels can prevail. In face of this situation, the Polish Government have remained calm, and His Majesty's Government hope that the Free City, with her ancient traditions, may again prove, as she has done before in her history, that different nationalities can work together when their real interests coincide. Meanwhile, I trust that all concerned will declare and show their determination not to allow any incidents in connection with Danzig to assume such a character as might constitute a menace to the peace of Europe.

36.

Sir N. Henderson to Viscount Halifax.

My Lord.   Berlin, July 15, 1939.

I took the opportunity of a visit to the State Secretary yesterday to mention to him that I had been informed that one of the Under-Secretaries at the Ministry for Foreign Affairs, Dr. Keppler, had said that Herr Hitler was convinced that England would never fight over Danzig.

2. I said to Baron von Weizsäcker that when I was in London I had assured your Lordship and the Prime Minister that Herr Hitler could not possibly be in any doubt as to the facts of the case, namely, that, if Germany by unilateral action at Danzig in any form compelled the Poles to resist, Britain would at once come to their assistance. He (Baron von Weizsäcker) could not himself be under any misapprehension on the subject, and it seemed to me highly undesirable that a member of his Department should talk in this misleading fashion.

That sort of remark would be repeated in London, and would once more make His Majesty's Government wonder what further steps they could take to convince Herr Hitler that they were in earnest. It was solely because they doubted whether Herr Hitler was correctly informed on this point that they continued to reiterate their determination to resist force by force in future. If Herr Hitler wanted war, it was quite simple. He had only to tell the Danzigers to proclaim the re-establishment of the Free City to Germany. Obviously that would put the onus of action on the Poles, but not even that would cause us to hesitate to support them, if Germany attacked them, since we would realise quite well that the Senate at Danzig would only adopt such a resolution on the direct order of the Chancellor.

3. Baron von Weizsäcker observed that he was not so certain that the Senate would not act one day of its own accord. I told him that I could not possibly believe that, especially as I clearly realised that the Senate would have already so acted if it had not been for Herr Hitler's orders to the contrary. That he had given those orders was one of the chief grounds for my belief that Herr Hitler still sought a peaceable solution of this question. Nor did the State Secretary demur to this.

4. As regards my general observations, Baron von Weizsäcker said that Dr. Keppler, who had been in the early days a kind of economic adviser of Herr Hitler's and still saw him occasionally at long intervals, was an honest man, who was also in fairly close relations with Herr von Ribbentrop. There were, Baron von Weizsäcker said, so many distinctions about a statement to the effect that England would not go to war over Danzig. Anybody, including Herr Hitler himself, might well say that England did not wish to fight about Danzig, and it would be true. Nor did Germany. Anybody, including Herr Hitler, might say that one day Danzig would revert without war to Germany, and that might equally be true as the result of a pacific settlement with the Poles in their own true interests.

5. I admitted that there were possibilities of twisting the facts. Yet these were, I said, plain enough, and His Majesty's Government could never be reproached this time, as they had been in 1914, of not having made their position clear beyond all doubt. If Herr Hitler wanted war, he knew exactly how he could bring it about. Baron von Weizsäcker replied to this that he would also draw a distinction about the position in 1914. He had never reproached Sir Edward Grey for not having publicly announced British intentions at that time. The fault, in his opinion, had been that His Majesty's Government had not made them known privately to the German Government before it was too late. Why did His Majesty's Government to-day insist all the time upon these public utterances? If something had to be said to Herr Hitler, why could it not be said privately without all the world being kept informed? That had been the mistake last year during the Czech crisis. Public warnings only made it more difficult for Herr Hitler to heed them.

6. Though I appreciate personally the force of this hint of the State Secretary's in favour of the private communicatior rather than the public warning, I confined myself to replying that one of our main causes for anxiety in England was our belief that disagreeable facts were withheld from Herr Hitler by those who were responsible for making them known to him. To this Baron von Weizsäcker replied that, while he could not tell me what reports the Chancellor read or did not read, Herr Hitler was influenced by nobody, but regarded situations as a whole and was guided by his own appreciations of them.

I have, &c.,

NEVILE HENDERSON.

Temporary easing in the Danzig situation.

37.

Mr. Shepherd to Viscount Halifax.

(Telegraphic.) *Danzig, July 19, 1939.*

Gauleiter Forster visited the High Commissioner at noon to-day. The latter has sent me, in a personal and confidential form, notes of conversation, of which the following is a translation: —

The Gauleiter told me the result of his interview with German Chancellor was as follows: —

1. There is no modification of German claims regarding Danzig and the Corridor as formulated in Chancellor's speech to Reichstag.

2. Nothing will be done on the German side to provoke a conflict on this question.

3. Question can wait if necessary until next year or even longer.

4. The Gauleiter said that the Senate would henceforth seek intervention of High Commissioner in difficult questions which might arise between the Senate and Polish representative. This would, he said, terminate a war of notes which only poisons the situation, but he added that "a single press indiscretion to the effect that the Senate and German Government are having recourse to politics would immediately terminate practice and more direct and consequently more dangerous method would again be applied." He said verbatim: "We are having recourse to High Commissioner and not to Geneva itself."

5. He requested High Commissioner to intervene officially at once in the matter of military trains not announced beforehand. Non-observance of this rule, which was established by an exchange of letters between the Senate and Polish representative in 1921, would have effect beyond local Danzig question and would, for example, entail a modification of German usage announcing to Polish Government visit of warships to port of Danzig. In addition, according to information at disposal of Senate, there were 300 men at Westerplatte in place of 100 agreed to. Herr Forster gave his word of honour that there were at Danzig only a few anti-aircraft guns, anti-tank guns and light infantry guns — no heavy guns, not an invading German soldier — nobody but Danzigers and four German officers. He claimed that a sharp watch at the frontier was necessary by the extensive importation of weapons for 3,000 Polish reservists resident in the district.

6. Herr Forster will publish an article which he had already read to me confidentially on the occasion of our last interview, when he said he would submit the question of publication to the Chancellor's decision. This article underlines point of view announced in Reichstag speech. Herr Forster declared that if repercussion of his article is not violent and if there is no incident, this will put an end to all Danzig-Polish polemics and press would be ordered to drop the subject of Danzig completely.

7. If there is a *détente* in situation, all military measures now taken in Danzig would be dropped.

8. The Gauleiter promised his loyal collaboration.

9. High Commissioner would be happy if it were possible to obtain from Poland a positive reaction in any formal matter which might arise in the near future so that new methods may be given a good initiation.

10. The Gauleiter said that Herr Hitler would have liked to take an opportunity to talk to the High Commissioner about the Danzig situation, but that Herr von Ribbentrop, who was present at the interview at Obersalzberg, had raised objections to which the Chancellor replied evasively: "Well, it will be a little later, I will let you know."

38.

Viscount Halifax to Mr. Norton (Warsaw).

(Telegraphic.) *Foreign Office, July 21, 1939.*

Danzig telegram of 19th July.*

I am most anxious that this tentative move from German side should not be compromised by publicity or by any disinclination on part of Polish Government to discuss in friendly and reasonable spirit any concrete question which may be taken up by Senate through High Commissioner.

2. Unless you see most serious objection, please approach M. Beck in following sense.

3. His Majesty's Government have learnt with great regret of further incident, but they hope that Polish Government will handle it with same restraint and circumspection which they have hitherto shown, more especially as there is some reason to think that German policy is now to work for a *détente* in the Danzig question. It is nevertheless essential not to destroy possibility of better atmosphere at outset, and I trust that more care than ever will be taken on Polish side to avoid provocation in any sphere and to restrain press. Above all, if any sign is forthcoming of more reasonable attitude on the part of Senate or German Government, it is important that from Polish side this should not be made occasion for provocative assertions that German Government are weakening. Moreover, I hope that if Senate show any sign of desiring to improve atmosphere by discussing concrete questions, the Polish Government for their part will not be slow to respond in a friendly and forthcoming manner.

4. For your own information, I hope to arrange that we shall be informed through High Commissioner and His Majesty's Consul-General in Danzig when any concrete question is to be taken up by High Commissioner at the request of Senate, and, of course, of the discussions, in order that we may have an opportunity of discreetly urging moderation on Polish Government.

5. Finally, when newspaper article referred to in telegram under

* No. 37.

82

reference appears, please do what you can to ensure that Polish Government and press treat it calmly, perhaps on the lines that it does not introduce any new element into the situation. You might also say that the publication of the proposed article does not modify impression of His Majesty's Government that Senate and the German Government, in fact, *détente* and an improvement in the atmosphere.

6. Whatever may be the import of this German move, position of Polish Government cannot be worsened in any respect by doing their utmost to make a success of procedure proposed by Gauleiter to High Commissioner.

39.

Mr. Norton to Viscount Halifax.

(Telegraphic.)   *Warsaw, July 25, 1939.*

Your telegram of 21st July.*

I developed your Lordship's ideas to M. Beck this morning.

2. M. Beck asked me to assure you that Polish Government were always on the look-out for signs of a German wish for a *détente*. They are inspired by the same principles as your Lordship, since it was in everyone's interest that temperature should be allowed to fall. Polish Commissioner in Danzig had received formal instructions to deal with each question in a purely practical and objective manner. Even shooting of Polish Customs guard, which Polish Government now considered to have been deliberate, was being treated as a local incident.

3. The most important question was whether new German tendency reported by M. Burckhardt was a manœuvre or not. M. Beck was naturally suspicious since Poland had much experience of German mentality and Germans real interest must be by any and every means to attempt to separate Poland from Great Britain. At one moment they tried to achieve this by threats, at another by talk of appeasement. In actual fact Polish Government had not received the slightest concrete sign of a desire for a relaxation of tension. For example, remilitarisation of Danzig was proceeding and identifications of fresh German troops on Polish frontier had been received. Marshal Smigly-Rydz had not decided to counter these for the moment since amongst other things Poland was not so rich as to be able to spend money for military purposes freely.

4. Words let fall by Herr Forster were not in themselves sufficient evidence of German intentions. Herr Forster had within the last few days complained to M. Burckhardt about Polish intention to put armed guards on their railways in Danzig.

M. Burckhardt had said that such complaint had better be made by Herr Greiser. Latter had at once said that he had no evidence of any such Polish intention. M. Beck feared that this allegation by Herr Forster was only a pretext for increasing militarisation of Danzig.

* No. 38.

83

5. All in all M. Beck, while entirely understanding and sharing your Lordship's general desire, did not at present see any facts on which to base a forecast of German change of policy.

6. He said incidentally that he had not given up the idea that *démarche* in the form of warning to Danzig Senate, supported by French and British representations, might be advisable.

40.

Mr. F. M. Shepherd to Viscount Halifax.

(Telegraphic.) *Danzig, July 25, 1939.*

Herr Forster informed High Commissioner yesterday that Danzig question could, if necessary, wait a year or more, and said that military precautions now being taken would be liquidated in the middle of September.

2. Meanwhile, there is increasing amount of horse and motor transport visible, and frequent reports reach me of men being called up and of arrival of men and material from East Prussia. While I cannot at present confirm these reports, it would be unwise to ignore them. There are numerous warehouses and other buildings in Danzig where material could be stored and men housed.

3. I learn that a certain Major-General Eberhard is now in command here.

41.

Sir H. Kennard to Viscount Halifax.

(Telegraphic.) *Warsaw, July 31, 1939.*

I asked Minister for Foreign Affairs to-day what impressions he had brought back from his visit to Gdynia and how far he thought that the *détente* at Danzig, foreshadowed in the conversation between the Gauleiter and the High Commissioner, should be taken seriously.

2. M. Beck said that, unfortunately, there were no indications that the Danzig Senate intended to behave more reasonably. They had just demanded that the Polish customs police who accompany the customs officials on their duties should be withdrawn, despite the fact that they have been employed in Danzig by the Polish customs authorities for some years past.

3. It was possible that the remilitarisation of Danzig was not proceeding so actively, and he had no information as to the intention of the German Government to send a General Officer Commanding to Danzig.

4. He, further, had no information of a serious increase in German concentrations on the Polish frontier, but he was somewhat perturbed by the reports which he had received from some eight Polish Consular representatives in Germany to the effect that an intensive official propaganda is now being conducted in Germany demonstrating the necessity of an isolated war against Poland without any British or French intervention. This, coupled with the notices which have been

sent to German reservists who are to be called up during the second fortnight in August, was somewhat ominous. He said that an intensive propaganda was also being conducted in East Prussia, where reservists up to 58 years old were being called up.

5. M. Beck did not think that the moment had yet come to convey a serious joint warning to the Danzig authorities, and felt that it would be well to await further developments and see how far the Gauleiter's suggestion of a *détente* was to be taken seriously.

6. The most essential thing was to show by every possible means the solidarity of the three Governments of Great Britain, France and Poland in their resistance to German aggression in any form.

42.

Sir H. Kennard to Viscount Halifax.

(Telegraphic.) *Warsaw, August 2, 1939.*

I discussed the situation at Danzig at some length informally with the Vice-Minister for Foreign Affairs to-day and asked him more especially for information regarding the controversy respecting the reduction of the Polish customs personnel in the Free State. M. Arciszewski said that three years ago there had only been about thirty Polish customs inspectors, and that in view of the numerous cases of smuggling and so forth, some eighty frontier guards had been added for the purpose of surveillance. The frontier guards wore a different uniform from the customs inspectors, and he thought that provided the Danzig Senate were acting in good faith and any concession would not be interpreted as a sign of weakness, it might be possible to come to some arrangement by which the customs officials and frontier guards should wear the same uniform and the number of the latter might be somewhat reduced. He did not think that any threat of a customs union with Germany should be taken too seriously as hitherto the Senate had never risked coming too far into the open. He admitted that the general situation might become critical towards the end of this month. He agreed that it was very difficult to fix a limit at which the Polish Government must react seriously to the accentuation of the surreptitious methods by which Germany was endeavouring to bring about a *fait accompli* at Danzig, but he still thought that she would hesitate before going to the length where a serious crisis must develop.

He admitted that the situation might develop within a few hours from the political to the military phase, but felt that the military preparations at Danzig were to some extent exaggerated. If the Reich really did not wish or intend to participate in a European war over the Danzig question, and there were real signs of a *détente*, it might be possible to resume conversations, but he thought that Herr Forster's assertions were in the present circumstances only a manœuvre, and that until there were serious indications that the German Government's intentions were reasonable, it would not be possible to discuss any practical solution.

Further deterioration in the situation at Danzig.

43.

Mr. Norton to Viscount Halifax.

(Telegraphic.) *Warsaw, August 4, 1939.*

M. Beck to-night, through his "chef de cabinet," informed me that at four customs posts on Danzig-East Prussian frontier Polish customs inspectors were to-day informed that by decision of Danzig Senate they would henceforth not be allowed to carry out their duties.

2. Polish Government take a very serious view of this step. Previous action of Danzig Senate has been clandestine, but this is an open challenge to Polish interests.

3. Polish Commissioner-General has therefore been instructed to deliver a note to-night requesting immediate confirmation that Polish customs inspectors will be allowed to carry out their duties, and warning to Senate that if they are interfered with Polish Government will react in the strongest manner. A reply is requested by to-morrow evening, 5th August.

4. "Chef de cabinet" could not say what steps the Polish Government would take. M. Beck proposed to give me further information to-morrow morning. Meanwhile, he was most anxious that his Majesty's Government should be informed at once of the serious turn events have taken.

5. Polish note is, I gather, not being published nor its contents revealed to press.

6. M. Burckhardt is being informed by the Polish Commissioner-General.

44.

Mr. F. M. Shepherd to Viscount Halifax.

(Telegraphic.) *Danzig, August 4, 1939.*

Polish representative saw the High Commissioner this morning on his return from Warsaw and read to him a translation of a note which he will hand to the Senate this afternoon. It is polite but firm, and ends on a conciliatory note. Referring to the threat to open the East Prussian frontier M. Chodacki requested the High Commissioner to give the President of the Senate a personal message to the effect that such a move would be for Poland a *casus belli*.

2. The President of the Senate complained to the High Com-

missioner that Gauleiter had not passed on to him the desire of the Führer to terminate the war of notes and to work towards a *détente*. Herr Greiser was incensed at having been placed in a false position, and said he would not have sent his notes of 29th July had he been kept *au courant*.

3. The President and Polish representative will meet at the High Commissioner's house on 7th August.

45.

Sir H. Kennard to Viscount Halifax.

(Telegraphic)   *Warsaw, August 9, 1939.*

Polish attitude towards the dispute over recent Danzig attempt to eliminate Polish customs inspection has been firm but studiously moderate. There was at first no attempt to represent the Danzig Senate as having climbed down, but, as was inevitable, the papers have since reproduced comment to this effect from the French and British press. The Polish Government said little to the press about what really passed, and even now nothing has been said of any time limit. Polish attitude to diplomatic conversations is also moderate.

2. It is true that on 7th August the independent Conservative *Czas*, in a commentary on Marshal Smigly-Rydz's speech, said that Poland was ready to fight for Danzig, and that if a *fait accompli* were attempted, then guns would fire. It also emphasised at length the Marshal's insistence that Poland had no aggressive intentions (the German press does not seem to be interested in that point).

3. The Polish Telegraph Agency to-day—in a message from its German correspondent—replies to attacks of Deutches Nachrichten-Büro and German press, pointing out that one sentence in the article in *Czas* had been singled out to give a distorted picture of Polish opinion in order to represent Poland as a potential aggressor. "Polish provocations" was the term used in Germany to describe Poland's attempts to defend her just interests. "A volley fired by German guns will be the closing point of the history of modern Poland," that was the pious desire of "peaceful and persecuted Germany." The message concluded by emphasising again that everyone knew that Poland had no aggressive intentions.

4. I fear that at times of strong national feeling it is almost inevitable that occasional remarks like that of *Czas* should occur in the press. Experience shows that the Germans can wax indignant with anyone and on any subject if Goebbels so desires. And the "provocation" of one article in a small and independent Warsaw newspaper compares strangely with the official utterances of Dr. Goebbels and Herr Forster in Danzig and the daily military and civil violation of all the treaties on which Poland's rights are based.

5. Possibly the German campaign is intended to cover up the

Senate's withdrawal in Danzig, where the situation is regarded as somewhat easier.

6. I shall, of course, continue to urge moderation here, both in official and press declarations.

<hr />

46.

Sir H. Kennard to Viscount Halifax.

(Telegraphic.)   *Warsaw, August 10, 1939.*

Minister for Foreign Affairs communicated to me to-day the text of a communication which was made to Polish Chargé d'Affaires at Berlin by State Secretary yesterday and of reply of the Polish Government which was made this afternoon. (Text of these communications, which are strictly confidential and are not being published at present, will be found in my immediately following telegram.*) Both these communications were made verbally though notes were taken of their contents in either case.

2. M. Beck drew my attention to the very serious nature of German *démarche* as it was the first time that the Reich had directly intervened in the dispute between Poland and Danzig Senate. He had already, through Polish Ambassador in London, warned your Lordship briefly of what he had communicated to me, but he asked me to request you to consider whether you could take any useful action in Berlin to reinforce Polish attitude. He would leave it to your Lordship to decide the nature of any such action, but would be glad in any case to learn your views as to the significance of this *démarche* on the part of the Reich. M. Beck has made a similar communication to my French colleague.

3. He further told me that the High Commissioner had communicated to him the tenor of a conversation which M. Burckhardt had had with Herr Forster this morning. Conversation was relatively moderate, and Herr Forster said Herr Hitler had told him that no incident should take place at Danzig at present time in view of gravity of the situation. Herr Forster said that he intended in his declaration which he is to make to-night to deal with aggressive tone of Polish press.

4. M. Beck finally said that he felt that a serious political crisis would develop during the last fortnight of this month, which while it need not necessarily lead to war would require very careful handling. No further military measures were being taken by the Polish Government for the moment, but he would at once inform me if they became necessary.

5. M. Beck stated that while he had not thought it necessary to refer, in his reply to the German Government, to the specific question

* No. 47.

of Polish customs inspectors, he could have refuted German allegations as the Polish Government had documentary proof that Danzig customs officials had definite instructions from authorities to inform Polish inspectors that they could no longer carry out their functions.

47.

Sir H. Kennard to Viscount Halifax.

(Telegraphic.) *Warsaw, August 10, 1939.*

My immediately preceding telegram.*

Following is translation of German *note verbale:*—

"German Government have learnt with lively surprise of tenor of note addressed by Polish Government to Senate of Free City of Danzig, in which Polish Government demand in the form of an ultimatum cancellation of an alleged measure whose existence was based on incorrect rumours. This measure, designed to prevent activity of Polish customs inspectors, was not, in fact, decreed by Senate. In case of refusal the threat was expressed that measures of reprisal would be taken.

"The German Government are compelled to call attention to the fact that repetition of such demands having the nature of an ultimatum and addressed to the Free City of Danzig as well as of threats of reprisals, would lead to an aggravation of Polish-German relations, for consequences of which responsibility will fall exclusively on Polish Government, German Government being obliged to disclaim here and now any responsibility in this respect.

"Further, the German Government call attention of Polish Government to the fact that steps which latter have taken to prevent export of certain Danzig goods to Poland are of such a nature as to cause heavy economic losses to the population of Danzig.

"Should Polish Government persist in maintaining such measures the German Government are of the opinion that in present state of affairs the Free City of Danzig would have no choice but to seek other opportunities of exporting, and, consequently, also of importing goods."

2. Following is translation of Polish reply:—

"The Government of Polish Republic have learnt with liveliest surprise of declaration made on 9th August, 1939, by State Secretary at German Ministry for Foreign Affairs to Polish Chargé d'Affaires *ad interim* at Berlin regarding existing relations between Poland and the Free City of Danzig. The Polish Government indeed perceive no juridical basis capable of justifying intervention of Germany in these relations.

* No. 46.

89

"If exchanges of views regarding the Danzig problem have taken place between Polish Government and German Government these exchanges were solely based on goodwill of Polish Government and arose from no obligation of any sort.

"In reply to above-mentioned declaration of the German Government the Polish Government are obliged to warn the German Government that in future, as hitherto, they will react to any attempt by authorities of the Free City which might tend to compromise the rights and interests which Poland possesses there in virtue of her agreements, by employment of such means and measures as they alone shall think fit to adopt, and will consider any future intervention by German Government to detriment of these rights and interests as an act of aggression."

48.

Sir N. Henderson to Viscount Halifax.

(Telegraphic.) *Berlin, August 16, 1939.*

State Secretary, whom I visited yesterday evening, said at once that the situation had very gravely deteriorated since 4th August. When I last saw him he had regarded the position as less dangerous than last year; now he considered it no less dangerous and most urgent. Deterioration was due firstly to Polish ultimatum to Danzig Senate of 4th August, and secondly to last sentence—which he quoted—of Polish reply to German Government of 10th August, but also in general to the unmistakable set policy of persecution and extermination of the German minority in Poland.

I told Baron von Weizsäcker that there was quite another side to the case. Polish note of 4th August had been necessitated by the succession of measures, and particularly military ones, undertaken in Danzig with view to undermining the Polish position there; Polish reply of 10th August had been provoked by German verbal note of 9th August, and moreover only described as aggression "acts to the detriment of Polish rights and interests"; and Polish Ambassador had only the day before complained to me of the number of cases of persecution of Polish minority in Germany.

State Secretary replied with some heat that though isolated cases of persecution of Poles had occurred, there was absolutely no comparison between them and what was being done in Poland. Hitherto, he said, not too much stress had been laid in the German papers on what was happening in this respect, but there was a limit to everything and that the limit had now been reached. As he put it the bottle was full to the top. (In other words Herr Hitler's patience was now exhausted.)

He admitted the militarisation of Danzig, but said that its object had been entirely defensive in order to protect the town against what should have been its protector.

As regards the Polish note of 10th August he said that if any German intervention to the detriment of Polish rights and interests in Danzig was to be regarded as an act of aggression, it meant asking Germany to disinterest herself altogether in the Free City, since the whole basis of her former negotiations with Poland had been with a view to modifying the position there in favour of Germany. It was a claim which made the whole situation intolerable and even His Majesty's Government had admitted that there might be modifications to be made.

I told Baron von Weizsäcker that the trouble was that Germany could never see but one side to any question, and always wanted everything modified in her favour. We disputed with acrimony about the rights and wrongs of the case without either apparently convincing the other. With these details I need not trouble you.

I eventually said that what was done could not now be undone. We seemed to be rapidly drifting towards a situation in which neither side would be in a position to give way and from which war would ensue. Did Herr Hitler want war? I was prepared to believe that Germany would not yield to intimidation. Nor certainly could His Majesty's Government. If Germany resorted to force, we would resist with force. There could be no possible doubt whatsoever about that. The position had been finally defined in your Lordship's speech at Chatham House on 29th June and by the Prime Minister's statement in the House of Commons on 10th July. From that attitude we could not deviate.

In reply to a suggestion of mine, State Secretary observed that whereas it might just have been possible before 5th August, it was absolutely out of the question now to imagine that Germany could be the first to make any gesture. Even apart from the recent Polish ultimatum and the verbal note about aggression, a German initiative could hardly have been possible in view of Colonel Beck's speech on 5th May in which he had deigned to say that if Germany accepted the principles laid down by him Poland would be ready to talk, but not otherwise. That was language which Germany could not admit. I made the obvious retort. State Secretary's only reply was that the fact remained that to talk of a German initiative now was completely academic.

Baron von Weizsäcker then proceeded to say that the trouble was that the German Government's appreciation of the situation was totally different from that of His Majesty's Government. Germany, with innumerable cases of the persecution of Germans before her eyes, could not agree that the Poles were showing calm and restraint: Germany believed that Poland was deliberately running with her eyes shut to ruin: Germany was convinced that His Majesty's Government did not realise whither their policy of encirclement and blind assistance to Poland were leading them and Europe: and that finally his own Government did not, would not and could not believe that Britain would fight under all circumstances whatever folly the Poles might commit.

I told Baron von Weizsäcker that the last was a very dangerous theory and sounded like Herr von Ribbentrop who had never been able to understand the British mentality. If the Poles were compelled by any act of Germany to resort to arms to defend themselves there was not a shadow of doubt that we would give them our full armed support. We had made that abundantly clear and Germany would be making a tragic mistake if she imagined the contrary.

State Secretary replied that he would put it differently (and he gave me to understand that the phrase was not his own). Germany believed that the attitude of the Poles would be or was such as to free the British Government from any obligation to follow blindly every eccentric step on the part of a lunatic.

I told the State Secretary that we were talking in a circle. The Polish Government had shown extreme prudence hitherto, and would, moreover, take no major step without previous consultation with us; just as in accordance with their military agreement I understood that the German Government would take no irrevocable step without prior consultation with the Italian Government. His Majesty's Government had given their word and must be sole judges of their action. It was consequently hypothetical to speak of "under all circumstances" or of blindly "following Poland's lead."

Baron von Weizsäcker's reply was that Poland had not consulted His Majesty's Government either before M. Chodacki, who could not have so acted without previous authority from Colonel Beck, had addressed his ultimatum to Danzig Senate, or before replying to the German verbal note of 9th August. Yet, in his opinion, both these were major steps fraught with the most serious consequences. He admitted that some of the Poles were, or wished to be, prudent, but they were, unfortunately, not the rulers of Poland to-day. The real policy of Poland, over which His Majesty's Government had no control and of which they probably were ignorant, was the thousands of cases of persecution and excesses against Germans in Poland. It was a policy based on the Polish belief in the unlimited support of the British and French Governments. Who, he asked, could now induce the Poles to abandon such methods? It was those methods, combined with the Polish press articles, which encouraged them, which made the situation no longer tenable and so extremely dangerous. The matter had since 4th August changed to one of the utmost seriousness and urgency. Things had drifted along till now, but the point had been reached when they could drift no longer.

There is no doubt that Baron von Weizsäcker was expressing, as he assured me very solemnly that he was, the considered views of his Government and the position as he himself sees it. He told me, though he admitted that he could not say anything for certain, that it was likely that Herr Hitler would in fact attend the Tannenberg celebration on 27th August. But he hinted that things might not only depend on a speech. Yet if nothing happens between now and then I fear that we must at least expect there on Herr Hitler's part a warlike pronouncement from which it may well be difficult for him later to withdraw. As Baron von Weizsäcker himself observed, the situation in one respect was even worse than last year as Mr. Chamberlain could not again come out to Germany.

I was impressed by one thing, namely, Baron von Weizsäcker's detachment and calm. He seemed very confident, and professed to believe that Russian assistance to the Poles would not only be entirely negligible, but that the U.S.S.R. would even in the end join in sharing in the Polish spoils. Nor did my insistence on the inevitability of British intervention seem to move him.

49.

Explanatory Note on Herr Hitler's Meeting with M. Burckhardt on August 11, 1939.

M. Burckhardt accepted an invitation from Herr Hitler to visit him at Berchtesgaden. M. Burckhardt accordingly had a conversation of a private character with Herr Hitler on the 11th August, in the course of which it is understood that the Danzig question in its relationship to the general European situation was discussed between them.

50.

Viscount Halifax to Sir H. Kennard (Warsaw).

(Telegraphic.) *Foreign Office, August 15, 1939.*

I have the impression that Herr Hitler is still undecided, and anxious to avoid war and to hold his hand if he can do so without losing face. As there is a possibility of him not forcing the issue, it is evidently essential to give him no excuse for acting, whether or not conversations about Danzig at some future time may be possible. It therefore seems of the first importance to endeavour to get the local issues (customs inspectors, margarine and herrings) settled at once, and not to let questions of procedure or "face" at Danzig stand in the way. It also seems essential that the Polish Government should make every effort to moderate their press, even in the face of a German press campaign and to intensify their efforts to prevent attacks on their German minority.

2. In dealing with local Danzig issues, I would beg M. Beck to work through the intermediary of the High Commissioner, or at all events after consultation with him, rather than direct with the Senate. I should like M. Beck to treat M. Burckhardt with the fullest confidence, as in my opinion he is doing his best in a very difficult situation.

3. While the present moment may not be opportune for negotiations on general issues as opposed to local differences, the Polish Government would in my judgment do well to continue to make it plain that, provided essentials can be secured, they are at all times ready to examine the possibility of negotiation over Danzig if there is a prospect of success. I regard such an attitude as important from the point of view of world opinion.

4. Before speaking to M. Beck on the above lines, please concert with your French colleague who will be receiving generally similar instructions in order that you may take approximately the same line with M. Beck.

51.

Sir H. Kennard to Viscount Halifax.

(Telegraphic.) *Warsaw, August 15, 1939.*

I spoke to the Minister for Foreign Affairs in the sense of your telegram of 15th August.* M. Beck agreed that Herr Hitler was probably still undecided as to his course of action. German military activity was nevertheless disturbing, though he did not take too alarmist a view at present.

2. M. Beck agreed that an effort should be made to settle local issues in Danzig and said that he was endeavouring to separate economic from political questions with a view to settling the former quickly and equitably. He hoped that to-morrow's conversation between Polish Commissioner-General and President of the Senate might lead to some results.

3. M. Beck said that if he could not arrive at a direct settlement of new incident which had occurred he would invoke M. Burckhardt's intervention.

4. This incident was as follows: Three Polish customs inspectors, while making their round of harbour in a motor hoat, discovered a German vessel entering the harbour without lights, and, as they suspected smuggling of munitions, turned their searchlight on her. On landing, they were arrested by Danzig police. Polish Commissioner-General has sent in a note demanding their release, though not in unduly energetic language. If he did not receive a reply shortly he would invite High Commissioner to settle this incident.

5. As regards press, he remarked that it was not the Poles but the British and other foreign press who first suggested that firmness of the Polish Government had caused the Senate to yield in the matter of Polish customs inspectors.

* No. 50.

Treatment of German minority in Poland.

52.

Sir H. Kennard to Viscount Halifax.

(Telegraphic.)   *Warsaw, August 24, 1939.*

While I am of course not in a position to check all the allegations made by the German press of minority persecutions here, I am satisfied from enquiries I have made that the campaign is a gross distortion and exaggeration of the facts.

2. Accusations of beating with chains, throwing on barbed wire, being forced to shout insults against Herr Hitler in chorus, &c., are merely silly, but many individual cases specified have been disproved.

3. M. Karletan, for instance, arrested in connexion with murder of Polish policeman on 15th August, was alleged by German press to have been beaten to death and his wife and children thrown out of the window. *Manchester Guardian* correspondent tells me that he visited him in prison on Sunday and found him in good health. He had not been beaten or physically injured at all. Story about wife and child was equally devoid of any foundation whatever.

4. It is true that many of the German minority have left Poland illegally, but I hear both from the Acting British Consul at Katowice and from British Vice-Consul at Lodz that the Germans themselves have told many to leave. There was an initial exodus last May. Many subsequently asked to come back, but the Poles were not anxious to have them, as they had no doubt been trained in propaganda, sabotage and espionage activities, such as Jungdeutsch Partei in Katowice have been conducting. In Lodz area some of those who left recently raised all the money and credit they could before leaving, and the Voivode told Vice-Consul on 20th August that from evidence available he was satisfied that German Consulate had transferred these funds to Germany and was no doubt privy to their departure. Many of those who left, especially from Lodz, are of the *intelligentsia,* and they are said to include Herr Witz, leader of Volksbund. British Vice-Consul at Lodz says many German organisations have been closed there, but they were notoriously conducting Nazi propaganda, and Polish author-ities could not ignore it altogether. I think, however, many Germans have lost their jobs, especially in factories of military or semi-military importance, and some 2,000 workmen have left Tomaszow.

5. Many of those who left their homes undoubtedly did so because they wished to be on German side of the front in event of war, and in general there is by common consent less individual friction with members of the minority now than last May.

6. Ministry for Foreign Affairs tell me that figure of 76,000 refugees quoted in German press is a gross exaggeration. I should say 17,000 was the absolute maximum. *Gazeta Polska* correspondent in Berlin has asked to be shown refugee camps of the 76,000 and apparently received no answer.

7. In Silesia the frontier is not fully open, but a special frontier card system is in force and considerable daily traffic is possible. The German authorities having closed frontier in Rybnik area where Poles cross to Poland, Polish authorities closed it elsewhere where Germans cross into Germany. In view of revelations of activities of Jung-deutsche Partei, the Polish authorities feel greater control of frontier traffic is in any case necessary.

8. Polish press has recently published many complaints of whole-sale removal of Poles from frontier districts in Silesia and East Prussia to the interior of Germany, smashing of property, especially in Allenstein district, closing of all Polish libraries in Silesia and other forms of persecution. According to semi-official *Gazeta Polska*, from April to June there were recorded 976 acts of violence against the minority, and since then the number of cases is stated to have increased beyond all bounds. For the last two days, however, no further information has been published, as M. Beck has damped the press down.

9. In general, responsible organs of the Polish press have not published violent tirades, still less claimed German territory for Poland, and *A.B.C.*, recently quoted in Germany, is a violent Opposition newspaper with little reputation and less influence.

53.

Sir H. Kennard to Viscount Halifax.

(Telegraphic.)   *Warsaw, August 26, 1939.*

Series of incidents again occurred yesterday on German frontier.

2. Polish patrol met party Germans 1 kilometre from East Prussian frontier near Pelta. Germans opened fire. Polish patrol replied, killing leader, whose body is being returned.

3. German bands also crossed Silesian frontier near Szczyglo, twice near Rybnik and twice elsewhere, firing shots and attacking blockhouses and customs posts with machine guns and hand grenades. Poles have protested vigorously to Berlin.

4. *Gazeta Polska*, in inspired leader to-day, says these are more than incidents. They are clearly prepared acts of aggression of para-military disciplined detachments supplied with regular army's arms, and in one case it was a regular army detachment. Attacks more or less continuous.

5. These incidents did *not* cause Poland to forsake calm and strong attitude of defence. Facts spoke for themselves and acts of aggression

came from German side. This was best answer to ravings of German press.

6. Ministry for Foreign Affairs state uniformed German detachment has since shot Pole across frontier and wounded another.

54.

Sir H. Kennard to Viscount Halifax.

(Telegraphic.) Warsaw, August 26, 1939.

Ministry for Foreign Affairs categorically deny story recounted by Herr Hitler to French Ambassador that twenty-four Germans were recently killed at Lodz and eight at Bielsko. Story is without any foundation whatever.

55.

Sir H. Kennard to Viscount Halifax.

(Telegraphic.) Warsaw, August 27, 1939.

So far as I can judge, German allegations of mass ill-treatment of German minority by Polish authorities are gross exaggerations, if not complete falsifications.

2. There is no sign of any loss of control of situation by Polish civil authorities. Warsaw (and so far as I can ascertain the rest of Poland) is still completely calm.

3. Such allegations are reminiscent of Nazi propaganda methods regarding Czecho-Slovakia last year.

4. In any case it is purely and simply deliberate German provocation in accordance with fixed policy that has since March exacerbated feeling between the two nationalities. I suppose this has been done with object of (a) creating war spirit in Germany, (b) impressing public opinion abroad, (c) provoking either defeatism or apparent aggression in Poland.

5. It has signally failed to achieve either of the two latter objects.

6. It is noteworthy that Danzig was hardly mentioned by Herr Hitler.

7. German treatment of Czech Jews and Polish minority is apparently negligible factor compared with alleged sufferings of Germans in Poland, where, be it noted, they do not amount to more than 10 per cent. of population in any commune.

8. In face of these facts, it can hardly be doubted that, if Herr Hitler decides on war, it is for the sole purpose of destroying Polish independence.

9. I shall lose no opportunity of impressing on Minister for Foreign Affairs necessity of doing everything possible to prove that Herr Hitler's allegations regarding German minority are false.

Developments leading immediately to the outbreak of hostilities between Great Britain and Germany on September 3, 1939.

56.

Letter of August 22, 1939, from the Prime Minister to the German Chancellor.

Your Excellency,　　　　　*10 Downing Street, August 22, 1939.*

Your Excellency will have already heard of certain measures taken by His Majesty's Government, and announced in the press and on the wireless this evening.

These steps have, in the opinion of His Majesty's Government, been rendered necessary by the military movements which have been reported from Germany, and by the fact that apparently the announcement of a German-Soviet Agreement is taken in some quarters in Berlin to indicate that intervention by Great Britain on behalf of Poland is no longer a contingency that need be reckoned with. No greater mistake could be made. Whatever may prove to be the nature of the German-Soviet Agreement, it cannot alter Great Britain's obligation to Poland which His Majesty's Government have stated in public repeatedly and plainly, and which they are determined to fulfil.

It has been alleged that, if His Majesty's Government had made their position more clear in 1914, the great catastrophe would have been avoided. Whether or not there is any force in that allegation, His Majesty's Government are resolved that on this occasion there shall be no such tragic misunderstanding.

If the case should arise, they are resolved, and prepared, to employ without delay all the forces at their command, and it is impossible to foresee the end of hostilities once engaged. It would be a dangerous illusion to think that, if war once starts, it will come to an early end even if a success on any one of the several fronts on which it will be engaged should have been secured.

Having thus made our position perfectly clear, I wish to repeat to you my conviction that war between our two peoples would be the greatest calamity that could occur. I am certain that it is desired neither by our people, nor by yours, and I cannot see that there is anything in the questions arising between Germany and Poland which could not and should not be resolved without the use of force, if only a situation of confidence could be restored to enable discussions to be carried on in an atmosphere different from that which prevails to-day.

We have been, and at all times will be, ready to assist in creating conditions in which such negotiations could take place, and in which it might be possible concurrently to discuss the wider problems affecting the future of international relations, including matters of interest to us and to you.

The difficulties in the way of any peaceful discussion in the present state of tension are, however, obvious, and the longer that tension is maintained, the harder will it be for reason to prevail.

These difficulties, however, might be mitigated, if not removed, provided that there could for an initial period be a truce on both sides—and indeed on all sides—to press polemics and to all incitement.

If such a truce could be arranged, then, at the end of that period, during which steps could be taken to examine and deal with complaints made by either side as to the treatment of minorities, it is reasonable to hope that suitable conditions might have been established for direct negotiations between Germany and Poland upon the issues between them (with the aid of a neutral intermediary, if both sides should think that that would be helpful).

But I am bound to say that there would be slender hope of bringing such negotiations to successful issue unless it were understood beforehand that any settlement reached would, when concluded, be guaranteed by other Powers. His Majesty's Government would be ready, if desired, to make such contribution as they could to the effective operation of such guarantees.

At this moment I confess I can see no other way to avoid a catastrophe that will involve Europe in war.

In view of the grave consequences to humanity, which may follow from the action of their rulers, I trust that Your Excellency will weigh with the utmost deliberation the considerations which I have put before you.

Yours sincerely,
NEVILE CHAMBERLAIN.

57.

Sir N. Henderson to Viscount Halifax (received August 24).

(Telegraphic.)   *Berlin, August 23, 1939.*

Two difficulties were raised last night before visit to Herr Hitler was actually arranged. In first place it was asked whether I would not be ready to wait until Herr von Ribbentrop's return. I said that I could not wait as my instructions were to hand letter myself as soon as possible. An hour or so later I was rung up again by State Secretary on the telephone asking for gist of letter and referring to publication of some private letter addressed to Herr Hitler last year. I told Baron von Weizsäcker that I had no recollection of publication of any private letter last year and assured him that there was no intention of publishing this one. As regards Prime Minister's letter I said that its three main points were (1) that His Majesty's Government was determined to fulfil their obligations to Poland, (2) that they were prepared, provided a peace atmosphere was created, to discuss all problems

99

affecting our two countries, and (3) that during period of truce they would welcome direct discussions between Poland and Germany in regard to minorities.

State Secretary appeared to regard these replies as likely to be satisfactory, but deferred a final answer till 8 A.M. this morning. At that hour he telephoned me to say that arrangements made had been confirmed and that he would accompany me to Berchtesgaden, leaving Berlin at 9.30 A.M.

We arrived Salzburg soon after 11 A.M. and motored to Berchtesgaden, where I was received by Herr Hitler shortly after 1 P.M. I had derived impression that atmosphere was likely to be most unfriendly and that probability was that interview would be exceedingly brief.

In order to forestall this I began conversation by stating that I had been instructed to hand to Chancellor personally a letter from Prime Minister on behalf of His Majesty's Government, but before doing so I wished to make some preliminary remarks. I was grateful to his Excellency for receiving me so promptly as it would have been impossible for me to wait for Herr von Ribbentrop's return inasmuch as the fact was that His Majesty's Government were afraid that the situation brooked no delay. I asked His Excellency to read the letter, not from the point of view of the past, but from that of the present and the future. What had been done could not now be undone, and there could be no peace in Europe without Anglo-German co-operation. We had guaranteed Poland against attack and we would keep our word. Throughout the centuries of history we had never, so far as I knew, broken our word. We could not do so now and remain Britain.

During the whole of this first conversation Herr Hitler was excitable and uncompromising. He made no long speeches but his language was violent and exaggerated both as regards England and Poland. He began by asserting that the Polish question would have been settled on the most generous terms if it had not been for England's unwarranted support. I drew attention to the inaccuracies of this statement, our guarantee having been given on 31st March and Polish reply on 26th March. He retorted by saying that the latter had been inspired by a British press campaign, which had invented a German threat to Poland the week before. Germany had not moved a man any more than she had done during the similar fallacious press campaign about Czecho-Slovakia on the 20th May last year.

He then violently attacked the Poles, talked of 100,000 German refugees from Poland, excesses against Germans, closing of German institutions and Polish systematic persecution of German nationals generally. He said that he was receiving hundreds of telegrams daily from his persecuted compatriots. He would stand it no longer, &c. I interrupted by remarking that while I did not wish to try to deny that persecutions occurred (of Poles also in Germany) the German press accounts were highly exaggerated. He had mentioned the castration of Germans. I happened to be aware of one case. The German in question was a sex-maniac, who had been treated as he

100

deserved. Herr Hitler's retort was that there had not been one case but six.

His next tirade was against British support of Czechs and Poles. He asserted that the former would have been independent to-day if England had not encouraged them in a policy hostile to Germany. He insinuated that the Poles would be to-morrow if Britain ceased to encourage them to-day. He followed this by a tirade against England, whose friendship he had sought for twenty years only to see every offer turned down with contempt. The British press was also vehemently abused. I contested every point and kept calling his statements inaccurate but the only effect was to launch him on some fresh tirade.

Throughout the conversation I stuck firmly to point (1) namely our determination to honour our obligations to Poland; Herr Hitler on the other hand kept harping on point (3), the Polish persecution of German nationals. Point (2) was not referred to at all and apparently did not interest him. (I had been warned that it would not.)

Most of the conversation was recrimination, the real points being those stressed in his reply in regard to the threat to Poland if persecutions continue and to England and France if they mobilise to such an extent as to constitute a danger to Germany.

At the end of this first conversation Herr Hitler observed, in reply to my repeated warnings that direct action by Germany would mean war, that Germany had nothing to lose and Great Britain much; that he did not desire war but would not shrink from it if it was necessary; and that his people were much more behind him than last September.

I replied that I hoped and was convinced that some solution was still possible without war and asked why contact with the Poles could not be renewed. Herr Hitler's retort was that, so long as England gave Poland a blank cheque, Polish unreasonableness would render any negotiation impossible. I denied the "blank cheque" but this only started Herr Hitler off again and finally it was agreed that he would send or hand me his reply in two hours' time.

58.

Sir N. Henderson to Viscount Halifax (received August 24).

(Telegraphic.) *Berlin, August 24, 1939.*

Following is continuation of my telegram of the 23rd August.*

After my first talk yesterday I returned to Salzburg on understanding that if Herr Hitler wished to see me again I would be at his disposal or, if he had nothing new to say, he could merely send me his reply to Prime Minister by hand.

As in the event he asked to see me, I went back to Berchtesgaden. He was quite calm the second time and never raised his voice once.

* No. 57.

101

Conversation lasted from 20 minutes to half an hour but produced little new, except that verbally he was far more categoric than in written reply as to his determination to attack Poland if "another German were ill-treated in Poland."

I spoke of tragedy of war and of his immense responsibility but his answer was that it would be all England's fault. I refuted this only to learn from him that England was determined to destroy and exterminate Germany. He was, he said, 50 years old: he preferred war now to when he would be 55 or 60. I told him that it was absurd to talk of extermination. Nations could not be exterminated and peaceful and prosperous Germany was a British interest. His answer was that it was England who was fighting for lesser races whereas he was fighting only for Germany: the Germans would this time fight to the last man: it would have been different in 1914 if he had been Chancellor then.

He spoke several times of his repeated offers of friendship to England and their invariable and contemptuous rejection. I referred to Prime Minister's efforts of last year and his desire for co-operation with Germany. He said that he had believed in Mr. Chamberlain's good will at the time, but, and especially since encirclement efforts of last few months, he did so no longer. I pointed out fallacy of this view but his answer was that he was now finally convinced of the rightness of views held formerly to him by others that England and Germany could never agree.

In referring to Russian non-aggression pact he observed that it was England which had forced him into agreement with Russia. He did not seem enthusiastic over it but added that once he made agreement it would be for a long period. (Text of agreement signed to-day confirms this and I shall be surprised if it is not supplemented later by something more than mere non-aggression).

I took line at end that war seemed to me quite inevitable if Herr Hitler persisted in direct action against Poland and expressed regret at failure of my mission in general to Berlin and of my visit to him. Herr Hitler's attitude was that it was England's fault and that nothing short of complete change of her policy towards Germany could now ever convince him of British desire for good relations.

59.

Sir N. Henderson to Viscount Halifax (received 8.30 P.M.).

(Telegraphic.)   *Berlin, August 24, 1939.*

I have hitherto not made particular reference to the underlined portion in Herr Hitler's reply* to the Prime Minister in regard to German general mobilisation as a counter to British and French mobilisations.

2. When Herr Hitler gave me his reply, readjusted, I asked him

* Given in *italics* in No. 60.

what exactly was intended by this sentence, as I would, I said, regard a general German mobilisation as the equivalent to war. The answer I got was confused, as was the actual German text. But the gist was that if the French and British mobilisations convinced Herr Hitler that the Western Powers meant to attack him he would mobilise in self-defence. I pointed out that any British military mobilisation would in any case fall far short of what already existed in Germany. Herr Hitler's reply was that this sentence was more particularly intended as a warning to France, and that, as I gathered, the French Government was being or would be so informed.

3. I feel that the main objects of inserting this underlined passage in his letter was (a) to indicate that Germany could not be intimidated; and (b) to serve as an excuse for general mobilisation if and when Herr Hitler decides on it.

60.

Communication from the German Chancellor to the Prime Minister, handed to His Majesty's Ambassador on August 23, 1939.

(Translation.)
Your Excellency,

The British Ambassador has just handed to me a communication in which your Excellency draws attention in the name of the British Government to a number of points which in your estimation are of the greatest importance.

I may be permitted to answer your letter as follows:—

1. Germany has never sought conflict with England and has never interfered in English interests. On the contrary, she has for years endeavoured—although unfortunately in vain—to win England's friendship. On this account she voluntarily assumed in a wide area of Europe the limitations on her own interests which from a national-political point of view it would have otherwise been very difficult to tolerate.

2. The German Reich, however, like other State possesses certain definite interests which it is impossible to renounce. These do not extend beyond the limits of the necessities laid down by former German history and deriving from vital economic pre-requisites. Some of these questions held and still hold a significance both of a national-political and a psychological character which no German Government is able to ignore.

To these questions belong the German City of Danzig, and the connected problem of the Corridor. Numerous statesmen, historians and men of letters even in England have been conscious of this at any rate up to a few years ago. I would add that all these territories lying in the aforesaid German sphere of interest and in particular those lands which returned to the Reich eighteen months ago received

103

their cultural development at the hands not of the English but exclusively of the Germans and this, moreover, already from a time dating back over a thousand years.

3. Germany was prepared to settle the questions of Danzig and of the Corridor by the method of negotiation on the basis of a proposal of truly unparalleled magnanimity. The allegations disseminated by England regarding a German mobilisation against Poland, the assertion of aggressive designs towards Roumania, Hungary, &c., as well as the so-called guarantee declarations which were subsequently given had, however, dispelled Polish inclination to negotiate on a basis of this kind which would have been tolerable for Germany also.

4. The unconditional assurance given by England to Poland that she would render assistance to that country in all circumstances regardless of the causes from which a conflict might spring, could only be interpreted in that country as an encouragement thenceforward to unloosen, under cover of such a charter, a wave of appalling terrorism against the one and a half million German inhabitants living in Poland. The atrocities which since then have been taking place in that country are terrible for the victims, but intolerable for a Great Power such as the German Reich which is expected to remain a passive onlooker during these happenings. Poland has been guilty of numerous breaches of her legal obligations towards the Free City of Danzig, has made demands in the character of ultimata, and has initiated a process of economic strangulation.

5. The Government of the German Reich therefore recently caused the Polish Government to be informed that it was not prepared passively to accept this development of affairs, that it will not tolerate further addressing of notes in the character of ultimata to Danzig, that it will not tolerate a continuance of the persecutions of the German minority, that it will equally not tolerate the extermination of the Free City of Danzig by economic measures, in other words, the destruction of the vital bases of the population of Danzig by a kind of Customs blockade, and that it will not tolerate the occurrence of further acts of provocation directed against the Reich. Apart from this, the questions of the Corridor and of Danzig must and shall be solved.

6. Your Excellency informs me in the name of the British Government that you will be obliged to render assistance to Poland in any such case of intervention on the part of Germany. I take note of this statement of yours and assure you that it can make no change in the determination of the Reich Government to safeguard the interests of the Reich as stated in paragraph 5 above. Your assurance to the effect that in such an event you anticipate a long war is shared by myself. Germany, if attacked by England, will be found prepared and determined. I have already more than once declared before the German people and the world that there can be no doubt concerning the determination of the new German Reich rather to accept, for

however long it might be, every sort of misery and tribulation than to sacrifice its national interests, let alone its honour.

7. The German Reich Government has received information to the effect that the British Government has the intention to carry out measures of mobilisation which, according to the statements contained in your own letter, are clearly directed against Germany alone. This is said to be true of France as well. Since Germany has never had the intention of taking military measures other than those of a defensive character against England or France, and, as has already been emphasised, has never intended, and does not in the future intend, to attack England or France, it follows that this announcement as confirmed by you, Mr. Prime Minister, in your own letter, can only refer to a contemplated act of menace directed against the Reich. *I therefore inform your Excellency that, in the event of these military announcements being carried into effect, I shall order immediate mobilisation of the German forces.*

8. The question of the treatment of European problems on a peaceful basis is not a decision which rests on Germany but primarily on those who since the crime committed by the Versailles dictate have stubbornly and consistently opposed any peaceful revision. Only after a change of spirit on the part of the responsible Powers can there be any real change in the relationship between England and Germany. I have all my life fought for Anglo-German friendship; the attitude adopted by British diplomacy—at any rate up to the present—has, however, convinced me of the futility of such an attempt. Should there be any change in this respect in the future nobody could be happier than I.

ADOLF HITLER.

61.

Non-Aggression Pact between Germany and the Union of Soviet Socialist Republics.

(Translation.)

The Government of the German Reich and the Government of the Union of Soviet Socialist Republics, guided by the desire to strengthen the cause of peace between Germany and the Union of Soviet Socialist Republics, and taking as a basis the fundamental regulations of the Neutrality Agreement concluded in April 1926 between Germany and the Union of Soviet Socialist Republics, have reached the following agreement:—

Article 1. The two Contracting Parties bind themselves to refrain from any act of force, any aggressive action and any attack on one another, both singly and also jointly with other Powers.

Art. 2. In the event of one of the Contracting Parties becoming the object of warlike action on the part of a third Power, the other Contracting Party shall in no manner support this third Power.

Art. 3. The Governments of the two Contracting Parties shall in future remain continuously in touch with one another, by way of consultation, in order to inform one another on questions touching their joint interests.

Art. 4. Neither of the two Contracting Parties shall participate in any grouping of Powers which is directed directly or indirectly against the other Party.

Art. 5. In the event of disputes or disagreements arising between the Contracting Parties on questions of this or that kind, both Parties would clarify these disputes or disagreements exclusively by means of friendly exchange of opinion or, if necessary, by arbitration committees.

Art. 6. The present Agreement shall be concluded for a period of ten years on the understanding that, in so far as one of the Contracting Parties does not give notice of termination one year before the end of this period, the period of validity of this Agreement shall automatically be regarded as prolonged for a further period of five years.

Art. 7. The present Agreement shall be ratified within the shortest possible time. The instruments of ratification shall be exchanged in Berlin. The Agreement takes effect immediately after it has been signed.

For the German Reich Government:
RIBBENTROP.
For the Government of the Union of
Soviet Socialist Republics:
MOLOTOV.

Moscow, August 23, 1939.

62.

Mr. F. M. Shepherd to Viscount Halifax.

(Telegraphic.) *Danzig, August 26, 1939.*

Following is translation of decree of Senate dated 23rd August: —

"*Decree: Article* 1.—Gauleiter of Danzig is Head of State ('Staatsoberhaupt') of the Free City of Danzig.

"*Article* 2.—This decree comes into force on 23rd August, 1939."

Following are translations of letters dated 24th August (*a*) from President of Senate to Herr Forster, and (*b*) of latter's reply: —

"(*a*) At its meeting yesterday the Senate passed a resolution according to which you have been declared Staatsoberhaupt of the Free City of Danzig as from yesterday. A copy of the certified resolution is enclosed. In addition, a legal decree has been prepared to-day and signed making the above-mentioned resolution of the Senate operative. By means of these two acts of the Government the Danzig Constitution has been altered in the above-mentioned sense.. The Senate has authorised me to request you, Herr Gauleiter, to accept this office forthwith in order in these difficult but wonderful last decisive days outwardly to give expression to the unity between party and State, which has so often been stressed and which outwardly has always existed.

"(b) I have taken cognisance of the contents of your letter of the 24th instant and of the enclosed certified copy of the decree regarding the Staatsoberhaupt of the Free City of Danzig of 23rd August, 1939, which was also enclosed. It, of course, goes without saying that in my capacity as Leader of the N.S.D.A.P. of the Danzig district I am prepared in days which are so fateful for Danzig also conduct the affairs of the State. With this decree promulgated on the 23rd August, 1939, a state of affairs is officially sanctioned which, since the accession to power by the National Socialists in 1933, has in practice been in force."

63.

Sir H. Kennard to Viscount Halifax.

(Telegraphic.)   *Warsaw, August 24, 1939.*

Following is translation of Polish note to the Danzig Senate:—

"Herr Staatsrat Boettcher to-day informed Councillor of the Polish Commissariat-General of the resolution of the Senate of the Free City conferring on Gauleiter Forster the functions and position of the head of the State ('Staatsoberhaupt') of the Free City, this being confirmed in today's Danzig press. I address myself to the Senate of the Free City as the body which, in accordsince with the legally binding Constitution of the Free City, exercises supreme authority in that territory, in order to make on behalf of my Government the following declaration:—

"My Government sees no legal foundation for the adoption by the Senate of the Free City of a resolution instituting a new State function for which there is no provision whatever in the Constitution of the Free City, and to which, as would appear, the authorities hitherto functioning in the Free City would be subordinated. The Polish Government reserve the right to adopt a further attitude in this respect.

"In this connexion the Polish Government consider it necessary to remind the authorities of the Free City that they have already more than once warned the Senate of the Free City in the most decisive fashion against a policy of *fait accompli*, the consequence of which might be most serious and the responsibility for which would fall exclusively upon the authorities of the Free City of Danzig."

64.

Speech by the Prime Minister in the House of Commons on August 24, 1939.

When at the beginning of this month Hon. Members separated for the summer recess, I think there can have been few among us who anticipated that many weeks would elapse before we should find ourselves meeting here again. Unfortunately, those anticipations have been fulfilled, and the Government have felt obliged to ask that Parliament should be summoned again, in order to take such new and drastic steps as are required by the gravity of the situation. In the last debate which we had upon foreign affairs, which took place on the 31st July, I observed that the Danzig situation required very careful watching. I expressed my anxiety about the pace at which the accumulation of war weapons was proceeding throughout Europe. I referred to the poisoning of public opinion by the propaganda which was going on, and I declared that if that could be stopped and if some action could be taken to restore confidence, I did not believe there was any question which could not be solved by peaceful discussion. I am sorry to say that there has been no sign since of any such action. On the contrary, the international position has steadily deteriorated until to-day we find ourselves confronted with the imminent peril of war.

At the beginning of August a dispute arose between the Polish Government and the Danzig Senate as to the position and functions of certain Polish Customs officials. It was not a question of major importance. Many more acute difficulties have been easily settled in the past under less tense conditions and even in this case discussions had actually begun between the parties last week. While those discussions were in progress, the German Press opened a violent campaign against the Polish Government. They declared that Danzig could not be the subject of any conference or any compromise and that it must come back to the Reich at once and unconditionally. They went further. They linked up with the Danzig question the question of the Corridor. They attacked the whole policy and the attitude of the Polish Government, and they published circumstantial accounts of the alleged ill-treatment of Germans living in Poland. Now we have no means of checking the accuracy of those stories, but we cannot help being struck by the fact that they bear a strong resemblance to similar allegations that were made last year in respect of the Sudeten Germans in Czecho-Slovakia. We must also remember that there is a large Polish minority in Germany and that the treatment of that minority has also been the subject of bitter complaints by the Polish Government.

There is no subject which is calculated to arouse ill-feeling in any country more than statements about the ill-treatment of people of their own race in another country. This is a subject which provides the most inflammable of all materials, the material most likely to cause a general conflagration. In those circumstances one cannot but deeply regret that such incidents, which, if they were established, would naturally excite sympathy for the victims and indignation against the authors of this alleged ill-treatment, should be treated in a way which is calculated still further to embitter the atmosphere and raise the temperature to the danger point. But I think it will be agreed that, in face of this campaign, declarations by Polish statesmen have shown great calm and self-restraint. The Polish leaders, while they have been firm in their determination to resist an attack upon their independence, have been unprovocative. They have always been ready, as I am sure they would be ready now, to discuss differences with the German Government, if they could be sure that those discussions would be carried on without threats of force or violence, and with some confidence that, if agreement were reached, its terms would be respected afterwards permanently, both in the letter and in the spirit. This Press campaign is not the only symptom which is ominously reminiscent of past experience. Military preparations have been made in Germany on such a scale that that country is now in a condition of complete readiness for war, and at the beginning of this week we had word that German troops were beginning to move towards the Polish frontier. It then became evident that a crisis of the first magnitude was approaching, and the Government resolved that the time had come when they must seek the approval of Parliament for further measures of defence.

That was the situation on Tuesday last, when in Berlin and Moscow it was announced that negotiations had been taking place, and were likely soon to be concluded, for a non-aggression pact between those two countries. I do not attempt to conceal from the House that that announcement came to the Government as a surprise, and a surprise of a very unpleasant character. For some time past there had been rumours about an impending change in the relations between Germany and the Soviet Union, but no inkling of that change had been conveyed either to us or to the French Government by the Soviet Government. The House may remember that on the 31st July I remarked that we had engaged upon steps almost unprecedented in character. I said that we had shown a great amount of trust and a strong desire to bring the negotiations with the Soviet Union to a successful conclusion when we agreed to send our soldiers, sailors and airmen to Russia to discuss military plans together before we had any assurance that we should be able to reach an agreement on political matters. Well, Sir, nevertheless, moved by the observation of the Russian Secretary for Foreign Affairs, that if we could come to a successful conclusion of our military discussions, political agreement should not present any insuperable difficulties, we sent the Mission.

The British and French Missions reached Moscow on the 11th August. They were warmly received, in friendly fashion, and discussions were actually in progress and had proceeded on a basis of mutual trust when this bombshell was flung down. It, to say the least of it, was highly disturbing to learn that while these conversations were proceeding on that basis, the Soviet Government were secretly negotiating a pact with Germany for purposes which, on the face of it, were inconsistent with the objects of their foreign policy, as we had understood it. I do not propose this afternoon to pass any final judgment upon this incident. That, I think, would be premature until we have had an opportunity of consulting with the French Government as to the meaning and the consequences of this agreement, the text of which was published only this morning. But the question that the Government had to consider when they learned of this announcement was what effect, if any, this changed situation would have upon their own policy. In Berlin the announcement was hailed, with extraordinary cynicism, as a great diplomatic victory which removed any danger of war, since we and France would no longer be likely to fulfil our obligations to Poland. We felt it our first duty to remove any such dangerous illusion.

The House will recollect that the guarantee which we had given to Poland was given before any agreement with Russia was talked of, and that it was not in any way made dependent upon any such agreement being reached. How, then, could we, with honour, go back upon such an obligation, which we had so often and so plainly repeated? Therefore, our first act was to issue a statement that our obligations to Poland and to other countries remained unaffected. Those obligations rest upon agreed statements made to the House of Commons, to which effect is being given in treaties which are at present in an advanced stage of negotiation. Those treaties, when concluded, will formally define our obligations, but they do not in any way alter, they do not add to or subtract from, the obligations of mutual assistance which have already been accepted. The communiqué which we issued to the Press after the meeting of the Cabinet this week spoke also of certain measures of defence which we had adopted. It will be remembered that, as I have said, Germany has an immense army of men already under arms and that military preparations of all kinds have been and are being carried on on a vast scale in that country.

The measures that we have taken up to now are of a precautionary and defensive character, and to give effect to our determination to put this country in a state of preparedness to meet any emergency, but I wish emphatically to repudiate any suggestion, if such a suggestion should be made, that these measures imply an act of menace. Nothing that we have done or that we propose to do menaces the legitimate interests of Germany. It is not an act of menace to prepare to help friends to defend themselves against force. If neighbours wishing to live together peacefully in friendly relations find that one of them is contemplating apparently an aggressive act of force against another of them, and is making open preparations for action, it is not a menace for the others to announce their intention of aiding the one who is the subject of this threat.

There is another action which has been taken to-day in the financial sphere. Hon. Members will have seen the announcement that the Bank Rate, which has remained at 2 per cent. for a long time past, has to-day been raised to 4 per cent., and the House will recognize that this is a normal protective measure adopted for the purpose of defending our resources in a period of uncertainty. There is in this connexion a contribution to be made by British citizens generally. The public can best co-operate in reducing as far as possible any demands which involve directly or indirectly the purchase of foreign exchange; next by scrupulously observing the request of the Chancellor of the Exchequer that capital should not at present be sent or moved out of the country; and, finally, by holding no more foreign assets than are strictly required for the normal purpose of business.

In view of the attitude in Berlin to which I have already referred, His Majesty's Government felt that it was their duty at this moment to leave no possible loophole for misunderstanding, and so that no doubt might exist in the mind of the German Government, His Majesty's Ambassador in Berlin was instructed to seek an interview with the German Chancellor and to hand him a message from me on behalf of the British Government. That message was delivered yesterday and the reply was received to-day. The object of my communication to the German Chancellor was to restate our position and to make quite sure that there was no misunderstanding. His Majesty's Government felt that this was all the more necessary having regard to reports which we had received as to the military movements taking place in Germany and as to the then projected German-Soviet Agreement. I therefore made it plain, as had been done in the communiqué issued after the Cabinet meeting on Tuesday, that if the case should arise His Majesty's Government were resolved and prepared to employ without delay all the forces at their command.

On numerous occasions I have stated my conviction that war between our two countries, admitted on all sides to be the greatest calamity that could occur, is not desired either by our own people or the German people. With this fact in mind I informed the German Chancellor that, in our view, there was nothing in the questions arising between Poland and Germany which could not be, and should not be, resolved without the use of force, if only a situation of confidence could be restored. We expressed our willingness to assist in creating the conditions in which such negotiations could take place. The present state of tension creates great difficulties, and I expressed the view that if there could be a truce on all sides to press polemics and all other forms of incitement suitable conditions might be established for direct negotiations between Germany and Poland upon the points at issue. The negotiations could, of course, deal also with the complaints made on either side about the protection of minorities.

The German Chancellor's reply includes what amounts to a restatement of the German thesis that Eastern Europe is a sphere in which Germany ought to have a free hand. If we—this is the thesis —or any country having less direct interest choose to interfere, the blame for the ensuing conflict will be ours. This thesis entirely misapprehends the British position. We do not seek to claim a special position for ourselves in Eastern Europe. We do not think of asking Germany to sacrifice her national interests, but we cannot agree that national interests can only be secured by the shedding of blood or the destruction of the independence of other States. With regard to the relations between Poland and Germany, the German Chancellor in his reply to me has referred again to the situation at Danzig, drawing attention to the position of that city and of the Corridor, and to the offer which he made early this year to settle these questions by methods of negotiations. I have repeatedly refuted the allegation that it was our guarantee to Poland that decided the Polish Government to refuse the proposals then made. That guarantee was not, in fact, given until after the Polish refusal had been conveyed to the German Government. In view of the delicacy of the situation I must refrain for the present from any further comment upon the communications which have just passed between the two Governments. Catastrophe has not yet come upon us. We must, therefore, still hope that reason and sanity may find a way to reassert themselves. The pronouncement we made recently and what I have said to-day reflects, I am sure, the views of the French Government, with whom we have maintained the customary close contact in pursuance of our well established cordial relations.

Naturally, our minds turn to the Dominions. I appreciate very warmly the pronouncements made by Ministers in other parts of the British Commonwealth. The indications that have been given from time to time, in some cases as recently as yesterday, of their sympathy with our patient efforts in the cause of peace, and of their attitude in the unhappy event of their proving unsuccessful, are a source of profound encouragement to us in these critical times. The House will, I am sure, share the appreciation with which His Majesty's Government have noted the appeal for peace made yesterday by King Leopold in the name of the heads of the Oslo States, after the meeting in Brussels yesterday of the representatives of those States. It will be evident from what I have said that His Majesty's Government share the hopes to which that appeal gave expression, and earnestly trust that effect will be given to it.

The Foreign Secretary, in a speech made on the 29th June to the Royal Institute of International Affairs,* set out the fundamental bases of British foreign policy. His observations on that subject were, I believe, received with general approval. The first basis is our determination to resist methods of force. The second basis is our recognition of the world desire to pursue the constructive work of building

* No. 25.

peace. If we were once satisfied, my noble Friend said, that the intentions of others were the same as our own, and if we were satisfied that all wanted peaceful solutions, then, indeed, we could discuss problems which are to-day causing the world so much anxiety. That definition of the basic fundamental ground of British policy still stands. We want to see established an international order based upon mutual understanding and mutual confidence, and we cannot build such an order unless it conforms to certain principles which are essential to the establishment of confidence and trust. Those principles must include the observance of international undertakings when they have once been entered into, and the renunciation of force in the settlement of differences. It is because those principles, to which we attach such vital importance, seem to us to be in jeopardy that we have undertaken these tremendous and unprecedented responsibilities.

If, despite all our efforts to find the way to peace—and God knows I have tried my best—if in spite of all that, we find ourselves forced to embark upon a struggle which is bound to be fraught with suffering and misery for all mankind and the end of which no man can foresee, if that should happen, we shall not be fighting for the political future of a far away city in a foreign land; we shall be fighting for the preservation of those principles of which I have spoken, the destruction of which would involve the destruction of all possibility of peace and security for the peoples of the world. This issue of peace or war does not rest with us, and I trust that those with whom the responsibility does lie will think of the millions of human beings whose fate depends upon their actions. For ourselves, we have a united country behind us, and in this critical hour I believe that we, in this House of Commons, will stand together, and that this afternoon we shall show the world that, as we think, so will we act, as a united nation.

65.

Speech by the Secretary of State for Foreign Affairs in the House of Lords on August 24, 1939.

My Lords, I am glad to accede to the invitation of the noble Lord opposite, and perhaps your Lordships will forgive me if I make a statement of somewhat greater length than is customary in answer to a formal question. It will perhaps be of some usefulness if I sketch in a word or two the background of the international developments which have led to the recall of Parliament. The events of this year are fresh in all our minds, and the cumulative effect of them had been to lead many countries of Europe to feel themselves confronted with an attempt on the part of Germany to dominate and control their destiny, and there were few which had not reason to fear that their liberties were in greater or less degree in danger. As a matter of history, successive British Governments have felt obliged to resist attempts by a single Power to dominate Europe at the expense of others, and the imposition of one country's will by force of arms. This country has stood for the maintenance of the independence of those States who both valued their liberties and were ready to defend them, and have endeavoured to uphold the principle that changes which must inevitably take place in the relations between nations can and should be effected peacefully and by free negotiation between those concerned.

His Majesty's Government accordingly entered into consultation with the countries who felt themselves to be more immediately threatened, for the sole purpose of concerting resistance to further aggression if such should be attempted. His Majesty's Government at the same time endeavoured to make clear their attitude both by word and deed so that no doubt might anywhere exist as to the policy which they were determined to pursue. They introduced compulsory service and made efforts unprecedented in times of peace to expand and equip the armed forces of the Crown and to place both the civil and military defences of the country in a state of full preparedness. The declarations of policy which have been made in this House and in another place have sought to set out both general principles of British policy and also the attitude of His Majesty's Government to particular questions, such as Danzig, which have from time to time held the forefront of the stage. The declarations which were thus made and the action which was taken met, I think, with the general approval both of Parliament and people.

Before the adjournment early this month my right honourable friend the Prime Minister said that the situation, in which the accumulation of the weapons of war was going on at such a pace, was one which could not but be regarded with anxiety. He referred to the bad feeling which was being created by poisonous propaganda, and said that if that could be stopped and if some action could be taken to restore confidence in Europe, there was no question which should not be capable of solution by a peaceful means. Of such action, however, there has unhappily been no sign, and since the House adjourned the international situation has deteriorated, until to-day we are confronted with the imminent peril of war.

At the beginning of August further differences arose between the Polish Government and the Danzig Senate concerning the position and functions of the Polish Customs Inspectors in the Free City. These differences were relatively unimportant in themselves and in an atmosphere of less tension would no doubt have been capable of being settled amicably, as similar differences have been settled in the past. Discussion of the questions at issue was in fact proceeding at the end of last week. But while efforts were being made to set the machinery of negotiation in motion, the German press opened a violent campaign against the Polish Government. This campaign, as noble Lords may have noticed, was not confined solely, or even principally, to the question of Danzig. On this question it was stated that there could be no compromise: Danzig must return unconditionally to the Reich. With it was linked the question of the so-called Corridor, and the attack on

114

Poland has extended to cover the general attitude and policy of the Polish Government, and in particular the position of the German minority in Poland.

In regard to the German minority I would say this. Every country must be concerned to secure just treatment for minorities, and must naturally feel particular interest in minorities allied to it by race. No one in this country, certainly, would wish to defend conditions under which such treatment was denied to any minority section, but if causes of complaint exist let them not be made the ground for such embitterment of the atmosphere as must make any settlement a hundred times more difficult, but let them be fairly and dispassionately brought to examination, so that before the public opinion of the world some ground may be established for their consideration and redress. It is impossible to ignore the fact that the accusations against Poland bear a strong resemblance to the accusations made last year against Czecho-Slovakia, and it is right also to remember that there is a large Polish minority in Germany, of whose treatment the Polish Government also bitterly complain.

Of the general attitude of Poland it must be admitted, I think, that in the face of a campaign which appears to threaten not only their independence of action, but also the existence of Poland as a nation, the declarations of the Polish leaders have been firm but quite unprovocative. I am confident that they have been, and are at all times, ready to discuss the differences between themselves and Germany, if they could be reasonably certain that the discussion would take place under free conditions, without the menace of force, and with assurance that the results of the discussion would be loyally and permanently observed. If at times the Polish newspapers have replied in kind to the onslaught of the German press, this has not been reflected in the attitude of the Polish Government. Concurrently with the press campaign there has been much active military preparation in Germany, and that country is being placed on a footing of complete readiness for war. At the beginning of this week there were indications that German troops were moving towards the Polish frontiers, and, in the face of what was obviously becoming a very menacing situation, His Majesty's Government decided that the time had come when they must seek the approval of Parliament for further measures of defence.

That, in outline, was the situation when on the 22nd August, the day before yesterday, it was officially stated in Berlin and Moscow that negotiations had been in progress, and were to be at once continued, for the signature of a non-aggression pact between the Soviet Union and Germany. I do not conceal the fact that this announcement came as a surprise to His Majesty's Government. For some time past there had been rumours of a change in the relations between the German and Soviet Governments, but no hint of such a change was conveyed by the Soviet Government to His Majesty's Government or the French Government, with whom they were in negotiation; and on the 31st July last the Prime Minister remarked in another place that His

115

Majesty's Government were showing a great degree of trust, and a strong desire to bring their negotiations with the Soviet Government to a successful issue, when, before any agreement had been finally reached on political matters, they agreed to send a Military Mission to Moscow to discuss military plans. The Military Missions of France and this country reached Moscow on the 11th August, and the conversations were proceeding to all appearance on a basis of mutual confidence, and it is, I do not conceal from your Lordships, certainly disturbing to learn that while these conversations were taking place the Soviet Government were secretly negotiating a pact with Germany for purposes which, on the face of it, were inconsistent with the objects, as we had understood them, of their foreign policy.

I would not now pass any final judgment on this matter. That would be premature until we have had time to consult with the French Government as to the meaning and the consequences of the agreement, the actual text of which has been published this morning, but one matter forces itself upon the immediate attention of His Majesty's Government. They had to consider what effect this changed situation should have on their policy. In Berlin the agreement was somewhat cynically welcomed as a great diplomatic victory which removed the danger of war, since, so it was alleged, Great Britain and France would no longer fulfil their obligations to Poland, and His Majesty's Government felt it their first duty to remove this dangerous illusion. It should be recalled, if it is not in mind, that our guarantee to Poland was given before any agreement with Russia was in prospect and without condition that such agreement should be reached. His Majesty's Government therefore at once issued a statement that their obligations to Poland and other countries remained unaffected; and throughout these days, as noble Lords will imagine, we have been in close and constant contact with the French Government, whose attitude is identical with our own. Our obligations rest on the agreed statements which were made in this House and in another place, and which are binding. Effect is being given to them in treaties, which are in an advanced stage of negotiation, and these treaties will formally define the mutual obligations of the parties, but they neither add to nor subtract from the obligations of mutual assistance which have been already accepted.

Certain necessary measures of precaution have already been taken. Some of these measures have already been announced, and other steps will be taken, as judged necessary, as soon as the legislation is passed, which I understand it is proposed to invite your Lordships to consider this afternoon. There is another action which has been taken to-day in the financial sphere. Your Lordships will have seen the announcement that the bank rate, which has remained for a long time past at 2 per cent., has to-day been raised to 4 per cent. The House will recognise that this is a normal protective measure, which is adopted for the purpose of defending our resources in a period of uncertainty. There is, in this connection, a contribution to be made generally by British citizens. The public can best co-operate by reducing, so far as possible, any demands which involve, directly or indirectly, the purchase of foreign exchange; next, by scrupulously observing the Chancellor of the Exchequer's request that capital should not at present be sent or moved out of the country; and, finally, by holding no more foreign assets than are strictly required for the normal purpose of business.

My Lords, I have said that His Majesty's Government have tried to make their position quite clear, but, in order that no possible doubt might exist in the mind of the German Government, His Majesty's Ambassador in Berlin was instructed yesterday to seek an interview with Herr Hitler and to give him a message on His Majesty's Government's behalf. The object of this message to the German Chancellor was to restate our position and to make quite sure that there was no misunderstanding. His Majesty's Government, as I have suggested, felt that that was all the more necessary having regard to the reports which we have received as to the military movements in Germany and as to the then projected German-Soviet Agreement. My right honourable Friend the Prime Minister, therefore, on behalf of His Majesty's Government, made it plain, as had, indeed, been made plain in the statement issued after the meeting of the Cabinet on Tuesday last, that if the case should arise His Majesty's Government were resolved and prepared to employ without delay all the forces at their command.

On numerous occasions the Prime Minister has stated his conviction, which is shared, I would suppose, by all people of this country, that war between the British and the German peoples—admitted on all sides to be the greatest calamity that could occur—was not desired either by our people or by the German people. And the Prime Minister further informed the German Chancellor that we did not see that there was anything in the questions arising between Germany and Poland which could not and should not be resolved without the use of force, if only a situation of confidence could be restored. We have expressed our willingness to assist in creating the conditions in which such negotiations could take place. It was obvious that the present state of tension created great difficulties, and the Prime Minister expressed the view that, if there could be a truce on all sides to press polemics and all incitements, a suitable condition might be established for direct negotiations between Germany and Poland upon the points between them. The negotiations could, of course, also deal with the complaints made on either side about the treatment of minorities.

The German Chancellor's reply includes what amounts to a restatement of the German thesis that Eastern Europe is a sphere in which Germany seeks to have a free hand; if we or any country having less direct interests choose to interfere, the blame for the ensuing conflict will be ours. The British position is, of course, that we do not in any way seek to claim a special position for ourselves; we do not think of asking Germany to sacrifice her national interests, but we do insist that the interests of other States should be respected. We cannot agree that national interests can only be secured by the shed-

117

ding of blood or by the destruction of the independence of other States; and, unfortunately, events such as those of last March make it difficult to accept assurances, even now repeated, about the limitations of German interests. Herr Hitler has often said that he has fought for a better Anglo-German understanding, but it has, as we see it, been the acts of Herr Hitler himself that have time and again destroyed our earnest and sincere endeavours to that end; and as regards relations between Germany and Poland, the German Chancellor has referred again to the situation at Danzig, drawing attention to the position of that City and of the Corridor, and to the offer which he made only this year to settle those questions by methods of negotiation. The allegation that it was our guarantee to Poland that decided the Polish Government to refuse the proposals then made has been repeatedly refuted. That guarantee was not, in fact, given until after the Polish refusal had been conveyed to the German Government.

My Lords, in view of the delicacy of the situation I would refrain at this time from any further comment upon the communications which have just passed between the two Governments. Catastrophe has not yet come upon Europe, and we must, therefore, still hope that reason and sanity may find means to reassert themselves. As to the military measures that we have taken, it must be remembered that, as I have said, Germany has already an immense number of men under arms, and has also made military preparations of all kinds on a vast scale. The measures taken in this country have so far been only of a precautionary and defensive kind, but no threats will affect our determination to do what is necessary to prepare the country for any emergency. I would with emphasis repudiate any suggestion that the measures we are taking imply a contemplated act of menace on our part. Nothing that we have done or propose to do constitutes a threat to any of Germany's legitimate interests. It is no act of menace to prepare oneself to help one's friends to defend themselves against the use of force.

In a speech that I made some six weeks or two months ago to the Royal Institute of International Affairs I tried to set out in terms which were fortunate enough to meet with almost unanimous approval the twin foundations of purpose on which British policy rests. The first was a determination to resist force, and the second was the recognition of the world's desire to get on with the constructive task of building peace. And if we could once, as I said, be satisfied that the intentions of others were the same as our own, and that we all really wanted peaceful solutions, then, I said, we could discuss all the problems that were causing the world anxiety. That definition of the policy of His Majesty's Government stands. Our object is, and has been, to build an international order based on mutual understanding and mutual confidence, but that order can only rest on the basis of certain moral principles which are widely recognised to be essential to the peaceful and the orderly life of nations, and among those principles I place high the renunciation of forcible solutions and the respect for the pledged word in international relationships. And, fundamentally, it is those principles which are to-day as we see it in danger, and it is those principles which we consider it vital to try and protect.

There are some who say that the fate of European nations is no concern of ours, and that we should not look far beyond our own frontiers. But those who thus argue forget, I think, that in failing to uphold the liberties of others we run great risk of betraying the principle of liberty itself, and with it our own freedom and independence. We have built up a society with values which are accepted not only in this country but over vast areas of the world. If we stand by and see these values set at nought the security of all those things on which life itself depends seems, to my judgment, to be undermined, and that is a fundamental matter on which I scarcely think that there will be any difference of opinion. I have no doubt that those with whom rest the issues of peace and war will measure their responsibilities to present and future generations before precipitating a struggle in which many nations of Europe must immediately be involved, of which the duration cannot be foreseen, and by which even those who stand aside from active participation will be vitally and dangerously affected. And I would earnestly hope that in face of all the certain consequences of a resort to force, and before any step is taken which cannot be retraced, reason may yet prevail. His Majesty's Government have noted with warm appreciation the appeal for peace made by King Leopold after the meeting at Brussels yesterday in the name of the heads of the Oslo States. It will be evident from what I have said that His Majesty's Government share the hopes to which that appeal gave such moving expression, and earnestly trust that effect may be given to it.

My Lords, in this moment of anxiety I trust that the ground on which His Majesty's Government have determined to take their stand will meet with the approval of all parties in this House. I believe it will, and I do not doubt that the Government may rely on the support of the whole country in any measures necessary to defend the cause of just dealing between the nations and to preserve secure the place of honourable freedom in the world.

66.

Sir H. Kennard to Viscount Halifax (received 8 P.M.)

(Telegraphic.) *Warsaw, August 24, 1939.*

M. Beck told me that he considered situation most grave. Attitude of Danzig authorities was becoming more provocative, though he had no intention for the moment of actually breaking off negotiations regarding customs inspectors and so forth.

2. M. Beck has, as requested, instructed Polish Ambassador in Berlin to seek immediate interview with State Secretary, and, unless he found attitude of Herr von Weizsäcker unsatisfactory, he would attempt to examine all points at issue with a view to ascertaining

whether anything can be done to relieve present tension.

3. M. Beck referred to certain incidents on the frontier, and I asked him more especially whether one which has caused great indignation here was true: it was reported in the press this morning that body of Polish frontier guard shot on 16th August was returned in a state of shocking and gruesome mutilation. M. Beck said that the facts were as stated in the press and that Commissioner-General was protesting to Danzig Senate without, however, demanding any reply.

4. As far as I can see, calm prevails, and M. Beck has assured me that strict orders have been given to prevent any provocative action either of military or any other nature. Frontier is still covered by ordinary frontier guards, and there would seem from M. Beck's attitude no necessity for warning which, nevertheless, I and my French colleague have given him to do nothing which would further aggravate present critical state of affairs.

67.

Sir H. Kennard to Viscount Halifax.
(Despatched at 2.35 A.M. on August 25 and received at
9.30 A.M. on August 25.)

(Telegraphic.)   *Warsaw, August 24, 1939.*
My telegram of 24th August.*

The Minister for Foreign Affairs informs me that Polish Ambassador in Berlin had an interview with Field-Marshal Göring this afternoon. The interview was most cordial and he told me the Marshal expressed his regret that his policy of maintaining friendly relations with Poland should have come to nought and admitted that he no longer had influence to do much in the matter. The Marshal had, however, no concrete suggestion to make beyond what had struck M. Beck as a most significant remark which he requested me to convey to you most confidentially. The Marshal stated that the question of Danzig and so forth were relatively small matters, but the main obstacle to any diminution of the tension between the two countries was Poland's alliance with Great Britain.

2. M. Beck had consulted the President and Marshal Smigly-Rydz, and it had been decided that if the German Government should put forward this suggestion in any other way the answer would be categorically in the negative. M. Beck feels that the German Government may make every effort to secure a free hand in Eastern Europe by such methods and he feels that it should be clearly understood that Poland will not be drawn into any intrigue of this nature.

3. I asked M. Beck about the proposed interview between M. Lipski and the State Secretary. M. Beck said that Herr von Weiz-

* No. 66.

120

säcker was in Berchtesgaden and would probably not return until the end of the week, but that M. Lipski had asked for an interview and was awaiting reply.

68.

Supplementary Communication from the German Chancellor handed to His Majesty's Ambassador on August 25, 1939.

The following is a translation of the text of a verbal communication made to Sir Nevile Henderson by Herr Hitler at his interview on the 25th August:—

"By way of introduction the Führer declared that the British Ambassador had given expression at the close of the last conversation to the hope that, after all, an understanding between Germany and England might yet be possible. He (the Führer) had therefore turned things over in his mind once more and desired to make a move as regards England which should be as decisive as the move as regards Russia which had led to the recent agreement. Yesterday's sitting in the House of Commons and the speeches of Mr. Chamberlain and Lord Halifax had also moved the Führer to talk once more to the British Ambassador. The assertion that Germany affected to conquer the world was ridiculous. The British Empire embraced 40 million square kilometres, Russia 19 million square kilometres, America 9½ million square kilometres, whereas Germany embraced less than 600,000 square kilometres. It is quite clear who it is who desires to conquer the world.

"The Führer makes the following communication to the British Ambassador:—

"1. Poland's actual provocations have become intolerable. It makes no difference who is responsible. If the Polish Government denies responsibility, that only goes to show that it no longer itself possesses any influence over its subordinate military authorities. In the preceding night there had been a further twenty-one new frontier incidents; on the German side the greatest discipline had been maintained. All incidents had been provoked from the Polish side. Furthermore, commercial aircraft had been shot at. If the Polish Government stated that it was not possible, it showed that it was no longer capable of controlling its own people.

"2. Germany was in all the circumstances determined to abolish these Macedonian conditions on her eastern frontier and, what is more, to do so in the interests of quiet and order, but also in the interests of European peace.

"3. The problem of Danzig and the Corridor must be solved.— The British Prime Minister had made a speech which was not in the least calculated to induce any change in the German attitude. At the most, the result of this speech could be a bloody and incalculable

121

war between Germany and England. Such a war would be bloodier than that of 1914 to 1918. In contrast to the last war, Germany would no longer have to fight on two fronts. Agreement with Russia was unconditional and signified a change in foreign policy of the Reich which would last a very long time. Russia and Germany would never again take up arms against each other. Apart from this, the agreements reached with Russia would also render Germany secure economically for the longest possible period of war.

"The Führer had always wanted an Anglo-German understanding. War between England and Germany could at the best bring some profit to Germany but none at all to England.

"The Führer declared that the German-Polish problem must be solved and will be solved. He is, however, prepared and determined after the solution of this problem to approach England once more with a large comprehensive offer. He is a man of great decisions, and in this case also he will be capable of being great in his action. He accepts the British Empire and is ready to pledge himself personally for its continued existence and to place the power of the German Reich at its disposal if—

"(1) His colonial demands which are limited and can be negotiated by peaceful methods are fulfilled and in this case he is prepared to fix the longest time limit.

"(2) His obligations towards Italy are not touched; in other words, he does not demand that England gives up her obligations towards France and similarly for his own part he cannot withdraw from his obligations towards Italy.

"(3) He also desires to stress the irrevocable determination of Germany never again to enter into conflict with Russia. The Führer is ready to conclude agreements with England which, as has already been emphasised, would not only guarantee the existence of the British Empire in all circumstances as far as Germany is concerned, but also if necessary an assurance to the British Empire of German assistance regardless of where such assistance should be necessary. The Führer would then also be ready to accept a reasonable limitation of armaments which corresponds to the new political situation, and which is economically tolerable. Finally, the Führer renewed his assurances that he is not interested in Western problems and that a frontier modification in the West does not enter into consideration. Western fortifications which have been constructed at a cost of milliards were final Reich frontier on the West.

"If the British Government would consider these ideas a blessing for Germany and also for the British Empire might result. If it rejects these ideas there will be war. In no case would Great Britain emerge stronger; the last war proved this.

"The Führer repeats that he is a man of *ad infinitum* decisions by which he himself is bound and that this is his last offer. Immediately after solution of the German-Polish question he would approach the British Government with an offer."

69.

Sir N. Henderson to Viscount Halifax (received 7 p.m.).

(Telegraphic.) *Berlin, August 25, 1939.*

In my immediately preceding telegram* I give text of a verbal communication which Chancellor made to me this morning. He was absolutely calm and normal and spoke with great earnestness and apparent sincerity. Minister for Foreign Affairs was present but took practically no part in the conversation.

2. Herr Hitler began by saying that he had always and still desired good relations with Great Britain, and his conscience compelled him to make this final effort to secure them. It was his last attempt. He suggested that I should fly to England myself in order to put the case to His Majesty's Government.

3. Conversation lasted an hour, my attitude being that Russian Pact in no way altered standpoint of His Majesty's Government, and that I must tell him quite honestly that Britain could not go back on her word to Poland and that I knew his offer would not be considered unless it meant a negotiated settlement of the Polish question. Herr Hitler refused to guarantee this on grounds that Polish provocation might at any moment render German intervention to protect German nationals inevitable. I again and again returned to this point but always got the same answer.

4. I told Herr Hitler that I could not discuss rights and wrongs of mutual provocation and incidents: that was for the Polish Ambassador to discuss with Herr von Ribbentrop and I suggested that he should do so. Herr Hitler's reply was that M. Lipski had seen Field-Marshal Göring, but had not been able to propose anything new.

5. I told Herr Hitler that we could not abandon Poland to her fate, but I made the entirely personal suggestion that M. Beck and Herr von Ribbentrop should meet somewhere and discuss the way out which alone might save Europe from war. Herr Hitler's reply was that he had invited M. Beck to come and talk the matter over last March only to have his invitation flatly refused. Only intervention by Herr von Ribbentrop in the discussion was to confirm this and to say that M. Lipski, who had had to convey this message, was obliged to put it in other words to soften the abruptness of it.

6. When I kept saying that His Majesty's Government could not in my opinion consider his offer unless it meant at the same time a peaceful settlement with Poland, Herr Hitler said: "If you think it useless then do not send my offer at all." He admitted the good

* Conveying the substance of No. 68.

123

intentions of M. Beck and M. Lipski, but said they had no control over what was happening in Poland. Only signs of excitement on Herr Hitler's part were when he referred to Polish persecutions. He mentioned that Herr von Ribbentrop on his return to Germany from Russia had had to fly from Königsberg over the sea to avoid being shot at by the Poles, who fired at every German aeroplane that flew over normal routes across Polish territory. He also said that there had been another case of castration.

7. Among various points mentioned by Herr Hitler were: that the only winner of another European war would be Japan; that he was by nature an artist not a politician, and that once the Polish question was settled he would end his life as an artist and not as a warmonger; he did not want to turn Germany into nothing but a military barracks and he would only do so if forced to do so; that once the Polish question was settled he himself would settle down; that he had no interest in making Britain break her word to Poland; that he had no wish to be small-minded in any settlement with Poland and that all he required for an agreement with her was a gesture from Britain to indicate that she would not be unreasonable.

8. After I had left, Herr von Ribbentrop sent Dr. Schmidt to the Embassy with text of verbal statement and also a message from him to the effect that Herr Hitler had always and still wished for an agreement with Britain and begging me to urge His Majesty's Government to take the offer very seriously.

70.

Viscount Halifax to Sir H. Kennard (Warsaw).

(Telegraphic.) *Foreign Office, August 25, 1939, 11 p.m.*

Please sound Polish Government on proposal for corps of neutral observers which, if accepted, would, of course, only come into operation if and when it was found possible to start any negotiations.

71.

Viscount Halifax to Sir H. Kennard (Warsaw).

(Telegraphic.) *Foreign Office, August 26, 1939, 5 p.m.*

It is clear that Herr Hitler is laying chief emphasis on ill-treatment of German minority, and may use this at any moment as an excuse for taking some irrevocable action.

2. Is it not possible for Polish Government to adopt suggestion that they should approach German Government with enquiry as to whether they would contemplate making exchange of populations an element to be considered in any negotiation? It is true this would afford no immediate safeguard as it is a remedy that would take some time to apply, but it would be a pledge that Polish Government

recognise the difficulty and are genuinely seeking means to overcome it, and it would give Polish Government some definite and new point on which to open up negotiation.

3. If action is to be taken by the Polish Government in this sense it ought to be done immediately.

72.

Sir H. Kennard to Viscount Halifax (received 5.5 p.m.)

(Telegraphic.)   *Warsaw, August 27, 1939.*

Your telegrams of 25th and 26th August.*

I discussed questions of exchange of populations and neutral observers with M. Beck this morning.

2. As regards first, he said that in principle he saw no objection and was prepared to convey to German Government that he was ready to consider such a proposal, possibly not directly to State Secretary, but in such a manner that he was sure it would reach the highest authorities.

3. As regards question of neutral observers, he had again consulted President of the Council, but he would let me know his decision in the course of the day.

4. As he told me that the Pope had during the night, through the Nuncio, asked if there was anything he could do, I suggested to M. Beck that he should inform His Holiness that he was prepared to consider an exchange of populations and also use of neutral observers in order to demonstrate that German accusations of maltreatment were completely without foundation. The Pope could then communicate these proposals to the German Government with approval of Polish Government. M. Beck seemed to consider this favourably and promised he would give it his immediate consideration. I warned him that there was no time to lose.

5. As regards Danzig, M. Beck did not from his latest information anticipate *fait accompli* there to-day or in very immediate future. For the moment all was quiet there as far as he knew.

6. I again emphasised to his Excellency importance of his giving sufficient warning to His Majesty's Government of any action which Polish Government or army contemplated taking as result of any *fait accompli* at Danzig. His Excellency again promised to do this, though he made reservation that situation might arise where immediate action would be necessary.

* Nos. 70 and 71.

73.

Viscount Halifax to Sir H. Kennard (Warsaw).

(Telegraphic.)   *Foreign Office, August 28, 1939, 2 p.m.*

Our proposed reply to Herr Hitler* draws a clear distinction between the method of reaching agreement on German-Polish differences and the nature of the solution to be arrived at. As to the method we wish to express our clear view that direct discussion on equal terms between the parties is the proper means.

2. Polish Government enjoy protection of Anglo-Polish Treaty.

3. His Majesty's Government have already made it plain and are repeating in their reply to Herr Hitler to-day that any settlement of German-Polish differences must safeguard Poland's essential interests and must be secured by international guarantee.

4. We have, of course, seen reports of Herr Hitler's reply to M. Daladier, but we should not consider intimation by Polish Government of their readiness to hold direct discussions as in any way implying acceptance of Herr Hitler's demands, which would, as made plain above, have to be examined in light of principles we have stated.

5. As Polish Government appear in their reply to President Roosevelt to accept idea of direct negotiations, His Majesty's Government earnestly hope that in the light of the considerations set forth in foregoing paragraphs Polish Government will authorise them to inform German Government that Poland is ready to enter at once into direct discussion with Germany.

6. Please endeavour to see M. Beck at once and telephone reply.

* No. 74.

74.

Reply of His Majesty's Government dated August 28, 1939, to the German Chancellor's Communications of August 23 and 25, 1939.*

His Majesty's Government have received the message conveyed to them from the German Chancellor by His Majesty's Ambassador in Berlin, and have considered it with the care which it demands.

They note the Chancellor's expression of his desire to make friendship the basis of the relations between Germany and the British Empire and they fully share this desire. They believe with him that if a complete and lasting understanding between the two countries could be established it would bring untold blessings to both peoples.

2. The Chancellor's message deals with two groups of questions: those which are the matters now in dispute between Germany and Poland and those affecting the ultimate relations of Germany and Great Britain. In connexion with these last, His Majesty's Government observe, that the German Chancellor has indicated certain proposals which, subject to one condition, he would be prepared to make to the

* Nos. 60 and 68.

British Government for a general understanding. These proposals are, of course, stated in very general form and would require closer definition, but His Majesty's Government are fully prepared to take them, with some additions, as subjects for discussion and they would be ready, if the differences between Germany and Poland are peacefully composed, to proceed so soon as practicable to such discussion with a sincere desire to reach agreement.

3. The condition which the German Chancellor lays down is that there must first be a settlement of the differences between Germany and Poland. As to that, His Majesty's Government entirely agree. Everything, however, turns upon the nature of the settlement and the method by which it is to be reached. On these points, the importance of which cannot be absent from the Chancellor's mind, his message is silent, and His Majesty's Government feel compelled to point out that an understanding upon both of these is essential to achieving further progress. The German Government will be aware that His Majesty's Government have obligations to Poland by which they are bound and which they intend to honour. They could not, for any advantage offered to Great Britain, acquiesce in a settlement which put in jeopardy the independence of a State to whom they have given their guarantee.

4. In the opinion of His Majesty's Government a reasonable solution of the differences between Germany and Poland could and should be effected by agreement between the two countries on lines which would include the safeguarding of Poland's essential interests, and they recall that in his speech of the 28th April last the German Chancellor recognised the importance of these interests to Poland.

But, as was stated by the Prime Minister in his letter to the German Chancellor of the 22nd August, His Majesty's Government consider it essential for the success of the discussions which would precede the agreement that it should be understood beforehand that any settlement arrived at would be guaranteed by other Powers. His Majesty's Government would be ready if desired to make their contribution to the effective operation of such a guarantee.

In the view of His Majesty's Government it follows that the next step should be the initiation of direct discussions between the German and Polish Governments on a basis which would include the principles stated above, namely, the safeguarding of Poland's essential interests and the securing of the settlement by an international guarantee.

They have already received a definite assurance from the Polish Government that they are prepared to enter into discussions on this basis, and His Majesty's Government hope the German Government would for their part also be willing to agree to this course.

If, as His Majesty's Government hope, such discussion led to agreement the way would be open to the negotiation of that wider and more complete understanding between Great Britain and Germany which both countries desire.

5. His Majesty's Government agree with the German Chancellor that one of the principal dangers in the German-Polish situation arises from the reports concerning the treatment of minorities. The present state of tension, with its concomitant frontier incidents, reports of maltreatment and inflammatory propaganda, is a constant danger to peace. It is manifestly a matter of the utmost urgency that all incidents of the kind should be promptly and rigidly suppressed and that unverified reports should not be allowed to circulate, in order that time may be afforded, without provocation on either side, for a full examination of the possibilities of settlement. His Majesty's Government are confident that both the Governments concerned are fully alive to these considerations.

6. His Majesty's Government have said enough to make their own attitude plain in the particular matters at issue between Germany and Poland. They trust that the German Chancellor will not think that, because His Majesty's Government are scrupulous concerning their obligations to Poland, they are not anxious to use all their influence to assist the achievement of a solution which may commend itself both to Germany and to Poland.

That such a settlement should be achieved seems to His Majesty's Government essential, not only for reasons directly arising in regard to the settlement itself, but also because of the wider considerations of which the German Chancellor has spoken with such conviction.

7. It is unnecessary in the present reply to stress the advantage of a peaceful settlement over a decision to settle the questions at issue by force of arms. The results of a decision to use force have been clearly set out in the Prime Minister's letter to the Chancellor of the 22nd August, and His Majesty's Government do not doubt that they are as fully recognised by the Chancellor as by themselves.

On the other hand, His Majesty's Government, noting with interest the German Chancellor's reference in the message now under consideration to a limitation of armaments, believe that, if a peaceful settlement can be obtained, the assistance of the world could confidently be anticipated for practical measures to enable the transition from preparation for war to the normal activities of peaceful trade to be safely and smoothly effected.

8. A just settlement of these questions between Germany and Poland may open the way to world peace. Failure to reach it would ruin the hopes of better understanding between Germany and Great Britain, would bring the two countries into conflict, and might well plunge the whole world into war. Such an outcome would be a calamity without parallel in history.

75

*Sir N. Henderson to Viscount Halifax (received
2.35 a.m. August 29).*

(Telegraphic.)   *Berlin, August 28, 1939.*

I saw the Chancellor at 10.30 this evening. He asked me to come
at 10 p.m., but I sent word that I could not have the translation ready
before the later hour. Herr von Ribbentrop was present, also Dr.
Schmidt. Interview lasted one and a quarter hours.

2. Herr Hitler began by reading the German translation. When
he had finished, I said that I wished to make certain observations from
notes which I had made in the conversations with the Prime Minister
and His Majesty's Secretary of State for Foreign Affairs. In the first
place I wished to say that we in England regarded it as absurd that
Britain should be supposed by the German Government to consider
the crushing of Germany as a settled policy. We held it to be no less
astonishing that anyone in Germany should doubt for a moment that
we would not fight for Poland if her independence or vital interests
were menaced.

3. Our word was our word, and we had never and would never
break it. In the old days Germany's word had the same value, and
I quoted a passage from a German book (which Herr Hitler had read)
about Marshal Blücher's exhortation to his troops when hurrying to
the support of Wellington at Waterloo: "Forward, my children, I have
given my word to my brother Wellington, and you cannot wish me to
break it."

4. Herr Hitler at once intervened to observe that things were
different 125 years ago. I said not so far as England was concerned.
He wanted, I said, Britain's friendship. What value would he place
on our friendship if we began it by disloyalty to a friend? Whatever
some people might say, the British people sincerely desired an understanding with Germany, and no one more so than the Prime Minister
(Herr von Ribbentrop remarked that Mr. Chamberlain had once said
to him that it was his dearest wish). To-day the whole British public
was behind the Prime Minister. The recent vote in the House of
Commons was an unmistakable proof of that fact. The Prime Minister
could carry through his policy of an understanding if, but only if, Herr
Hitler were prepared to co-operate. There was absolutely no truth in
the idea sometimes held in Germany that the British Cabinet was
disunited or that the country was not unanimous. It was now or
never, and it rested with Herr Hitler. If he was prepared to sacrifice
that understanding in order to make war or immoderate demands on
Poland, the responsibility was his. We offered friendship but only on
the basis of a peaceful and freely negotiated solution of the Polish
question.

5. Herr Hitler replied that he would be willing to negotiate, if
there was a Polish Government which was prepared to be reasonable

and which really controlled the country. He expatiated on misdoings of the Poles, referred to his generous offer of March last, said that it could not be repeated and asserted that nothing else than the return of Danzig and the whole of the Corridor would satisfy him, together with a rectification in Silesia, where 90 per cent. of the population had voted for Germany at the post-war plebiscite but where, as a result of Haller-Korfani *coup*, what the Plebiscite Commission had allotted had nevertheless been grabbed by Poland.

6. I told Herr Hitler that he must choose between England and Poland. If he put forward immoderate demands there was no hope of a peaceful solution. Corridor was inhabited almost entirely by Poles. Herr Hitler interrupted me here by observing that this was only true because a million Germans had been driven out of that district since the war. I again said the choice lay with him. He had offered a Corridor over the Corridor in March, and I must honestly tell him that anything more than that, if that, would have no hope of acceptance. I begged him very earnestly to reflect before raising his price. He said his original offer had been contemptuously refused and he would not make it again. I observed that it had been made in the form of a dictate and therein lay the whole difference.

7. Herr Hitler continued to argue that Poland could never be reasonable: she had England and France behind her, and imagined that even if she were beaten she would later recover, thanks to their help, more than she might lose. He spoke of annihilating Poland. I said that reminded me of similar talk last year of annihilation of the Czechs. He retorted that we were incapable of inducing Poland to be reasonable. I said that it was just because we remembered the experience of Czecho-Slovakia last year that we hesitated to press Poland too far to-day. Nevertheless, we reserved to ourselves the right to form our own judgment as to what was or what was not reasonable so far as Poland or Germany were concerned. We kept our hands free in that respect.

8. Generally speaking, Herr Hitler kept harping on Poland, and I kept on just as consistently telling Herr Hitler that he had to choose between friendship with England which we offered him and excessive demands on Poland which would put an end to all hope of British friendship. If we were to come to an understanding it would entail sacrifices on our part. If he was not prepared to make sacrifices on his part there was nothing to be done. Herr Hitler said that he had to satisfy the demands of his people, his army was ready and eager for battle, his people were united behind him, and he could not tolerate further ill-treatment of Germans in Poland, &c.

9. It is unnecessary to recall the details of a long and earnest conversation in the course of which the only occasion in which Herr Hitler became at all excited was when I observed that it was not a question of Danzig and the Corridor, but one of our determination to resist force by force. This evoked a tirade about the Rhineland,

130

Austria and Sudeten and their peaceful reacquisition by Germany. He also resented my references to 15th March.

10. In the end I asked him two straight questions. Was he willing to negotiate direct with the Poles and was he ready to discuss the question of an exchange of populations? He replied in the affirmative as regards the latter (though I have no doubt that he was thinking at the same time of a rectification of frontiers). As regards the first, he said he could not give me an answer until after he had given reply of His Majesty's Government the careful consideration which such a document deserved. In this connexion he turned to Herr von Ribbentrop and said: "We must summon Field-Marshal Göring to discuss it with him."

11. I finally repeated to him very solemnly the main note of the whole conversation so far as I was concerned, namely, that it lay with him as to whether he preferred a unilateral solution which would mean war as regards Poland, or British friendship. If he were prepared to pay the price of the latter by a generous gesture as regards Poland, he could at a stroke change in his favour the whole of public opinion not only in England but in the world. I left no doubt in his mind as to what the alternative would be, nor did he dispute the point.

12. At the end Herr von Ribbentrop asked me whether I could guarantee that the Prime Minister could carry the country with him in a policy of friendship with Germany. I said that was no possible doubt whatever that he could and would, provided Germany co-operated with him. Herr Hitler asked whether England would be willing to accept an alliance with Germany. I said, speaking personally, I did not exclude such a possibility provided the developments of events justified it.

13. Conversation was conducted in quite a friendly atmosphere, in spite of absolute firmness on both sides. Herr Hitler's general attitude was that he could give me no real reply until he had carefully studied the answer of His Majesty's Government. He said that he would give me a written reply to-morrow, Tuesday. I told him that I would await it, but was quite prepared to wait. Herr Hitler's answer was that there was no time to wait.

14. I did not refer to the question of a truce. I shall raise that point to-morrow if his answer affords any real ground for hope that he is prepared to abandon war for the sake of British understanding.

76.

Sir N. Henderson to Viscount Halifax (received 4.55 p.m.)

(Telegraphic.) *Berlin, August 29, 1939.*

Following are additional points in amplification of my telegram of 28th August*: —

Herr Hitler insisted that he was not bluffing, and that people would

* No. 75.

make a great mistake if they believed that he was. I replied that I was fully aware of the fact and that we were not bluffing either. Herr Hitler stated that he fully realised that that was the case. In answer to a suggestion by him that Great Britain might offer something at once in the way of colonies as evidence of her good intentions, I retorted that concessions were easier of realisation in a good rather than a bad atmosphere.

77.

Speech by the Prime Minister in the House of Commons on August 29, 1939.

The Prime Minister (Mr. Chamberlain): Since the House met on Thursday last there has been little change in the main features of the situation. The catastrophe, as I said then, is- not yet on us, but I cannot say that the danger of it has yet in any way receded. In these circumstances it might perhaps have seemed that it was unnecessary to ask the House to meet again before the date which had been fixed, but in times like these we have felt that it was right that the House should be kept as far as possible continuously informed of all the developments in the situation as they took place. That will continue to be the principle which will guide us in further meetings of this House.

There is one thing that I would like to say at this moment with regard to the press. I think it is necessary once more to urge the press to exercise the utmost restraint at a time when it is quite possible for a few thoughtless words in a paper, perhaps not of particular import- ance, to wreck the whole of the efforts which are being made by the Government to obtain a satisfactory solution. I have heard that an account purporting to be a verbatim description of the communication of the British Government to Herr Hitler was telegraphed to another country last night or this morning. Such an account could only be an invention from beginning to end. It is, I think, very unfortunate that journalists in the exercise of their profession should take such respon- sibilities upon themselves, responsibilities which affect not only them- selves, but the inhabitants, perhaps, of all the countries in the world.

I hope that it will not be necessary this afternoon to have any long Debate. I will attempt to give the House an account of the events of the last few days, but, of course, there has been no change in the policy of the Government, and, therefore, there would not appear to be any necessity for any lengthy discussion. On the day after the House adjourned—on Friday, that is—we received information in the course of the morning that the German Chancellor had asked the British Ambassador in Berlin to call upon him at half-past one that day, and in the course of the afternoon we were told by telephone that Sir Nevile Henderson had had an interview lasting about an hour and a half with Herr Hitler, that he was sending us an account of that interview, and that Herr Hitler had suggested to him that it would be a good thing if he were to fly over to this country the next morning in order to give us a verbal and more extended account of the conversation. We received the record of the interview from our Ambassador on that evening, on Friday evening, but it was not completely deciphered until after midnight, and I did not myself see the whole of it until the next morning, Saturday morning. On Saturday Sir Nevile Henderson arrived by plane from Berlin shortly before lunch, and we understood from him that in Berlin it was not considered to be necessary that he should go back the same day, as the German Government were very anxious that we should give careful study to the communication he had to make to us. Accordingly, we devoted the whole of Saturday and the Sunday morning to a very careful, exhaustive and thorough consideration of the document which was brought to us by the British Ambassador and of the reply that we proposed to send back, and our final answer was taken by the Ambassador yesterday afternoon, when he flew back to Berlin and delivered it to the Chancellor last night.

I should be glad if I could disclose to the House the fullest information as to the contents of the communications exchanged with Herr Hitler, but hon. members will understand that in a situation of such extreme delicacy, and when issues so grave hang precariously in the balance, it is not in the public interest to publish these confidential communications or to comment on them in detail at this stage. I am, however, able to indicate in quite general terms some of the main points with which they deal. Herr Hitler was concerned to impress upon His Majesty's Government his wish for an Anglo-German understanding of a complete and lasting character. On the other hand, he left His Majesty's Government in no doubt of his views as to the urgency of settling the German-Polish question. His Majesty's Government have also frequently expressed their desire to see the realisation of such an Anglo-German understanding, and as soon as circumstances permit they would naturally welcome an opportunity of discussing with Germany the several issues a settlement of which would have to find a place in any permanent agreement. But everything turns upon the manner in which the immediate differences between Germany and Poland can be handled and the nature of the proposals which might be made for any settlement. We have made it plain that our obligations to Poland, cast into formal shape by the agreement which was signed on 25th August, on Friday last, will be carried out. The House will remember that the Government have said more than once, publicly, that the German-Polish differences should be capable of solution by peaceful means.

Meanwhile, the first prerequisite, if there is to be any general and useful discussion, is that the tension created by frontier clashes and by reports of incidents on both sides of the border should be diminished. His Majesty's Government accordingly hope that both Governments will use their best endeavours to prevent the occurrence of such incidents, the circulation of exaggerated reports, and all other activities that result in dangerous inflammation of opinion. His Majesty's Government would hope that if an equitable settlement of Polish-German differences could be reached by free negotiation, this might in turn lead on to a wider agreement which would accrue to the lasting benefit of Europe and of the world at large. At this moment the position is that we are waiting for the reply of Herr Hitler to our communication. On the nature of that reply depends whether further time can be given for the exploration of the situation and for the operation of the many forces which are working for peace. A waiting period of that kind is often very trying, but nothing, I think, can be more remarkable than the calm which characterises the attitude of the whole British people. It seems to me that there are two explanations of that attitude. The first is that none of us has any doubt of where our duty lies. There is no difference of opinion among us; there is no weakening of our determination. The second explanation is our confidence that we are ready for any eventuality.

The House might like to hear one or two particulars of the preparations which have been made. Obviously, there are many things which I cannot very well say here because they could not be confined to those whom I see before me. My statement must, therefore, be in very general terms. Some of the measures which we had to take, such as those in connexion with requisitioning, necessarily must cause some degree of inconvenience to the public. I am confident that the people of the country generally recognise that the nation's needs must now be paramount and that they will submit willingly, and even cheerfully, to any inconvenience or hardships that may be involved. At any rate, we have not had to begin here by issuing rationing cards. To deal first with the active defence of the country, the air defence of Great Britain has been placed in a state of instant readiness. The ground anti-aircraft defences have been deployed and they are mannered by territorial anti-aircraft units. The regular squadrons of the Royal Air Force have been brought up to war strength by the addition of the necessary reservists, including a portion of the Volunteer Reserve. The fighter and general reconnaissance squadrons of the Auxiliary Air Force have been called up and are standing ready and the balloon barrage is in position. The Observer Corps are at their posts, and, indeed, the whole warning system is ready night and day to be brought into instant operation. The coast defences are ready and are manned by the coast defence units of the Territorial Army. Arrangements have also been made for the protection by the National Defence companies, by the Militia and by units of the Territorial Army of a very large number of important points whose safety is essential for the national war effort.

As to the Navy, the House will remember that in July last it was announced that the Reserve Fleet would be called up at the beginning of August in order to take part in combined Fleet and Air exercises. For that purpose a number of reservists were called up under the provisions of the Reserves and Auxiliary Forces Act. As a result, the Navy was in an advanced state of preparedness when the present crisis arose, and the whole of our fighting Fleet is now ready at a moment's notice to take up the dispositions which would be necessary in war. A number of other measures have been taken during the past week to increase the state of our naval preparedness. I need not go into all the details, but the naval officers in charge of the various commercial ports have been appointed and have taken up their duties, and the naval ports and bases have been put into an advanced state of preparedness. As hon. members will be aware, the Admiralty has also assumed control of merchant shipping, acting under the powers conferred by the Emergency Powers Act, and written instructions have already been issued to merchant shipping on various routes. A considerable number of movements have been carried out of units of the armed land forces both at home and overseas. These movements are part of prearranged plans to provide that in order to ensure a greater state of readiness a number of units should; if possible, move to their war stations before the outbreak of war. The Civil Defence regional organisation has been placed on war footing. Regional commissioners and their staffs are at their war stations.

The main responsibility for the organisation of Civil Defence measures generally rests with the local authorities. Instructions have been sent to the local authorities to complete all the preparatory steps so that action can be taken at the shortest notice. Plans for the evacuation of school children, mothers with young children, expectant mothers and blind persons from certain congested areas — plans which have involved an immense amount of detailed thinking— are ready. Those who have to carry out those plans have been recalled for duty, school teachers in evacuation areas have been kept in easy reach of school assembly points since Saturday, and a rehearsal of the arrangements for evacuating school children was carried out yesterday. Nearly a week ago local authorities were warned to make arrangements for the extinction of public lighting and to prepare the necessary aids to movement when the lighting has been extinguished. Arrangements have been completed for calling up at very short notice of the personnel of the Air-Raid Precautions Service, and duty officers are available throughout the twenty-four hours at key posts. The last item I mention is that the necessary preliminary steps have been taken to prepare hospitals for the reception of casualties.

I have given a number of instances of steps which have been taken over and above the measures which have already been put into operation. A complete and continuous survey is being carried out over the whole range of our defence preparations, and preparatory measures are being taken in order to ensure that further precautionary measures, if and when they should be found necessary, can be given effect to as rapidly as possible. The instances I have given to the House are merely illustrations of the general state of readiness, of

which the House and the country are aware. I think that they justify
and partly account for the general absence of fear, or, indeed, of any
violent emotion. The British people are said sometimes to be slow to
make up their minds, but, having made them up, they do not readily
let go. The issue of peace or war is still undecided, and we still will
hope, and still will work, for peace; but we will abate no jot of our
resolution to hold fast to the line which we have laid down for
ourselves.

78.

Reply of the German Chancellor to the Communication of August 28,
1939, from His Majesty's Government.* This reply was handed to
Sir N. Henderson by Herr Hitler during the evening of August
29, 1939.

(Translation.)

The British Ambassador in Berlin has submitted to the British
Government suggestions which I felt bound to make in order—

(1) to give expression once more to the will of the Reich Government for sincere Anglo-German understanding, co-operation
and friendship;

(2) to leave no room for doubt as to fact that such an understanding could not be bought at the price of a renunciation of vital
German interests, let alone the abandonment of demands
which are based as much upon common human justice as
upon the national dignity and honour of our people.

The German Government have noted with satisfaction from the
reply of the British Government and from the oral explanations given
by the British Ambassador that the British Government for their part
are also prepared to improve the relationship between Germany and
England and to develop and extend it in the sense of the German
suggestion.

In this connexion, the British Government are similarly convinced
that the removal of the German-Polish tension, which has become
unbearable, is the pre-requisite for the realisation of this hope.

Since the autumn of the past year, and on the last occasion in
March, 1939, there were submitted to the Polish Government proposals,
both oral and written, which, having regard to the friendship then
existing between Germany and Poland, offered the possibility of a
solution of the questions in dispute acceptable to both parties. The
British Government are aware that the Polish Government saw fit, in
March last, finally to reject these proposals. At the same time, they
used this rejection as a pretext or an occasion for taking military
measures which have since been continuously intensified. Already in
the middle of last month Poland was in effect in a state of mobilisation.

* No. 74.

This was accompanied by numerous encroachments in the Free City of Danzig due to the instigation of the Polish authorities; threatening demands in the nature of ultimata, varying only in degree, were addressed to that City. A closing of the frontiers, at first in the form of a measure of customs policy but extended later in a military sense affecting also traffic and communications, was imposed with the object of bringing about the political exhaustion and economic destruction of this German community.

To this were added barbaric actions of maltreatment which cry to Heaven, and other kinds of persecution of the large German national group in Poland which extended even to the killing of many resident Germans or to their forcible removal under the most cruel conditions. This state of affairs is unbearable for a Great Power. It has now forced Germany, after remaining a passive onlooker for many months, in her turn to take the necessary steps for the safeguarding of justified German interests. And indeed the German Government can but assure the British Government in the most solemn manner that a condition of affairs has now been reached which can no longer be accepted or observed with indifference.

The demands of the German Government are in conformity with the revision of the Versailles Treaty in regard to this territory which has always been recognised as being necessary: viz., return of Danzig and the Corridor to Germany, the safeguarding of the existence of the German national group in the territories remaining to Poland.

The German Government note with satisfaction that the British Government also are in principle convinced that some solution must be found for the new situation which has arisen.

They further feel justified in assuming that the British Government too can have no doubt that it is a question now of conditions, for the elimination of which there no longer remain days, still less weeks, but perhaps only hours. For in the disorganized state of affairs obtaining in Poland, the possibility of incidents intervening, which it might be impossible for Germany to tolerate, must at any moment be reckoned with.

While the British Government may still believe that these grave differences can be resolved by way of direct negotiations, the German Government unfortunately can no longer share this view as a matter of course. For they have made the attempt to embark on such peaceful negotiations, but, instead of receiving any support from the Polish Government, they were rebuffed by the sudden introduction of measures of a military character in favour of the development alluded to above.

The British Government attach importance to two considerations: (1) that the existing danger of an imminent explosion should be eliminated as quickly as possible by direct negotiation, and (2) that the existence of the Polish State, in the form in which it would then continue to exist, should be adequately safeguarded in the economic and political sphere by means of international guarantees.

On this subject the German Government makes the following declaration:—

Though sceptical as to the prospects of a successful outcome, they are nevertheless prepared to accept the English proposal and to enter into direct discussions. They do so, as has already been emphasised, solely as the result of the impression made upon them by the written statement received from the British Government that they too desire a pact of friendship in accordance with the general lines indicated to the British Ambassador.

The German Government desire in this way to give the British Government and the British nation a proof of the sincerity of Germany's intentions to enter into a lasting friendship with Great Britain.

The Government of the Reich felt, however, bound to point out to the British Government that in the event of a territorial rearrangement in Poland they would no longer be able to bind themselves to give guarantees or to participate in guarantees without the U.S.S.R. being associated therewith.

For the rest, in making these proposals the German Government have never had any intention of touching Poland's vital interests or questioning the existence of an independent Polish State. The German Government, accordingly, in these circumstances agree to accept the British Government's offer of their good offices in securing the despatch to Berlin of a Polish Emissary with full powers. They count on the arrival of this Emissary on Wednesday, the 30th August, 1939.

The German Government will immediately draw up proposals for a solution acceptable to themselves and will, if possible, place these at the disposal of the British Government before the arrival of the Polish negotiator.

79.

Sir N. Henderson to Viscount Halifax (received 9.15 p.m.)

(Telegraphic.) *Berlin, August 29, 1939.*

Herr Hitler handed me German reply at 7.15 this evening. Translation of full text will follow as soon as possible.

2. In reply to two British proposals, namely, for direct German-Polish negotiations and international guarantee of any settlement, German Government declares:—

(1) That, in spite of its scepticism as to the prospect of their success, it accepts direct negotiation solely out of desire to ensure lasting friendship with Britain, and

(2) In the case of any modifications of territory German Government cannot undertake or participate in any guarantees without consulting the U.S.S.R.

3. Note observes that German proposals have never had for their object any diminution of Polish vital interests, and declares that German Government accepts mediation of Great Britain with a view to visit to Berlin of some Polish plenipotentiary. German Government, note adds, counts on arrival of such plenipotentiary to-morrow, Wednesday, 30th August.

4. I remarked that this phrase sounded like an ultimatum, but after some heated remarks both Herr Hitler and Herr von Ribbentrop assured me that it was only intended to stress urgency of the moment when the two fully mobilised armies were standing face to face.

5. I said that I would transmit this suggestion immediately to His Majesty's Government, and asked whether, if such Polish plenipotentiary did come, we could assume that he would be well received and that discussions would be conducted on footing of complete equality. Herr Hitler's reply was "of course."

6. German demands are declared to be revision of Versailles Treaty; namely, return of Danzig and the Corridor to Germany, security for lives of German national minorities in the rest of Poland; note concludes with statement that the German Government will immediately elaborate proposals for an acceptable solution, and inform British Government, if possible, before arrival of Polish plenipotentiary.

80.

Sir N. Henderson to Viscount Halifax (received 10.25 p.m.)

(Telegraphic.)   *Berlin, August 29, 1939.*

Interview this evening was of a stormy character and Herr Hitler far less reasonable than yesterday. Press announcement this evening that five more Germans had been killed in Poland and news of Polish mobilisation had obviously excited him.

2. He kept saying that he wanted British friendship more than anything in the world, but he could not sacrifice Germany's vital interests therefor, and that for His Majesty's Government to make a bargain over such a matter was an unendurable proposition. All my attempts to correct this complete misrepresentation of the case did not seem to impress him.

3. In reply to his reiterated statement that direct negotiations with Poland, though accepted by him, would be bound to fail, I told his Excellency that their success or failure depended on his goodwill or the reverse, and that the choice lay with him. It was, however, my bounden duty to leave him in no doubt that an attempt to impose his will on Poland by force would inevitably bring him into direct conflict with us.

4. It would have been useless to talk of a truce, since that can only depend on whether M. Beck or some other Polish representative came to Berlin or not.

81

Viscount Halifax to Sir N. Henderson (Berlin).

(Telegraphic.) *Foreign Office, August 30, 1939, 2 a.m.*

We shall give careful consideration to German Government's reply,* but it is, of course, unreasonable to expect that we can produce a Polish representative in Berlin to-day, and German Government must not expect this.

It might be well for you at once to let this be known in proper quarters through appropriate channels. We hope you may receive our reply this afternoon.

* No. 78.

82.

Sir N. Henderson to Viscount Halifax (received 1 p.m.)

(Telegraphis.) *Berlin, August 30, 1939.*

Your message* was conveyed to the Minister for Foreign Affairs at 4 a.m. this morning. I had made similar observation to Herr Hitler yesterday evening, his reply being that one could fly from Warsaw to Berlin in one and a half hours.

2. I repeated the message this morning by telephone to State Secretary, who said that it had already been conveyed to Herr Hitler. He added that something must be done as soon as possible.

3. While I still recommend that the Polish Government should swallow this eleventh-hour effort to establish direct contact with Herr Hitler, even if it be only to convince the world that they were prepared to make their own sacrifice for preservation of peace, one can only conclude from the German reply that Herr Hitler is determined to achieve his ends by so-called peaceful fair means if he can, but by force if he cannot. Much, of course, may also depend on detailed plan referred to in the last paragraph of the German reply.

4. Nevertheless, if Herr Hitler is allowed to continue to have the initiative, it seems to me that result can only be either war or once again victory for him by a display of force and encouragement thereby to pursue the same course again next year or the year after.

* No. 81.

83.

Viscount Halifax to Sir N. Henderson (Berlin).

(Telegraphic.) *Foreign Office, August 30, 1939, 2.45 p.m.*

We are considering German note* with all urgency and shall send official reply later in afternoon.

* No. 78.

We are representing at Warsaw how vital it is to reinforce all instructions for avoidance of frontier incidents, and I would beg you to confirm similar instructions on German side.

I welcome the evidence in the exchanges of views, which are taking place, of that desire for Anglo-German understanding of which I spoke yesterday in Parliament.

84.

Sir H. Kennard to Viscount Halifax (received 10 a.m.)

(Telegraphic.)   *Warsaw, August 30, 1939.*

I feel sure that it would be impossible to induce the Polish Government to send M. Beck or any other representative immediately to Berlin to discuss a settlement on basis proposed by Herr Hitler. They would certainly sooner fight and perish rather than submit to such humiliation, especially after examples of Czecho-Slovakia, Lithuania and Austria.

2. I would suggest that if negotiations are to be between equals it is essential that they should take place in some neutral country or even possibly Italy, and that the basis for any negotiations should be some compromise between the clearly defined limits of March proposals on the German side and *status quo* on the Polish side.

3. Considering that the Polish Government, standing alone and when they were largely unprepared for war, refused the March terms it would surely be impossible for them to agree to proposals which appear to go beyond the March terms now that they have Great Britain as their ally, France has confirmed her support and world public opinion is clearly in favour of direct negotiations on equal terms and is behind Poland's resistance to a dictated settlement.

4. I am, of course, expressing no views to the Polish Government, nor am I communicating to them Herr Hitler's reply* till I receive instructions which I trust will be without delay.

* No. 78.

85.

Viscount Halifax to Sir H. Kennard (Warsaw).

(Telegraphic.)   *Foreign Office, August 30, 1939, 5.30 p.m.*

Atmosphere may be improved if strict instructions are given or confirmed by Polish Government to all their military and civil authorities: —

   (1) Not to fire on fugitives or members of the German minority who cause trouble, but to arrest them;

   (2) To abstain themselves from personal violence to members of German minority, and to prevent similar violence on the part of the population;

(3) To allow members of the German minority wishing to leave Poland to pass freely;

(4) To stop inflammatory radio propaganda.

Please inform M. Beck, adding that I realise that Herr Hitler is using reports to justify immoderate action, but I am anxious to deprive him of this pretext. I am requesting German Government to reciprocate; and warning them that Polish Government can only be expected to maintain such instructions if no provocation is offered by members of the German minority.

86.

Sir H. Kennard to Viscount Halifax (received 8.15 p.m.)

(Telegraphic.)   *Warsaw, August 30, 1939.*

M. Beck has asked me to say:—

1. His Majesty's Government may rest absolutely assured that Polish Government have no intention of provoking any incidents. On the other hand, they point out that German provocation at Danzig is becoming more and more intolerable.

2. In connexion with proposed British answer to Herr Hitler, Polish Government feel sure that His Majesty's Government will not express any definite views on problems concerning Poland without consulting Polish Government.

87.

Viscount Halifax to Sir N. Henderson (Berlin).

(Telegraphic.)   *Foreign Office, August 30, 1939, 5.30 p.m.*

In informing German Government of the renewed representations which have been made in Warsaw, please make it clear that Polish Government can only be expected to maintain an attitude of complete restraint if German Government reciprocate on their side of frontier and if no provocation is offered by members of German minority in Poland. Reports are current that Germans have committed acts of sabotage which would justify the sternest measures.

88.

Viscount Halifax to Sir N. Henderson (Berlin).

(Telegraphic.)   *Foreign Office, August 30, 1939, 6.50 p.m.*

We understand that German Government are insisting that a Polish representative with full powers must come to Berlin to receive German proposals.

2. We cannot advise Polish Government to comply with this procedure, which is wholly unreasonable.

3. Could you not suggest to German Government that they adopt the normal procedure, when their proposals are ready, of inviting Polish Ambassador to call and handing proposals to him for transmission to Warsaw and inviting suggestions as to conduct of negotiations.

4. German Government have been good enough to promise they will communicate proposals also to His Majesty's Government. If latter think they offer reasonable basis they can be counted on to do their best in Warsaw to facilitate negotiations.

89.

Reply of His Majesty's Government to the German Chancellor's Communication of August 29, 1939.* This reply was handed by Sir N. Henderson to Herr von Ribbentrop at Midnight on August, 30, 1939.

His Majesty's Government appreciate the friendly reference in the Declaration contained in the reply of the German Government to the latter's desire for an Anglo-German understanding and to their statement of the influence which this consideration has exercised upon their policy.

2. His Majesty's Government repeat that they reciprocate the German Government's desire for improved relations, but it will be recognised that they could not sacrifice the interests of other friends in order to obtain that improvement. They fully understand that the German Government cannot sacrifice Germany's vital interests, but the Polish Government are in the same position and His Majesty's Government believe that the vital interests of the two countries are not incompatible.

3. His Majesty's Government note that the German Government accept the British proposal and are prepared to enter into direct discussions with the Polish Government.

4. His Majesty's Government understand that the German Government accept in principle the condition that any settlement should be made the subject of an international guarantee. The question of who shall participate in this guarantee will have to be discussed further, and His Majesty's Government hope that to avoid loss of time the German Government will take immediate steps to obtain the assent of the U.S.S.R., whose participation in the guarantee His Majesty's Government have always assumed.

5. His Majesty's Government also note that the German Government accept the position of the British Government as to Poland's vital interests and independence.

6. His Majesty's Government must make an express reservation in regard to the statement of the particular demands put forward by the German Government in an earlier passage in their reply. They

* No. 78.

understand that the German Government are drawing up proposals for a solution. No doubt these proposals will be fully examined during the discussions. It can then be determined how far they are compatible with the essential conditions which His Majesty's Government have stated and which in principle the German Government have expressed their willingness to accept.

7. His Majesty's Government are at once informing the Polish Government of the German Government's reply. The method of contact and arrangements for discussions must obviously be agreed with all urgency between the German and Polish Governments, but in His Majesty's Government's view it would be impracticable to establish contact so early as to-day.

8. His Majesty's Government fully recognise the need for speed in the initiation of discussion, and they share the apprehensions of the Chancellor arising from the proximity of two mobilised armies standing face to face. They would accordingly most strongly urge that both parties should undertake that, during the negotiations, no aggressive military movements will take place. His Majesty's Government feel confident that they could obtain such an undertaking from the Polish Government if the German Government would give similar assurances.

9. Further, His Majesty's Government would suggest that a temporary *modus vivendi* might be arranged for Danzig, which might prevent the occurrence of incidents tending to render German-Polish relations more difficult.

90.

Viscount Halifax to Sir H. Kennard (Warsaw).

(Sent to Sir H. Kennard on August 30 and acted on in the early morning of August 31.)

(Telegraphic.) *Foreign Office, August 30, 1939.*

My telegram to Berlin gives the text of the reply of His Majesty's Government* to the German communication† which has been repeated to you.

2. Please communicate it to M. Beck. In doing so, you should point out that, whilst the first part of the German Government's reply consists of an indefensible and misleading presentation of the German case, the really important part of the reply consists of Germany's acceptance of the proposal for direct discussion, of the suggestion of the proposed international guarantee, and Germany's assertion that she intends to respect Poland's vital interests.

3. It is perhaps unnecessary to take exception at this stage to much that finds place in the German reply, of which His Majesty's Government would be as critical as, they have no doubt, would be the Polish Government, but His Majesty's Government have made an express reservation in regard to statement of the particular demands put forward in the German note. The point that seemed to call for

* No. 89. † No. 78.

144

immediate comment was the German demand that a Polish representative should present himself at Berlin to-day. M. Beck will see the line we took last night on this (see my telegram to Berlin‡) and the further reference we have made to point in our reply to German Government's latest communication. German Government are now drawing up proposals for a solution, and it will be in the light of these, and of other developments, that the decision as to future procedure, including place and conditions of discussion, will have to be taken.

4. M. Beck will see from the reply of His Majesty's Government that the proposal has been made for a military standstill during discussions, to which His Majesty's Government earnestly hope that the Polish Government will have no objection.

5. His Majesty's Government would be glad to have the views of the Polish Government urgently. In view of the fact that the Polish Government have authorised His Majesty's Government to say that they are prepared to enter into direct discussions with the German Government, His Majesty's Government hope that, provided method and general arrangement for discussions can be satisfactorily agreed, Polish Government will be prepared to do so without delay. We regard it as most important from the point of view of the internal situation in Germany and of world opinion that, so long as the German Government profess themselves ready to negotiate, no opportunity should be given them for placing the blame for a conflict on Poland.

6. You should, of course, emphasise that His Majesty's Government have made it quite clear to Herr Hitler that they are irrevocably determined to implement their obligations without reserve. On this point there is no misunderstanding in Berlin. The position of the Polish Government is very different from that which they occupied last March, since it is now supported both by direct British guarantee and promise of British participation in guarantee of any settlement reached on bases we have indicated, and the conversations would be carried on against this background.

‡ No. 81.

91.

Sir N. Henderson to Viscount Halifax (received 2.45 a.m. August 31).
(Telegraphic.) *Berlin, August 30, 1939.*

I informed Herr von Ribbentrop to-night of the advice given to the Polish Government in your telegram of 30th August to Warsaw.*

2. Practically his only comment was that all provocation came from the side of Poland. I observed that His Majesty's Government had constantly warned the Polish Government that all provocative action should be vigorously discouraged and that I had reason to believe that the German press accounts were greatly exaggerated. Herr von Ribbentrop replied that His Majesty's Government's advice had had cursed ("verflucht") little effect. I mildly retorted that I was surprised to hear such language from a Minister for Foreign Affairs.

* No. 85.

92

Sir N. Henderson to Viscount Halifax (received 9.30 a.m. August 31).

(Telegraphic.) *Berlin, August 30, 1939.*

I told Herr von Ribbentrop this evening that His Majesty's Government found it difficult to advise Polish Government to accept procedure adumbrated in German reply, and suggested that he should adopt normal contact, *i.e.*, that when German proposals were ready to invite Polish Ambassador to call and to hand him proposals for transmission to his Government with a view to immediate opening of negotiations. I added that if basis afforded prospect of settlement His Majesty's Government could be counted upon to do their best in Warsaw to temporize negotiations.

2. Herr von Ribbentrop's reply was to produce a lengthy document which he read out in German aloud at top speed. Imagining that he would eventually hand it to me I did not attempt to follow too closely the sixteen or more articles which it contained. Though I cannot therefore guarantee accuracy the main points were: restoration of Danzig to Germany; southern boundary of Corridor to be line Marienwerder, Graudenz, Bromberg, Schönlanke; plebiscite to be held in the Corridor on basis of population on 1st January, 1919, absolute majority to decide; international commission of British, French, Italian and Russian members to police the Corridor and guarantee reciprocal communications with Danzig and Gdynia pending result of the plebiscite; Gdynia to be reserved to Poland; Danzig to be purely commercial city and demilitarised.

3. When I asked Herr von Ribbentrop for text of these proposals in accordance with undertaking in the German reply of yesterday, he asserted that it was now too late as Polish representative had not arrived in Berlin by midnight.

4. I observed that to treat matter in this way meant that request for Polish representative to arrive in Berlin on 30th August constituted, in fact, an ultimatum in spite of what he and Herr Hitler had assured me yesterday. This he denied, saying that idea of an ultimatum was figment of my imagination. Why then I asked could he not adopt normal procedure and give me copy of proposals and ask Polish Ambassador to call on him, just as Herr Hitler had summoned me a few days ago, and hand them to him for communication to Polish Government? In the most violent terms Herr von Ribbentrop said that he would never ask the Ambassador to visit him. He hinted that if Polish Ambassador asked him for interview it might be different. I said that I would naturally inform my Government so at once. Whereupon he said while those were his personal views he would bring all that I had said to Herr Hitler's notice. It was for Chancellor to decide.

5. We parted on that note, but I must tell you that Herr von Ribbentrop's whole demeanour during an unpleasant interview was aping Herr Hitler at his worst. He inveighed incidentally against Polish

mobilisation, but I retorted that it was hardly surprising since Germany had also mobilised as Herr Hitler himself had admitted to me yesterday.

93.

Sir H. Kennard to Viscount Halifax (received 8 a.m.)

(Telegraphic.) *Warsaw, August 31, 1939.*

I have communicated to M. Beck the reply of His Majesty's Government to Herr Hitler and made the comments therein in the sense of your telegram of 30th August.* M. Beck stated that before giving me a definite reply he would have to consult his Government but he could tell me at once that he would do everything possible to facilitate the efforts of His Majesty's Government which he greatly appreciated. I think he was greatly relieved to know that His Majesty's Government had not in any way committed themselves as regards demands put forward by German Government and he fully realised the main importance which His Majesty's Government attaches to the necessity for not giving the German Government any opportunity for placing the blame on Poland in any refusal to enter into direct negotiations.

2. He has promised me the considered reply of his government by mid-day to-morrow.†

3. I took the opportunity of impressing upon him again the necessity of avoiding any incidents in the meantime and asked him whether any had recently occurred. He said he had just heard that there had been a clash between German and Polish military forces but as at present informed he did not think it had amounted to more than an exchange of shots without serious casualties.

* No. 90.
† *i.e.*, meaning August 31.

94.

Viscount Halifax to Sir H. Kennard (Warsaw).

(Telegraphic.) *Foreign Office, August 31, 1939, 12 noon.*

You should concert with your French colleague in suggesting to Polish Government that they should now make known to the German Government, preferably direct, but if not, through us, that they have made aware of our last reply to German Government and that they confirm their acceptance of the principle of direct discussions.

French Government fear that German Government might take advantage of silence on part of Polish Government.

Viscount Halifax to Sir H. Kennard (Warsaw).

(Telegraphic.)   *Foreign Office, August 31, 1939, 1.45 p.m.*

Berlin telegram of 30th August.*

Please at once inform Polish Government and advise them, in view of fact that they have accepted principle of direct discussions, immediately to instruct Polish Ambassador in Berlin to say to German Government that, if latter have any proposals, he is ready to transmit them to his Government so that they may at once consider them and make suggestions for early discussions.

* No. 92

96.

Sir H. Kennard to Viscount Halifax (received 7.15 p.m.)

(Telegraphic.)   *Warsaw, August 31, 1939.*

My telegram of 31st August.*

M. Beck has just handed me in writing Polish reply to my *démarche* last night†; translation is in my immediately following telegram.‡ He particularly asked that it should be treated as most confidential.

2. I asked M. Beck what steps he proposed to take in order to establish contact with the German Government. He said he would now instruct M. Lipski to seek an interview either with the Minister for Foreign Affairs or State Secretary in order to say Poland had accepted British proposals. I urged him to do this without delay.

3. I then asked him what attitude Polish Ambassador would adopt if Herr von Ribbentrop or whoever he saw handed him the German proposals. He said that M. Lipski would not be authorised to accept such a document as, in view of past experience, it might be accompanied by some sort of ultimatum. In his view it was essential that contact should be made in the first instance, and that then details should be discussed as to where, with whom, and on what basis negotiations should be commenced.

4. As regards Danzig he pointed out that the situation there was becoming extremely serious. Polish officials were being arrested, railway traffic was suspended, and he thought it essential that immediate steps should be taken to secure a *modus vivendi* as a result of which those arrested would be released and railway traffic would be resumed. He suggested M. Burckhardt might be able to effect this.

5. He confirmed that no other serious incidents had occurred, but stated that he feared that in connexion with any negotiations he would have to appeal to the intervention of His Majesty's Government.

6. He added that if invited to go to Berlin he would of course not go, as he had no intention of being treated like President Hacha.

* No. 93.   † i.e., the night of August 30/31.   ‡ No. 97.

97

Sir H. Kennard to Viscount Halifax (received 6.30 p.m.)

(Telegraphic.) *Warsaw, August 31, 1939.*

Following is text of Poland's reply dated 31st August, 1939:—

"(1) Polish Government confirm their readiness which has previously been expressed for a direct exchange of views with the German Government on the basis proposed by British Government and communicated to me by Lord Halifax's telegram of 28th August addressed to the British Ambassador, Warsaw.*

"(2) Polish Government are also prepared on a reciprocal basis to give a formal guarantee that in the event of negotiations taking place Polish troops will not violate the frontiers of the German Reich provided a corresponding guarantee is given regarding non-violation of frontiers of Poland by troops of the German Reich.

"(3) In the present situation it is also essential to create a simple provisional *modus vivendi* in the Free City of Danzig.

"(4) As regards the suggestions communicated to Polish Government on 28th August through the intermediary of the British Ambassador at Warsaw, an explanation of what the British Government understands by international guarantee would be required in regard to relations between Poland and the German Reich. In default of an answer to this fundamental question the Polish Government are obliged completely to reserve their attitude towards this matter until such time as full explanations are received.

"(5) Polish Government express hope that in the event of conversations with the German Reich being initiated, they will continue to be able to take advantage of good offices of His Majesty's Government."

* Conveying the substance of No. 74.

98.

Message which was communicated to H.M. Ambassador in Berlin by the State Secretary on August 31, 1939, at 9.15 p.m.

(Translation.)

His Majesty's Government informed the German Government, in a note dated the 28th August, 1939,* of their readiness to offer their mediation towards direct negotiations between Germany and Poland over the problems in dispute. In so doing they made it abundantly clear that they, too, were aware of the urgent need for progress in view of the continuous incidents and the general European tension. In a reply dated the 29th August, † the German Government, in spite

* No. 74. † No. 78.

of being sceptical as to the desire of the Polish Government to come to an understanding, declared themselves ready in the interests of peace to accept the British mediation or suggestion. After considering all the circumstances prevailing at the time, they considered it necessary in their note to point out that, if the danger of a catastrophe was to be avoided, then action must be taken readily and without delay. In this sense they declared themselves ready to receive a personage appointed by the Polish Government up to the evening of the 30th August, with the proviso that the latter was, in fact, empowered not only to discuss but to conduct and conclude negotiations.

Further, the German Government pointed out that they felt able to make the basic points regarding the offer of an understanding available to the British Government by the time the Polish negotiator arrived in Berlin.

Instead of a statement regarding the arrival of an authorized Polish personage, the first answer the Government of the Reich received to their readiness for an understanding was the news of the Polish mobilisation, and only towards 12 o'clock on the night of the 30th August, 1939, did they receive a somewhat general assurance of British readiness to help towards the commencement of negotiations.

Although the fact that the Polish negotiator expected by the Government of the Reich did not arrive removed the necessary condition for informing His Majesty's Government of the views of the German Government as regards possible bases of negotiation, since His Majesty's Government themselves had pleaded for *direct* negotiations between Germany and Poland, the German Minister for Foreign Affairs, Herr von Ribbentrop, gave the British Ambassador on the occasion of the presentation of the last British note precise information as to the text of the German proposals which would be regarded as a basis of negotiation in the event of the arrival of the Polish plenipotentiary.

The Government of the German Reich considered themselves entitled to claim that in these circumstances a Polish personage would immediately be nominated, at any rate retroactively.

For the Reich Government cannot be expected for their part continually not only to emphasise their willingness to start negotiations, but actually to be ready to do so, while being from the Polish side merely put off with empty subterfuges and meaningless declarations.

It has once more been made clear as a result of a *démarche* which has meanwhile been made by the Polish Ambassador that the latter himself has no plenary powers either to enter into any discussion, or even to negotiate.

The Führer and the German Government have thus waited two days in vain for the arrival of a Polish negotiator with plenary powers.

In these circumstances the German Government regard their

proposals as having this time too been to all intents and purposes rejected, although they considered that these proposals, in the form in which they were made known to the British Government also, were more than loyal, fair and practicable.

The Reich Government consider it timely to inform the public of the bases for negotiation which were communicated to the British Ambassador by the Minister for Foreign Affairs, Herr von Ribbentrop.

The situation existing between the German Reich and Poland is at the moment of such a kind that any further incident can lead to an explosion on the part of the military forces which have taken up their position on both sides. Any peaceful solution must be framed in such a way as to ensure that the events which lie at the root of this situation cannot be repeated on the next occasion offered, and that thus not only the East of Europe, but also other territories shall not be brought into such a state of tension. The causes of this development lie in: (1) the impossible delineation of frontiers, as fixed by the Versailles dictate; (2) the impossible treatment of the minority in the ceded territories.

In making these proposals, the Reich Government are, therefore, actuated by the idea of finding a lasting solution which will remove the impossible situation created by frontier delineation, which may assure to both parties their vitally important line of communication, which may—as far as it is at all possible—remove the minority problem and, in so far as this is not possible, may give the minorities the assurance of a tolerable future by means of a reliable guarantee of their rights.

The Reich Government are content that in so doing it is essential that economic and physical damage done since 1918 should be exposed and repaired in its entirety. They, of course, regard this obligation as being binding for both parties.

These considerations lead to the following practical proposals: —

(1) The Free City of Danzig shall return to the German Reich in view of its purely German character, as well as of the unanimous will of its population;

(2) The territory of the so-called Corridor which extends from the Baltic Sea to the line Marienwerder-Graudenz-Kulm-Bromberg (inclusive) and thence may run in a westerly direction to Schönlanke, shall itself decide as to whether it shall belong to Germany or Poland;

(3) For this purpose a plebiscite shall take place in this territory. The following shall be entitled to vote: all Germans who were either domiciled in this territory on the 1st January, 1918, or who by that date have been born there, and similarly of Poles, Kashubes, &c., domiciled in this territory on the above day (the 1st January, 1918) or born there up to that date. The Germans who have been driven from this territory shall return to it in order to exercise their vote with a view to ensuring an objective plebiscite, and also with a view to ensuring the extensive preparation necessary therefor. The above territory

shall, as in the case of the Saar territory, be placed under the supervision of an international commission to be formed immediately, on which shall be represented the four Great Powers—Italy, the Soviet Union, France and England. This commission shall exercise all the rights of sovereignty in this territory. With this end in view, the territory shall be evacuated within a period of the utmost brevity, still to be agreed upon, by the Polish armed forces, the Polish police, and the Polish authorities;

(4) The Polish port of Gdynia, which fundamentally constitutes Polish sovereign territory so far as it is confined territorially to the Polish settlement, shall be excluded from the above territory. The exact frontiers of this Polish port should be determined between Germany and Poland, and, if necessary, delimited by an international committee of arbitration;

(5) With a view to assuring the necessary time for the execution of the extensive work involved in the carrying out of a just plebiscite, this plebiscite shall not take place before the expiry of twelve months;

(6) In order to guarantee unrestricted communication between Germany and East Prussia and between Poland and the sea during this period, roads and railways shall be established to render free transit traffic possible. In this connexion only such taxes as are necessary for the maintenance of the means of communication and for the provision of transport may be levied;

(7) The question as to the party to which the area belongs is to be decided by simple majority of the votes recorded;

(8) In order to guarantee to Germany free communication with her province of Danzig-East Prussia, and to Poland her connexion with the sea after the execution of the plebiscite—regardless of the results thereof—Germany shall, in the event of the plebiscite area going to Poland, receive an extra-territorial traffic zone, approximately in a line from Bütow to Danzig or Dirschau, in which to lay down an autobahn and a 4-track railway line. The road and the railway shall be so constructed that the Polish lines of communication are not affected, i.e., they shall pass either over or under the latter. The breadth of this zone shall be fixed at 1 kilometre, and it is to be German sovereign territory. Should the plebiscite be favourable to Germany, Poland is to obtain rights, analogous to those accorded to Germany, to a similar extra-territorial communication by road and railway for the purpose of free and unrestricted communication with her port of Gdynia;

(9) In the event of the Corridor returning to the German Reich, the latter declares its right to proceed to an exchange of population with Poland to the extent to which the nature of the Corridor lends itself thereto;

(10) Any special right desired by Poland in the port of Danzig would be negotiated on a basis of territory against similar rights to be granted to Germany in the port of Gdynia;

(11) In order to remove any feeling in this area that either side was being threatened, Danzig and Gdynia would have the character of exclusively mercantile towns, that is to say, without military installations and military fortifications;

(12) The peninsula of Hela, which as a result of the plebiscite might go either to Poland or to Germany, would in either case have similarly to be demilitarised;

(13) Since the Government of the German Reich has the most vehement complaints to make against the Polish treatment of minorities, and since the Polish Government for their part feel obliged to make complaints against Germany, both parties declare their agreement to have these complaints laid before an international committee of enquiry, whose task would be to examine all complaints as regards economic or physical damage, and any other acts of terrorism. Germany and Poland undertake to make good economic or other damage done to minorities on either side since the year 1918, or to cancel expropriation as the case may be, or to provide complete compensation to the persons affected for this and any other encroachments on their economic life;

(14) In order to free the Germans who may be left in Poland and the Poles who may be left in Germany from the feeling of being outlawed by all nations, and in order to render them secure against being called upon to perform action or to render services incompatible with their national sentiments, Germany and Poland agree to guarantee the rights of both minorities by means of the most comprehensive and binding agreement, in order to guarantee to these minorities the preservation, the free development and practical application of their nationality (Volkstum), and in particular to permit for this purpose such organisation as they may consider necessary. Both parties undertake not to call upon members of the minority for military service;

(15) In the event of agreement on the basis of these proposals, Germany and Poland declare themselves ready to decree and to carry out the immediate demobilisation of their armed forces;

(16) The further measures necessary for the more rapid execution of the above arrangement shall be agreed upon by both Germany and Poland conjointly.

99.

Viscount Halifax to Sir N. Henderson (Berlin).

(Telegraphic.)　　　　　　　*Foreign Office, August 31, 1939, 11 p.m.*

Please inform German Government that we understand that Polish Government are taking steps to establish contact with them through Polish Ambassador in Berlin.

2. Please also ask them whether they agree to the necessity for securing an immediate provisional *modus vivendi* as regards Danzig. (We have already put this point to German Government.) Would

they agree that M. Burckhardt might be employed for this purpose if it were possible to secure his services?

100.

Viscount Halifax to Sir H. Kennard (Warsaw).

(Telegraphic.) *Foreign Office, September 1, 1939, 12.50 a.m.*

Your telegrams of 31st August*:—

1. I am glad to learn that Polish Ambassador at Berlin is being instructed to establish contact with German Government.

2. I fully agree as to the necessity for discussing detailed arrangements for the negotiations and as to the undesirability of a visit by M. Beck to Berlin.

3. On the other hand, I do not see why the Polish Government should feel difficulty about authorising Polish Ambassador to accept a document from the German Government, and I earnestly hope that they may be able to modify their instructions to him in this respect. There was no mention of any ultimatum in the report on the German proposals which has been furnished to us, and the suggestion that the demand for the presence of a Polish plenipotentiary at Berlin on 30th August amounted to an ultimatum was vigorously repudiated by Herr von Ribbentrop in conversation with His Majesty's Ambassador. If the document did contain an ultimatum, the Polish Government would naturally refuse to discuss it until the ultimatum was withdrawn. On the other hand, a refusal by them to receive proposals would be gravely misunderstood by outside opinion.

4. I should have thought that the Polish Ambassador could surely be instructed to receive and transmit a document and to say (a) if it contained anything like an ultimatum, that he anticipated that the Polish Government would certainly be unable to discuss on such a basis, and (b) that, in any case, in the view of the Polish Government, questions as to the venue of the negotiations, the basis on which they should be held, and the persons to take part in them, must be discussed and decided between the two Governments.

5. If negotiations are initiated, His Majesty's Government will at all times be ready, if desired, to lend any assistance in their power to achieve a just settlement.

6. As regards an international guarantee, this will no doubt have to be fully discussed. What His Majesty's Government had in mind was a guarantee of the full and proper observance of any settlement reached.

7. As regards Danzig, we fully share the view of M. Beck as to the importance of establishing some *modus vivendi*. We have already made a suggestion in this sense to the German Government and will in the light of paragraph 4 of your telegram of 31st August† do so

* Nos. 96 and 97. † No. 96.

again. If German Government agree, I will at once approach M. Burckhardt .

8. Please speak to M. Beck immediately in the above sense.

101.

Sir H. Kennard to Viscount Halifax (dated 7.43 p.m. September 1 and received 2 a.m. September 2).

(Telegraphic.)   *Warsaw, September 1, 1939.*

Your telegram of 1st September* was decyphered at 4 *a.m.* to-day.

2. M. Lipski had already called on the German Foreign Minister at 6.30 *p.m.* yesterday. In view of this fact, which was followed by German invasion of Poland at dawn to-day, it was clearly useless for me to take the action suggested.

* No. 100.

102.

Sir N. Henderson to Viscount Halifax (received 12.10 a.m., September 1).

(Telegraphic.)   *Berlin, August 31, 1939.*

Following is translation from text of communication handed by Polish Ambassador to German Minister for Foreign Affairs this evening: —

"During the course of the night the Polish Government received from the British Government news of the exchange of information with the German Government regarding the possibility of direct discussion between the Government of the Reich and the Polish Government.

"The Polish Government are weighing favourably the British Government's suggestion; a formal answer in this matter will be communicated to them in the immediate future."

I understand that no discussion took place.

103.

Sir N. Henderson to Viscount Halifax (received in the early hours of September 1, 1939).

(Telegraphic.)   *Berlin, September 1, 1939.*

Written communication was made to the Ministry for Foreign Affairs early this morning in the sense of paragraph 2 of your telegram of 31st August.*

* No. 99.

104.

Explanatory Note upon the actual Course of Events.

The reply to the German Government of 28th August was, before its delivery, communicated to the French and Polish Governments. The Polish Government authorised His Majesty's Government to inform the German Government that Poland was ready at once to enter into direct discussions with Germany. It will be seen that paragraph 4 of the British reply of 28th August made plain the attitude of the Polish Government on this point.

The British reply was handed to Herr Hitler at 10.30 *p.m.* on 28th August, and he promised to give a written reply the following day.

The German reply in writing was handed to His Majesty's Ambassador at 7.15 *p.m.* on 29th August. Apart from the complete distortion of events leading up to the crisis, the German Government's reply demanded the arrival in Berlin of a Polish emissary with full powers during the course of the following day.

The reply of the British Government is self-explanatory. It was communicated by His Majesty's Ambassador to the German Minister for Foreign Affairs at midnight on 30th August. Herr von Ribbentrop's reply was to produce a long document which he read out rapidly in German. It was apparently the sixteen-point plan which the German Government have since published. When Sir N. Henderson asked for the text of these proposals in accordance with the undertaking in the German reply of 29th August Herr von Ribbentrop asserted that it was now too late as the Polish plenipotentiary had not arrived in Berlin by midnight, as had been demanded by the German Government in their communication of the previous evening.

The Polish Government on learning of these developments informed His Majesty's Government during the afternoon of 31st August that they would authorise their Ambassador to inform the German Government that Poland had accepted the British proposals for negotiations.

The Polish Ambassador in Berlin (M. Lipski) was not received by Herr von Ribbentrop until the evening of 31st August. After this interview the German Government broadcast their proposals forthwith. M. Lipski at once tried to establish contact with Warsaw but was unable to do so because all means of communication between Poland and Germany had been closed by the German Government.

105.

*Speech by the Prime Minister in the House of Commons on
September 1, 1939.*

The Prime Minister (Mr. Chamberlain): I do not propose to say many words to-night. The time has come when action rather than speech is required. Eighteen months ago in this House I prayed that the responsibility might not fall upon me to ask this country to accept the awful arbitrament of war. I fear that I may not be able to avoid that responsibility. But, at any rate, I cannot wish for conditions in which such a burden should fall upon me in which I should feel clearer than I do to-day as to where my duty lies. No man can say that the Government could have done more to try to keep open the way for an honourable and equitable settlement of the dispute between Germany and Poland. Nor have we neglected any means of making it crystal clear to the German Government that if they insisted on using force again in the manner in which they had used it in the past we were resolved to oppose them by force. Now that all the relevant documents are being made public we shall stand at the bar of history knowing that the responsibility for this terrible catastrophe lies on the shoulders of one man—the German Chancellor, who has not hesitated to plunge the world into misery in order to serve his own senseless ambitions.

I would like to thank the House for the forbearance which they have shown on two recent occasions in not demanding from me information which they recognised I could not give while these negotiations were still in progress. I have now had all the correspondence with the German Government put into the form of a White Paper. On account of mechanical difficulties I am afraid there are still but a few copies available, but I understand that they will be coming in in relays while the House is sitting. I do not think it is necessary for me to refer in detail now to these documents, which are already past history. They make it perfectly clear that our object has been to try and bring about discussions of the Polish-German dispute between the two countries themselves on terms of equality, the settlement to be one which safeguarded the independence of Poland and of which the due observance would be secured by international guarantees. There is just one passage from a recent communication, which was dated the 30th August, which I should like to quote, because it shows how easily the final clash might have been avoided had there been the least desire on the part of the German Government to arrive at a peacful settlement. In this document we said:—

"His Majesty's Government fully recognises the need for speed in the initiation of discussions and they share the apprehensions of the Chancellor arising from the proximity of two mobilised armies standing face to face. They would accordingly most strongly urge that both parties should undertake that during the negotiations no aggressive military movements should take place. His Majesty's Government feel confident that they could obtain such an undertaking from the Polish Government if the German Government would give similar assurances."

That telegram, which was repeated to Poland, brought an instantaneous reply from the Polish Government, dated the 31st August, in which they said:—

"The Polish Government are also prepared on a reciprocal basis

157

to give a formal guarantee in the event of negotiations taking place that Polish troops will not violate the frontiers of the German Reich provided a corresponding guarantee is given regarding the non-violation of the frontiers of Poland by troops of the German Reich."

We never had any reply from the German Government to that suggestion, one which, if it had been followed, might have saved the catastrophe which took place this morning. In the German broadcast last night, which recited the 16 points of the proposals which they have put forward, there occurred this sentence: —

"In these circumstances the Reich Government considers its proposals rejected."

I must examine that statement. I must tell the House what are the circumstances. To begin with let me say that the text of these proposals has never been communicated by Germany to Poland at all. The history of the matter is this. On Tuesday, the 29th August, in replying to a Note which we had sent to them, the German Government said, among other things, that they would immediately draw up proposals for a solution acceptable to themselves and

"will, if possible, place these at the disposal of the British Government before the arrival of the Polish negotiator."

It will be seen by examination of the White Paper that the German Government had stated that they counted upon the arrival of a plenipotentiary from Poland in Berlin on the 30th, that is to say, on the following day. In the meantime, of course, we were awaiting these proposals. The next evening, when our Ambassador saw Herr von Ribbentrop, the German Foreign Secretary, he urged upon the latter that when these proposals were ready—for we had heard no more about them—he should invite the Polish Ambassador to call and should hand him the proposals for transmission to his Government. Thereupon, reports our Ambassador, in the most violent terms Herr von Ribbentrop said he would never ask the Ambassador to visit him. He hinted that if the Polish Ambassador asked him for an interview it might be different.

The House will see that this was on Wednesday night, which, according to the German statement of last night, is now claimed to be the final date after which no negotiation with Poland was acceptable. It is plain, therefore, that Germany claims to treat Poland as in the wrong because she had not by Wednesday night entered upon discussions with Germany about a set of proposals of which she had never heard.

Now what of ourselves? On that Wednesday night, at the interview to which I have just referred, Herr von Ribbentrop produced a lengthy document which he read out in German, aloud, at top speed. Naturally, after this reading our Ambassador asked for a copy of the document, but the reply was that it was now too late, as the Polish representative had not arrived in Berlin by midnight. And so, Sir, we never got a copy of those proposals, and the first time we heard them—*we* heard them—was on the broadcast last night. Well, Sir, those are the circumstances in which the German Government said that they would consider that their proposals were rejected. It is not clear that their conception of a negotiation was that on almost instantaneous demand a Polish plenipotentiary should go to Berlin—where others had been before him—and should there receive a statement of demands to be accepted in their entirety or refused? I am not pronouncing any opinion upon the terms themselves, for I do not feel called upon to do so. The proper course, in our view—in the view of all of us—was that these proposals should have been put before the Poles, who should have been given time to consider them and to say whether, in their opinion, they did or did not infringe those vital interests of Poland which Germany had assured us on a previous occasion she intended to respect. Only last night the Polish Ambassador did see the German Foreign Secretary, Herr von Ribbentrop. Once again he expressed to him what, indeed, the Polish Government had already said publicly, that they were willing to negotiate with Germany about their disputes on an equal basis. What was the reply of the German Government? The reply was that without another word the German troops crossed the Polish frontier this morning at dawn and are since reported to be bombing open towns. [An Hon. Member: "Gas?"] In these circumstances there is only one course open to us. His Majesty's Ambassador in Berlin and the French Ambassador have been instructed to hand to the German Government the following document:—

"Early this morning the German Chancellor issued a proclamation to the German Army which indicated clearly that he was about to attack Poland. Information which has reached His Majesty's Government in the United Kingdom and the French Government indicates that German troops have crossed the Polish frontier and that attacks upon Polish towns are proceeding. In these circumstances it appears to the Governments of the United Kingdom and France that by their action the German Government have created conditions, namely, an aggressive act of force against Poland threatening the independence of Poland, which call for the implementation by the Governments of the United Kingdom and France of the undertaking to Poland to come to her assistance. I am accordingly to inform your Excellency that unless the German Government are prepared to give His Majesty's Government satisfactory assurances that the German Government have suspended all aggressive action against Poland and are prepared promptly to withdraw their forces from Polish .territory, His Majesty's Government in the United Kingdom will without hesitation fulfil their obligations to Poland."

[An Hon. Member: "Time limit?".] If a reply to this last warning is unfavourable, and I do not suggest that it is likely to be otherwise, His Majesty's Ambassador is instructed to ask for his passports. In that case we are ready. Yesterday, we took further steps towards the completion of our defensive preparations. This morning we ordered complete mobilisation of the whole of the Royal Navy, Army and Royal Air Force. We have also taken a number of other measures, both at home and abroad, which the House will not perhaps expect me to specify in detail. Briefly, they represent the final steps in accordance with pre-arranged plans. These last can be put into force rapidly, and are of such a nature that they can be deferred until war seems inevitable. Steps have also been taken under the powers conferred by the House last week to safeguard the position in regard to stocks of commodities of various kinds.

The thoughts of many of us must at this moment inevitably be turning back to 1914, and to a comparison of our position now with that which existed then. How do we stand this time? The answer is that all three Services are ready, and that the situation in all directions is far more favourable and reassuring than in 1914, while behind the fighting Services we have built up a vast organization of Civil Defence under our scheme of Air Raid Precautions. As regards the immediate man-power requirements, the Royal Navy, the Army and the Royal Air Force are in the fortunate position of having almost as many men as they can conveniently handle at this moment. There are, however, certain categories of service in which men are immediately required, both for Military and Civil Defence. These will be announced in detail through the Press and the B.B.C. The main and most satisfactory point to observe is that there is to-day no need to make an appeal in a general way for recruits such as was issued by Lord Kitchener 25 years ago. That appeal has been anticipated by many months, and the men are already available.

So much for the immediate present. Now we must look to the future. It is essential in the face of the tremendous task which confronts us, more especially in view of our past experiences in this matter, to organise our man-power this time upon as methodical, equitable and economical a basis as possible. We, therefore, propose immediately to introduce legislation directed to that end. A Bill will be laid before you which for all practical purposes will amount to an expansion of the Military Training Act. Under its operation all fit men between the ages of 18 and 41 will be rendered liable to military service if and when called upon. It is not intended at the outset that any considerable number of men other than those already liable shall be called up, and steps will be taken to ensure that the man-power essentially required by industry shall not be taken away.

There is one other allusion which I should like to make before I end my speech, and that is to record my satisfaction, and the satisfaction of His Majesty's Government, that throughout these last days of crisis Signor Mussolini also has been doing his best to reach a solution.

It now only remains for us to set our teeth and to enter upon this struggle, which we ourselves earnestly endeavoured to avoid, with determination to see it through to the end. We shall enter it with a clear conscience, with the support of the Dominions and the British Empire, and the moral approval of the greater part of the world. We have no quarrel with the German people, except that they allow themselves to be governed by a Nazi Government. As long as that Government exists and pursues the methods it has so persistently followed during the last two years, there will be no peace in Europe. We shall merely pass from one crisis to another, and see one country after another attacked by methods which have now become familiar to us in their sickening technique. We are resolved that these methods must come to an end. If out of the struggle we again re-establish in the world the rules of good faith and the renunciation of force, why, then even the sacrifices that will be entailed upon us will find their fullest justification.

106.

Speech by Herr Hitler to the Reichstag on September 1, 1939.

(Translation.)

For months we have been suffering under the torture of a problem which the Versailles *Diktat* created—a problem which has deteriorated until it becomes intolerable for us. Danzig was and is a German city. The Corridor was and is German. Both these territories owe their cultural development exclusively to the German people. Danzig was separated from us, the Corridor was annexed by Poland. As in other German territories of the East, all German minorities living there have been ill-treated in the most distressing manner. More than 1,000,000 people of German blood had in the years 1919-20 to leave their homeland.

As always, I attempted to bring about, by the peaceful method of making proposals for revision, an alteration of this intolerable position. It is a lie when the outside world says that we only tried to carry through our revisions by pressure. Fifteen years before the National Socialist Party came to power there was the opportunity of carrying out these revisions by peaceful settlements and understanding. On my own initiative I have, not once but several times, made proposals for the revision of intolerable conditions. All these proposals, as you know, have been rejected—proposals for limitation of armaments and even, if necessary, disarmament, proposals for the limitation of war-making, proposals for the elimination of certain methods of modern warfare. You know the proposals that I have made to fulfil the necessity of restoring German sovereignty over German territories. You know the endless attempts I made for a peaceful clarification and understanding of the problem of Austria, and later of the problem of the Sudetenland, Bohemia, and Moravia. It was all in vain.

It is impossible to demand that an impossible position should be cleared up by peaceful revision and at the same time constantly reject peaceful revision. It is also impossible to say that he who undertakes to carry out these revisions for himself transgresses a law, since the Versailles *Diktat* is not law to us. A signature was forced out of us with pistols at our head and with the threat of hunger for millions of people. And then this document, with our signature, obtained by force, was proclaimed as a solemn law.

In the same way, I have also tried to solve the problem of Danzig, the Corridor, &c., by proposing a peaceful discussion. That the problems had to be solved was clear. It is quite understandable to us that the time when the problem was to be solved had little interest for the Western Powers. But that time is not a matter of indifference to us. Moreover, it was not and could not be a matter of indifference to those who suffer most.

In my talks with Polish statesmen I discussed the ideas which you recognise from my last speech to the Reichstag. No one could say that this was in any way an inadmissible procedure or undue pressure. I then naturally formulated at last the German proposals, and I must once more repeat that there is nothing more modest or loyal than these proposals. I should like to say this to the world. I alone was in the position to make such proposals, for I know very well that in doing so I brought myself into opposition to millions of Germans. These proposals have been refused. Not only were they answered first with mobilisation, but with increased terror and pressure against our German compatriots and with a slow strangling of the Free City of Danzig—economically, politically, and in recent weeks by military and transport means.

Poland has directed its attacks against the Free City of Danzig. Moreover, Poland was not prepared to settle the Corridor question in a reasonable way which would be equitable to both parties, and she did not think of keeping her obligations to minorities.

I must here state something definitely; Germany has kept these obligations; the minorities who live in Germany are not persecuted. No Frenchman can stand up and say that any Frenchman living in the Saar territory is oppressed, tortured, or deprived of his rights. Nobody can say this.

For four months I have calmly watched developments, although I never ceased to give warnings. In the last few days I have increased these warnings. I informed the Polish Ambassador three weeks ago that if Poland continued to send to Danzig notes in the form of ultimata, if Poland continued its methods of oppression against the Germans, and if on the Polish side an end was not put to Customs measures destined to ruin Danzig's trade, then the Reich could not remain inactive. I left no doubt that people who wanted to compare the Germany of to-day with the former Germany would be deceiving themselves.

An attempt was made to justify the oppression of the Germans by claiming that they had committed acts of provocation. I do not know in what these provocations on the part of women and children consist, if they themselves are maltreated, in some cases killed. One

162

thing I do know—that no great Power can with honour long stand by passively and watch such events.

I made one more final effort to accept a proposal for mediation on the part of the British Government. They proposed, not that they themselves should carry on the negotiations, but rather that Poland and Germany should come into direct contact and once more to pursue negotiations.

I must declare that I accepted this proposal, and I worked out a basis for these negotiations which are known to you. For two whole days I sat with my Government and waited to see whether it was convenient for the Polish Government to send a plenipotentiary or not. Last night they did not send us a plenipotentiary, but instead informed us through their Ambassador that they were still considering whether and to what extent they were in a position to go into the British proposals. The Polish Government also said that they would inform Britain of their decision.

Deputies, if the German Government and its Leader patiently endured such treatment Germany would deserve only to disappear from the political stage. But I am wrongly judged if my love of peace and my patience are mistaken for weakness or even cowardice. I therefore, decided last night and informed the British Government that in these circumstances I can no longer find any willingness on the part of the Polish Government to conduct serious negotiations with us.

These proposals for mediation have failed because in the meanwhile there, first of all, came as an answer the sudden Polish general mobilisation, followed by more Polish atrocities. These were again repeated last night. Recently in one night there were as many as twenty-one frontier incidents; last night there were fourteen, of which three were quite serious. I have, therefore, resolved to speak to Poland in the same language that Poland for months past has used towards us. This attitude on the part of the Reich will not change.

The other European States understand in part our attitude. I should like here above all to thank Italy, which throughout has supported us, but you will understand that for the carrying on of this struggle we do not intend to appeal to foreign help. We will carry out this task ourselves. The neutral States have assured us of their neutrality, just as we had already guaranteed it to them.

When statesmen in the West declare that this affects their interests, I can only regret such a declaration. It cannot for a moment make me hesitate to fulfil my duty. What more is wanted? I have solemnly assured them, and I repeat it, that we ask nothing of these Western States and never will ask anything. I have declared that the frontier between France and Germany is a final one. I have repeatedly offered friendship and, if necessary, the closest co-operation to Britain, but this cannot be offered from one side only. It must find response on the other side. Germany has no interests in the West, and our western wall is for all time the frontier of the Reich on the west. Moreover, we have no aims of any kind there for the future. With this assurance we are in solemn earnest, and as long as others do not violate their neutrality we will likewise take every care to respect it.

I am happy particularly to be able to tell you of one event. You know that Russia and Germany are governed by two different doctrines. There was only one question that had to be cleared up. Germany has no intention of exporting its doctrine. Given the fact that Soviet Russia has no intention of exporting its doctrine to Germany, I no longer see any reason why we should still oppose one another. On both sides we are clear on that. Any struggle between our people would only be of advantage to others. We have, therefore, resolved to conclude a pact which rules out for ever any use of violence between us. It imposes the obligation on us to consult together in certain European questions. It makes possible for us economic co-operation, and above all it assures that the powers of both these powerful States are not wasted against one another. Every attempt of the West to bring about any change in this will fail.

At the same time I should like here to declare that this political decision means a tremendous departure for the future, and that it is a final one. Russia and Germany fought against one another in the World War. That shall and will not happen a second time. In Moscow, too, this pact was greeted exactly as you greet it. I can only endorse word for word the speech of the Russian Foreign Commissar, Molofov.

I am determined to solve (1) the Danzig question; (2) the question of the Corridor; and (3) to see to it that a change is made in the relationship between Germany and Poland that shall ensure a peaceful co-existence. In this I am resolved to continue to fight until either the present Polish Government is willing to bring about this change or until another Polish Government is ready to do so. I am resolved to remove from the German frontiers the element of uncertainty, the everlasting atmosphere of conditions resembling civil war. I will see to it that in the East there is, on the frontier, a peace precisely similar to that on our other frontiers.

In this I will take the necessary measures to see that they do not contradict the proposals I have already made known in the Reichstag itself to the rest of the world, that is to say, I will not war against women and children. I have ordered my air force to restrict itself to attacks on military objectives. If, however, the enemy thinks he can from that draw *carte blanche* on his side to fight by the other methods he will receive an answer that will deprive him of hearing and sight.

This night for the first time Polish regular soldiers fired on our own territory. Since 5.45 *a.m.* we have been returning the fire, and from now on bombs will be met with bombs. Whoever fights with poison gas will be fought with poison gas. Whoever departs from the rules of humane warfare can only expect that we shall do the same. I will continue this struggle, no matter against whom, until the safety of the Reich and its rights are secured.

For six years now I have been working on the building up of the

164

German defences. Over 90 milliards have in that time been spent on the building up of these defence forces. They are now the best equipped and are above all comparison with what they were in 1914. My trust in them is unshakable. When I called up these forces and when I now ask sacrifices of the German people and if necessary every sacrifice, then I have a right to do so, for I also am to-day absolutely ready, just as we were formerly, to make every personal sacrifice.

I am asking of no German man more than I myself was ready throughout four years at any time to do. There will be no hardships for Germans to which I myself will not submit. My whole life henceforth belongs more than ever to my people. I am from now on just first soldier of the German Reich. I have once more put on that coat that was the most sacred and dear to me. I will not take it off again until victory is secured, or I will not survive the outcome.

Should anything happen to me in the struggle then my first successor is Party Comrade Göring; should anything happen to Party Comrade Göring my next successor is Party Comrade Hess. You would then be under obligation to give to them as Führer the same blind loyalty and obedience as to myself. Should anything happen to Party Comrade Hess, then by law the Senate will be called, and will choose from its midst the most worthy—that is to say the bravest—successor.

As a National Socialist and as German soldier I enter upon this struggle with a stout heart. My whole life has been nothing but one long struggle for my people, for its restoration, and for Germany. There was only one watchword for that struggle: faith in this people. One word I have never learned: that is, surrender.

If, however, anyone thinks that we are facing a hard time, I should ask him to remember that once a Prussian King, with a ridiculously small State, opposed a stronger coalition, and in three wars finally came out successful because that State had that stout heart that we need in these times. I would, therefore, like to assure all the world that a November 1918 will never be repeated in German history. Just as I myself am ready at any time to stake my life—anyone can take it for my people and for Germany—so I ask the same of all others.

Whoever, however, thinks he can oppose this national command, whether directly or indirectly, shall fall. We have nothing to do with traitors. We are all faithful to our old principle. It is quite unimportant whether we ourselves live, but it is essential that our people shall live, that Germany shall live. The sacrifice that is demanded of us is not greater than the sacrifice that many generations have made. If we form a community closely bound together by vows, ready for anything, resolved never to surrender, then our will will master every hardship and difficulty. And I would like to close with the declaration that I once made when I began the struggle for power in the Reich. I then said: "If our will is so strong that no hardship and suffering can subdue it, then our will and our German might shall prevail."

107

Herr Hitler's Proclamation to the German Army on September 1, 1939.

(Translation.)

The Polish State has refused the peaceful settlement of relations which I desired, and has appealed to arms. Germans in Poland are persecuted with bloody terror and driven from their houses. A series of violations of the frontier, intolerable to a great Power, prove that Poland is no longer willing to respect the frontier of the Reich.

In order to put an end to this lunacy, I have no other choice than to meet force with force from now on. The German Army will fight the battle for the honour and the vital rights of reborn Germany with hard determination. I expect that every soldier, mindful of the great traditions of eternal German soldiery, will ever remain conscious that he is a representative of the National-Socialist Greater Germany. Long live our people and our Reich!

108.

Proclamation by Herr Forster and Exchange of Telegrams between Herr Forster and Herr Hitler, September 1, 1939.

Herr Forster's proclamation to the people of Danzig, as given over the German wireless, was as follows:—

(Translation.)

"Men and women of Danzig: The hour for which you have been longing for twenty years has come. This day Danzig has returned to the great German Reich. Our Führer, Adolf Hitler, has freed us.

"The Swastika flag, the flag of the German Reich, is flying to-day for the first time from the public buildings of Danzig. It also flies from the former Polish buildings, and everywhere in the harbour, the towers of the ancient town hall and St. Mary's Church. The bells ring in Danzig's hour of liberation.

"We thank our God that He gave the Führer the power and the opportunity of freeing us from the evil of the Versailles *Diktat*. We Danzigers are happy to be able to become now citizens of the Reich. Men and women of Danzig, we wish to stand together in this solemn hour and stretch out our hand and take a solemn oath to the Führer to do everything that lies in our power for our glorious Greater Germany. Long live German Danzig, which has been liberated and returned again to the Reich! Long live our great German fatherland!"

Herr Forster also sent the following telegram to Herr Hitler:—

(Translation.)

"My Führer, I have just signed the following constitutional law concerning the reunion of Danzig with the Reich, and I have put it into force:—

"The constitutional law concerning the reunion of the Free City of Danzig with the German Reich from September 1:—

"Article 1. The Constitution of the Free City of Danzig is cancelled with immediate effect.

"Art. 2. All legislative and executive power is in the hands of the head of the State.

"Art. 3. The Free City of Danzig with its territory and population shall immediately form part of the territory of the German Reich.

"Art. 4. Until the Führer makes a definite decision about the introduction of German Reich law, all legal provisions of the Constitution remain in force as they are at the moment of the issue of this constitutional law.

"I ask you, my Führer, in the name of Danzig and its population, to agree to this constitutional law and to carry out the re-incorporation of Danzig by a law of the German Reich. The eternal gratitude and everlasting faith of Danzig is devotedly pledged to you, my Führer."

Herr Hitler sent the following telegram in reply:—

(Translation.)

"I accept the proclamation of the Free State of Danzig concerning the return to the German Reich.

"I thank you, Gauleiter Forster, and all Danzig men and women for the resolute loyalty which you and they have preserved for so many years. Greater Germany greets you with overflowing heart. The law for reunion is ratified forthwith. I appoint you herewith as head of the civil administration of Danzig."

109.

Viscount Halifax to Sir N. Henderson (Berlin).

(Telegraphic.)   *Foreign Office, September 1, 1939, 4.45 p.m.*

My immediately following telegram contains the text of a communication that you should, in conjunction with your French colleague, make at once to the German Government.

2. You should ask for immediate reply and report result of your interview. I shall then send you further instructions.

3. In reply to any question you may explain that the present communication is in the nature of warning and is not to be considered as an ultimatum.

4. For your own information. If the German reply is unsatisfactory the next stage will be either an ultimatum with time limit or an immediate declaration of war.

110.

Viscount Halifax to Sir N. Henderson (Berlin).

(Telegraphic.) *Foreign Office, September 1, 1939, 5.45 p.m.*

Following is text referred to in my immediately preceding telegram:—

On the instructions of His Majesty's Principal Secretary of State for Foreign Affairs, I have the honour to make the following communication:—

Early this morning the German Chancellor issued a proclamation to the German army which indicated clearly that he was about to attack Poland.

Information which has reached His Majesty's Government in the United Kingdom and the French Government indicates that German troops have crossed the Polish frontier and that attacks upon Polish towns are proceeding.

In these circumstances, it appears to the Governments of the United Kingdom and France that by their action the German Government have created conditions (viz., an aggressive act of force against Poland threatening the independence of Poland) which call for the implementation by the Governments of the United Kingdom and France of the undertaking to Poland to come to her assistance.

I am accordingly to inform your Excellency that unless the German Government are prepared to give His Majesty's Government satisfactory assurances that the German Government have suspended all aggressive action against Poland and are prepared promptly to withdraw their forces from Polish territory, His Majesty's Government in the United Kingdom will without hesitation fulfil their obligations to Poland.

111.

Sir N. Henderson to Viscount Halifax (received 10.30 p.m.)

(Telegraphic.) *Berlin, September 1, 1939.*

Your telegrams of 1st September.*

I was received by Herr von Ribbentrop at 9.30 this evening, and handed him the communication from His Majesty's Government. After reading it, he said that he wished to state that it was not Germany who had aggressed Poland, that on the contrary it was Poland who had provoked Germany for a long time past; that it was the Poles who had first mobilised and that yesterday it was Poland that had invaded German territory with troops of the regular army.

I said that I was instructed to ask for immediate answer. The

* Nos. 109 and 110.

Minister replied that he would submit the British communication to the Head of the State.

I replied that I realised that this would be necessary, and that I was at his disposal at whatever time he might be in a position to give the Chancellor's answer.

Herr von Ribbentrop then remarked that if His Majesty's Government had been as active, *vis-à-vis* Poland, as they had been *vis-à-vis* Germany, a settlement would have been reached at an early stage.

French Ambassador saw Herr Von Ribbentrop immediately after and received an identic reply.

As I was leaving Herr von Ribbentrop gave me long explanation of why he had been unable to give me text of German proposals two nights ago. I told him that his attitude on that occasion had been most unhelpful and had effectively prevented me from making a last effort for peace, and that I greatly deplored it.

He was courteous and polite this evening. I am inclined to believe that Herr Hitler's answer will be an attempt to avoid war with Great Britain and France, but not likely to be one which we can accept.

112.

Sir H. Kennard to Viscount Halifax (received 2 p.m.).

(Telegraphic.) *Warsaw, September 1, 1939.*

Minister for Foreign Affairs has just telephoned to me in the middle of an air raid to beg me to point out to your Lordship that various cases of armed German aggression, which have occurred this morning on Polish soil, cannot be taken longer as mere isolated cases but constitute acts of war. Various open towns have been bombed from the air, with heavy civilian casualties, and his Excellency drew my attention to desirability of some military action from the air this afternoon.

2. His Excellency pointed out that at 6.30 *p.m.* Polish Ambassador saw Herr von Ribbentrop and expressed readiness of Polish Government to enter into direct negotiations. At dawn this morning, without any further diplomatic development or declaration of war, Germany had committed various acts of unprovoked aggression on a major scale, and thus, while Polish Government had made every effort to avoid serious clashes, German forces had deliberately attacked Polish territory and already caused deaths of numerous innocent civilians. Polish Government had, therefore, no course but to break off relations with German Government, and Polish Ambassador at Berlin has asked for his passports.

3. His Excellency failed to see what measures could now be taken to prevent European war, and while he did not say so in so many words it is obvious that he hopes His Majesty's Government will take some action of a military character to relieve the pressure on this field of operations.

4. M. Beck has also given me a categorical and official denial that any Polish act of aggression occurred last night as stated by Deutsches Nachrichten-Büro.

5. French Ambassador has suggested to me that French and British wireless should repeatedly point out that Germany has openly and flagrantly attacked Poland without warning.

113.

Viscount Halifax to Sir H. Kennard (Warsaw).

Sir,   *Foreign Office, September 1, 1939.*

The Polish Ambassador called to see me at his request at 10.30 this morning. Count Raczynski said that he had been officially informed from Paris that German forces had crossed the frontier at four points. He added that the towns of Vilno, Grodno, Brest-Litovsk, Lodz, Katowice and Cracow were being bombed and that at 9 *a.m.* an air attack had been made on Warsaw, as a result of which there were many civilian victims, including women and children. As regards the German attack, he understood, although he had no official information, that the points at the frontier which had been crossed were near Danzig, in East Prussia and Upper Silesia. His Excellency said that he had few words to add, except that it was a plain case as provided for by the treaty. I said that I had no doubt on the facts as he had reported them that we should take the same view.

I am, &c.

HALIFAX.

114.

Viscount Halifax to Sir N. Henderson (Berlin).

Sir,   *Foreign Office, September 1, 1939.*

I asked the German Chargé d'Affaires to call on me at 10, Downing Street at 10.50 this morning, and informed him that I had done this because we had received a good many reports to the effect that German forces had crossed the Polish frontier at several points. Dr. Kordt interrupted me to ask whether I meant the Polish frontier or that of the Danzig Free State. I replied that the Polish Ambassador had mentioned four points, but that I did not know which points these were. We also had information that several Polish towns, including Warsaw, had been bombed.

2. I asked Dr. Kordt whether he had any information which would enable him to cast any light upon these reports. He replied that he had no information whatsoever. I then said that I assumed, therefore, that he had no communication to make to us from his Government. Dr. Kordt replied that he had none with the exception of two notes which he had sent in earlier in the morning relating to the limitation

of shipping and of the passage of aircraft in the Gulf of Danzig. Dr. Kordt explained that this related to the whole gulf and not only to the port of Danzig. I informed Dr. Kordt that I had not yet seen these notes.

3. I went on to inform Dr. Kordt that the reports to which I had drawn his attention created a very serious situation. It was not necessary for me to say anything more at the present except to let him know that the Cabinet would meet later in the morning and that any further communication which we might have to make would be addressed to his Government in Berlin, but we should inform him of the character of that communication.

4. Before he left, Dr. Kordt stated that he had just listened on the wireless to the beginning of the Führer's speech in the Reichstag. He had not heard the latter mention any of the points to which I have drawn attention. The Führer had said, however, that the situation was intolerable and that he was obliged to draw the necessary consequences.

5. Dr. Kordt subsequently telephoned at 11.30 *a.m.* to say that he had received a telephone message from the News Department in the German Ministry for Foreign Affairs to the effect that the news that Warsaw and other towns were being bombed was untrue. He also repeated to me a sentence from the Führer's speech to the effect that since this morning shooting was taking place from the Polish side, and the Germans were shooting back.

I am, &c.
HALIFAX.

115.

Sir H. Kennard to Viscount Halifax (received 8 p.m.).

(Telegraphic.)   *Warsaw, September 2, 1939.*

M. Beck requested French Ambassador and me to see him to-day and points out while the Polish army was sternly resisting the German attack it found itself much hampered by German superiority in the air. It was possible for German Air Force to throw whole of their weight on this front at present, and he very discreetly suggested it was essential that there should be some diversion as soon as possible in the West.

2. He hoped, therefore, we would inform him as soon as possible of entry of the two countries into the war and that our aircraft would find it possible to draw off a considerable proportion of German aircraft operating on this front.

3. His Excellency also drew our attention to the fact that German aircraft had not confined themselves strictly to military objectives. They have bombed factories not engaged in war work, villages not near military objectives, and have caused severe losses among civilian population.

4. I trust I may be informed at the earliest possible moment of our declaration of war and that our air force will make every effort to show activity on western front with a view to relieving pressure here.

116.

Speech by the Prime Minister in the House of Commons on September 2, 1399.

The Prime Minister: Sir Nevile Henderson was received by Herr von Ribbentrop at half-past nine last night, and he delivered the warning message which was read to the House yesterday. Herr von Ribbentrop replied that he must submit the communication to the German Chancellor. Our Ambassador declared his readiness to receive the Chancellor's reply. Up to the present no reply has been received.

It may be that the delay is caused by consideration of a proposal which, meanwhile, had been put forward by the Italian Government, that hostilities should cease and that there should then immediately be a conference between the five Powers, Great Britain, France, Poland, Germany and Italy. While appreciating the efforts of the Italian Government, His Majesty's Government, for their part, would find it impossible to take part in a conference while Poland is being subjected to invasion, her towns are under bombardment and Danzig is being made the subject of a unilateral settlement by force. His Majesty's Government will, as stated yesterday, be bound to take action unless the German forces are withdrawn from Polish territory. They are in communication with the French Government as to the limit of time within which it would be necessary for the British and French Governments to know whether the German Government were prepared to effect such a withdrawal. If the German Government should agree to withdraw their forces then His Majesty's Government would be willing to regard the position as being the same as it was before the German forces crossed the Polish frontier. That is to say, the way would be open to discussion between the German and Polish Governments on the matters at issue between them, on the understanding that the settlement arrived at was one that safeguarded the vital interests of Poland and was secured by an international guarantee. If the German and Polish Governments wished that other Powers should be associated with them in the discussion, His Majesty's Government for their part would be willing to agree.

There is one other matter to which allusion should be be made in order that the present situation may be perfectly clear. Yesterday Herr Forster who, on 23rd August, had, in contravention of the Danzig constitution, become the head of the State, decreed the incorporation of Danzig in the Reich and the dissolution of the Constitution. Herr Hitler was asked to give effect to this decree by German law. At a meeting of the Reichstag yesterday morning a law was passed for the reunion of Danzig with the Reich. The international status of Danzig as a Free City is established by a treaty of which His Majesty's Government are a signatory, and the Free City was placed under the protection of the League of Nations. The rights given to Poland in Danzig by treaty are defined and confirmed by agreement concluded between Danzig and Poland. The action taken by the Danzig authorities and the Reichstag yesterday is the final step in the unilateral repudiation of these international instruments, which could only be modified by negotiation. His Majesty's Government do not, therefore, recognise either the validity of the grounds on which the action of the Danzig authorities was based, the validity of this action itself, or of the effect given to it by the German Government.

Later in the debate, the Prime Minister said: I think the House recognizes that the Government is in a somewhat difficult position. I suppose it always must be a difficulty for allies who have to communicate with one another by telephone to synchronise their thoughts and actions as quickly as those who are in the same room; but I should be horrified if the House thought for one moment that the statement that I have made to them betrayed the slightest weakening either of this Government or of the French Government in the attitude which we have already taken up. I am bound to say that I myself share the distrust which the right hon. Gentleman expressed of manœuvres of this kind. I should have been very glad had it been possible for me to say to the House now that the French Government and ourselves were agreed to make the shortest possible limit to the time when action should be taken by both of us.

It is very possible that the communications which we have had with the French Government will receive a reply from them in the course of the next few hours. I understand that the French Cabinet is in session at this moment, and I feel certain that I can make a statement to the House of a definite character to-morrow when the House meets again. I am the last man to neglect any opportunity which I consider affords a serious chance of avoiding the great catastrophe of war even at the last moment, but I confess that in the present case I should have to be convinced of the good faith of the other side in any action which they took before I could regard the proposition which has been made as one to which we could expect a reasonable chance of a successful issue. I anticipate that there is only one answer I shall be able to give to the House to-morrow. I hope that the issue will be brought to a close at the earliest possible moment so that we may know where we are, and I trust that the House, realising the position which I have tried to put before it, will believe me that I speak in complete good faith and will not prolong the discussion which, perhaps, might make our position more embarrassing than it is.

117.

Mr. Preston to Viscount Halifax.

(Telegraphic.) *Kovno, September 2, 1939.*

Following from M. Burckhardt:—

"I arrived here by car evening of 1st September. From midnight 30th August until midnight 31st August I was under surveillance of agents of Gestapo in Danzig. On 1st September at 8 *a.m.* I was visited by Herr Forster and Vice-President of Danzig Senate. Herr Forster informed me that he considered my functions as High Commissioner had terminated and that he intended to fly Haken-kreuz from building of High Commission. If I wished to leave before he did so I had better depart within two hours. During these two hours I was constantly visited by agents of Gestapo who endeavoured to induce me to expedite my departure. I am remaining at Kovno for the present intending to leave for Geneva."

118.

Viscount Halifax to Sir N. Henderson (Berlin).

(Telegraphic.) *Foreign Office, September 3, 1939, 5 a.m.*

Please seek interview with Minister for Foreign Affairs at 9 *a.m.* to-day, Sunday or, if he cannot see you then, arrange to convey at that time to representative of German Government the following communication:—

"In the communication which I had the honour to make to you on 1st September I informed you, on the instructions of His Majesty's Principal Secretary of State for Foreign Affairs, that, unless the German Government were prepared to give His Majesty's Government in the United Kingdom satisfactory assurances that the German Government had suspended all aggressive action against Poland and were prepared promptly to withdraw their forces from Polish territory, His Majesty's Government in the United Kingdom would, without hesitation, fulfil their obligations to Poland.

"Although this communication was made more than twenty-four hours ago, no reply has been received but German attacks upon Poland have been continued and intensified. I have accordingly the honour to inform you that, unless not later than 11 *a.m.*, British Summer Time, to-day 3rd September, satisfactory assurances to the above effect have been given by the German Government and have reached His Majesty's Government in London, a state of war will exist between the two countries as from that hour."

If the assurance referred to in the above communication is received, you should inform me by any means at your disposal before 11 *a.m.* to-day, 3rd September. If no such assurances is received here by 11 *a.m.*, we shall inform the German representative that a state of war exists as from that hour.

119.

Memorandum handed to Sir N. Henderson at 11.20 a.m. on September 3, 1939, by Herr von Ribbentrop.

(Translation.)

The German Government have received the British Government's ultimatum of the 3rd September, 1939.* They have the honour to reply as follows:—

1. The German Government and the German people refuse to receive, accept, let alone to fulfil, demands in the nature of ultimata made by the British Government.

2. On our eastern frontier there has for many months already reigned a condition of war. Since the time when the Versailles Treaty first tore Germany to pieces, all and every peaceful settlement was refused to all German Governments. The National Socialist Government also has since the year 1933 tried again and again to remove by peaceful negotiations the worst rapes and breaches of justice of this treaty. The British Government have been among those who, by their intransigent attitude, took the chief part in frustrating every practical revision. Without the intervention of the British Government—of this the German Government and German people are fully conscious—a reasonable solution doing justice to both sides would certainly have been found between Germany and Poland. For Germany did not have the intention nor had she raised the demands of annihilating Poland. The Reich demanded only the revision of those articles of the Versailles Treaty which already at the time of the formulation of that Dictate had been described by understanding statesmen of all nations as being in the long run unbearable, and therefore impossible for a great nation and also for the entire political and economic interests of Eastern Europe. British statesmen, too, declared the solution in the East which was then forced upon Germany as containing the germ of future wars. To remove this danger was the desire of all German Governments and especially the intention of the new National Socialist People's Government. The blame for having prevented this peaceful revision lies with the British Cabinet policy.

3. The British Government have—an occurrence unique in history —given the Polish State full powers for all actions against Germany which that State might conceivably intend to undertake. The British Government assured the Polish Government of their military support

* No. 118.

in all circumstances, should Germany defend herself against any provocation or attack. Thereupon the Polish terror against the Germans living in the territories which had been torn from Germany immediately assumed unbearable proportions. The Free City of Danzig was, in violation of all legal provisions, first threatened with destruction economically and by measures of customs policy, and was finally subjected to a military blockade and its communications strangled. All these violations of the Danzig Statute, which were well known to the British Government, were approved and covered by the blank cheque given to Poland. The German Government, though moved by the sufferings of the German population which was being tortured and treated in an inhuman manner, nevertheless remained a patient onlooker for five months, without undertaking even on one single occasion any similar aggressive action against Poland. They only warned Poland that these happenings would in the long run be unbearable, and that they were determined, in the event of no other kind of assistance being given to this population, to help them themselves. All these happenings were known in every detail to the British Government. It would have been easy for them to use their great influence in Warsaw in order to exhort those in power there to exercise justice and humaneness and to keep to the existing obligations. The British Government did not do this. On the contrary, in emphasising continually their obligation to assist Poland under all circumstances, they actually encouraged the Polish Government to continue in their criminal attitude which was threatening the peace of Europe. In this spirit, the British Government rejected the proposal of Signor Mussolini, which might still have been able to save the peace of Europe, in spite of the fact that the German Government had declared their willingness to agree to it. The British Government, therefore, bear the responsibility for all the unhappiness and misery which have now overtaken and are about to overtake many peoples.

4. After all efforts at finding and concluding a peaceful solution had been rendered impossible by the intransigence of the Polish Government covered as they were by England, after the conditions resembling civil war, which had existed already for months at the eastern frontier of the Reich, had gradually developed into open attacks on German territory, without the British Government raising any objections, the German Government determined to put an end to this continual threat, unbearable for a great Power, to the external and finally also to the internal peace of the German people, and to end it by those means which, since the Democratic Governments had in effect sabotaged all other possibilities of revision, alone remained at their disposal for the defence of the peace, security and honour of the Germans. The last attacks of the Poles threatening Reich territory they answered with similar measures. The German Government do not intend, on account of any sort of British intentions or obligations in the East, to tolerate conditions which are identical with those conditions which we observe in Palestine, which is under British

protection. The German people, however, above all do not intend to allow themselves to be ill-treated by Poles.

5. The German Government, therefore, reject the attempts to force Germany, by means of a demand having the character of an ultimatum, to recall its forces which are lined up for the defence of the Reich, and thereby to accept the old unrest and the old injustice. The threat that, failing this, they will fight Germany in the war, corresponds to the intention proclaimed for years past by numerous British politicians. The German Government and the German people have assured the English people countless times how much they desire an understanding, indeed close friendship, with them. If the British Government hitherto always refused these offers and now answer them with an open threat of war, it is not the fault of the German people and of their Government, but exclusively the fault of the British Cabinet or of those men who for years have been preaching the destruction and extermination of the German people. The German people and their Government do not, like Great Britain, intend to dominate the world, but they are determined to defend their own liberty, their independence and above all their life. The intention, communicated to us by order of the British Government by Mr. King-Hall, of carrying the destruction of the German people even further than was done through the Versailles Treaty is taken note of by us, and we shall therefore answer any aggressive action on the part of England with the same weapons and in the same form.

120.

Speech by the Prime Minister in the House of Commons on September 3, 1939.

The Prime Minister: When I spoke last night to the House I could not but be aware that in some parts of the House there were doubts and some bewilderment as to whether there had been any weakening, hesitation or vacillation on the part of His Majesty's Government. In the circumstances, I make no reproach, for if I had been in the same position as hon. members not sitting on this Bench and not in possession of all the information which we have, I should very likely have felt the same. The statement which I have to make this morning will show that there were no grounds for doubt. We were in consultation all day yesterday with the French Government and we felt that the intensified action which the Germans were taking against Poland-allowed no delay in making our own position clear. Accordingly, we decided to send to our Ambassador in Berlin instructions which he was to hand at 9 o'clock this morning to the German Foreign Secretary and which read as follows:—

177

"Sir,

"In the communication which I had the honour to make to you on the 1st September, I informed you, on the instructions of His Majesty's Principal Secretary of State for Foreign Affairs, that unless the German Government were prepared to give His Majesty's Government in the United Kingdom satisfactory assurances that the German Government had suspended all aggressive action against Poland and were prepared promptly to withdraw their forces from Polish territory, His Majesty's Government in the United Kingdom would, without hesitation, fulfil their obligations to Poland.

"Although this communication was made more than twenty-four hours ago, no reply has been received but German attacks upon Poland have been continued and intensified. I have accordingly the honour to inform you that, unless not later than 11 *a.m.*, British Summer Time, to-day 3rd September, satisfactory assurances to the above effect have been given by the German Government and have reached His Majesty's Government in London, a state of war will exist between the two countries as from that hour."

That was the final Note. No such undertaking was received by the time stipulated, and, consequently, this country is at war with Germany. I am in a position to inform the House that, according to arrangements made between the British and French Governments, the French Ambassador in Berlin is at this moment making a similar *démarche,* accompanied also by a definite time limit. The House has already been made aware of our plans. As I said that other day, we are ready.

This is a sad day for all of us, and to none is it sadder than to me. Everything that I have worked for, everything that I have hoped for, everything that I have believed in during my public life, has crashed into ruins. There is only one thing left for me to do; that is, to devote what strength and powers I have to forwarding the victory of the cause for which we have to sacrifice so much. I cannot tell what part I may be allowed to play myself; I trust I may live to see the day when Hitlerism has been destroyed and a liberated Europe has been re-established.

121.

Herr Hitler's Proclamations of September 3, 1939, to the German People and the German Army.

(Translation.)

Appeal to the German People.

Great Britain has for centuries pursued the aim of rendering the peoples of Europe defenceless against the British policy of world

178

conquest by proclaiming a balance of power, in which Great Britain claimed the right to attack on threadbare pretexts and destroy that European State which at the moment seemed most dangerous. Thus, at one time, she fought the world power of Spain, later the Dutch, then the French, and, since the year 1871, the German.

We ourselves have been witnesses of the policy of encirclement which has been carried on by Great Britain against Germany since before the war. Just as the German nation had begun, under its National Socialist leadership, to recover from the frightful consequences of the *Diktat* of Versailles, and threatened to survive the crisis, British encirclement immediately began once more.

The British war inciters spread the lie before the War that the battle was only against the House of Hohenzollern or German militarism; that they had no design on German colonies; that they had no intention of taking the German mercantile fleet. They then oppressed the German people under the Versailles *Diktat,* the faithful fulfilment of which would have sooner or later exterminated 20 million Germans.

I undertook to mobilise the resistance of the German nation against this, and to assure work and bread for them. But as the peaceful revision of the Versailles *Diktat* of force seemed to be succeeding, and the German people again began to live, the new British encirclement policy was resumed. The same lying inciters appeared as in 1914. I have many times offered Great Britain and the British people the understanding and friendship of the German people. My whole policy was based on the idea of this understanding. I have always been repelled. I had for years been aware that the aim of these war inciters had for long been to take Germany by surprise at a favourable opportunity.

I am more firmly determined than ever to beat back this attack. Germany shall not again capitulate. There is no sense in sacrificing one life after another and submitting to an even worse Versailles *Diktat.* We have never been a nation of slaves and will not be one in the future. Whatever Germans in the past had to sacrifice for the existence of our realm, they shall not be greater than those which we are to-day prepared to make.

This resolve is an inexorable one. It necessitates the most thorough measures, and imposes on us one law above all others: If the soldier is fighting at the front, no one shall profit by the war. If the soldier falls at the front no one at home shall evade his duty.

As long as the German people was united it has never been conquered. It was the lack of unity in 1918 that led to collapse. Whoever offends against this unity need expect nothing else than annihilation as an enemy of the nation. If our people fulfils its highest duty in this sense, that God will help us who has always bestowed His mercy on him who was determined to help himself.

Appeal to the German Army on the Western Front.

Soldiers of the Western Army; just as before the War, so after the War Great Britain has pursued the policy of Germany's encirclement. In spite of the fact that Germany has no demands to make on any other State to the West of the Reich; in spite of the fact that Germany claims no territorial revision in this territory; and in spite of the fact that Germany has made, above all to Great Britain just as to France, the offer of a cordial understanding, indeed of friendship. The British Government, driven on by those warmongers whom we knew in the last War, have resolved to let fall their mask and to proclaim war on a threadbare pretext.

The German people and your comrades in the East now expect from you, soldiers of the Western Front, that you shall protect the frontiers of the Reich, unshakable as a wall of steel and iron, against every attack, in an array of fortifications which is a hundred times stronger than that western front of the Great War, which was never conquered.

If you do your duty, the battle in the East will have reached its successful conclusion in a few months, and then the power of the whole National Socialist State stands behind you. As an old soldier of the World War, and as your Supreme Commander, I am going, with confidence in you, to the Army on the East. Our plutocratic enemies will realise that they are now dealing with a different Germany from that of the year 1914.—(Signed) ADOLF HITLER.

Attempted Mediation by other States.

*Message from the President of the United States of America to His
Majesty the King of Italy of August 23, and His Majesty's Reply
of August 30, 1939.*

122.

*From the President of the United States of America to the King of
Italy.*

Again a crisis in world affairs makes clear the responsibility of
heads of nations for the fate of their own people, and, indeed, of
humanity itself.

It is because of the traditional accord between Italy and the United
States and the ties of consanguinity between the millions of our citizens
that I feel I can address your Majesty on behalf of the maintenance of
world peace.

It is my belief, and that of the American people, that your Majesty
and your Majesty's Government can greatly influence the averting of
an outbreak of war.

Any general war would cause to suffer all the nations, whether
belligerent or neutral, whether victors or vanquished, and would
clearly bring devastation to the peoples and perhaps the Governments
of some nations most directly concerned.

The friends of the Italian people, and among them the American
people, could only regard with grief the destruction of the great
achievements which European nations and the Italian nation in particular have attained in the past generation.

We in America, having welded a homogeneous nation out of many
nationalities, often find it difficult to visualise the animosities which
so often have created a crisis among nations of Europe which are
smaller than ours in population and territory, but we accept the fact
that these nations have an absolute right to maintain their national
independence if they so desire.

If that is a sound doctrine, then it must apply to the weaker nations
as well as the stronger. The acceptance of this means peace, because
fear of aggression ends.

The alternative, which means of necessity efforts by the strong to
dominate the weak, will lead not only to war but to long future years
of oppression on the part of the victors and rebellion on the part of
the vanquished—so history teaches us.

181

On the 14th April last I suggested, in essence, an understanding that no armed forces should attack or invade the territory of any other independent nation, and that, this being assured, discussions should be undertaken to seek progressive relief from the burden of armaments and open the avenue of international trade, including the sources of raw materials necessary for the peaceful economic life of each nation.

I said that in these discussions the United States would gladly take part, and such peaceful conversations would make it wholly possible for Governments other than the United States to enter into peaceful discussions of the political and territorial problems in which they are directly concerned.

Were it possible for your Majesty's Government to formulate proposals for a pacific solution of the present crisis along these lines, you are assured of the earnest sympathy of the United States.

The Governments of Italy and the United States can to-day advance those ideals of Christianity which of late seem so often to have been obscured.

The unheard voices of countless millions of human beings ask that they shall not be vainly sacrificed again.

123.

From the King of Italy to the President of the United States of America.

I am grateful for your interest. I immediately transmitted your message to my Government. As is known to all, we have done and are doing everything possible to bring about peace with justice.

Messages sent by the President of the United States of America to Herr Hitler and the President of Poland and the reply of the President of Poland.

124.

The following is the text of the message from President Roosevelt to Herr Hitler of August 24, 1939:

In the message which I sent you on the 14th April, I stated that it appeared to be that the leaders of great nations had it in their power to liberate their peoples from the disaster that impended, but that, unless the effort were immediately made, with good will on all sides, to find a peaceful and constructive solution to existing controversies, the crisis which the world was confronting must end in catastrophe. To-day that catastrophe appears to be very near—at hand, indeed.

To the message which I sent you last April I have received no reply, but because my confident belief that the cause of world peace—which is the cause of humanity itself—rises above all other considerations I am again addressing myself to you, with the hope that the war which impends and the consequent disaster to all peoples may yet be averted.

I therefore urge with all earnestness—and I am likewise urging the President of the Republic of Poland—that the Governments of Germany and Poland agree by common accord to refrain from any positive act of hostility for a reasonable stipulated period, and that they agree, likewise by common accord, to solve the controversies which have arisen between them by one of the three following methods:—

First, by direct negotiation;

Second, by the submission of these controveries to an impartial arbitration in which they can both have confidence; or

Third, that they agree to the solution of these controversies through the procedure of conciliation, selecting as a conciliator or moderator a national of one of the American Republics, which are all of them free from any connexion with, or participation in, European political affairs.

Both Poland and Germany being sovereign Governments, it is understood, of course, that, upon resort to any one of the alternatives I suggest, each nation will agree to accord complete respect to the independence and territorial integrity of the other.

The people of the United States are as one in their opinion to policies of military conquest and domination. They are as one in rejecting the thesis that any ruler or any people possess the right to achieve their ends or objectives through the taking of action which will plunge countless of millions into war, and which will bring distress and suffering to every nation of the world, belligerent and neutral, when such ends and objectives, so far as they are just and reasonable, can be satisfied through the processes of peaceful negotiation or by resort to judicial arbitration.

I appeal to you in the name of the people of the United States, and I believe in the name of peace-loving men and women everywhere, to agree to a solution of the controversies existing between your Government and that of Poland through the adoption of one of the alternative methods I have proposed.

I need hardly reiterate that should the Governments of Germany and Poland be willing to solve their differences in the peaceful manner suggested, the Government of the United States still stands prepared to contribute its share to the solution of the problems which are endangering world peace in the form set forth in my message of the 14th April.

125.

The following is the text of the message from President Roosevelt to the President of Poland of August 24, 1939:—

The manifest gravity of the existing crisis imposes the urgent obligation upon all to examine every possible means which might prevent the outbreak of a general war. With this in mind I feel justified in suggesting that certain possible avenues of solution be considered. [Mr. Roosevelt then mentions the three methods described in his message to Herr Hitler.]

Should you determine to attempt a solution by any of these methods you are assured of the earnest and complete sympathy of the United States and of their people. During exploration of the avenues I appeal to you, as I have likewise appealed to the Government of the German Reich, to agree to refrain from any positive act of hostility.

It is, I think, well known to you that, speaking on behalf of the United States, I have exerted, and will continue to exert, every influence on behalf of peace. The rank and file of the population of every nation—large and small—want peace. They do not seek military conquest. They recognise that disputes, claims and counterclaims will always arise from time to time between nations, but that all such controversies, without exception, can be solved by a peaceful procedure, if the will on both sides exists so to do.

126.

The following is the text of the reply of August 25, 1939, to President Roosevelt from President Moscicki:—

I appreciate the noble message which your Excellency has been kind enough to send me. I should like to emphasise that the Polish Government have ever considered direct talks between Governments to be the most suitable method of resolving difficulties which may arise between States. We consider that this method is all the more suitable where neighbouring States are concerned. On the basis of these principles Poland concluded non-aggression pacts with Germany and Russia. We consider also that the method of conciliation through the intermediary of a disinterested and impartial third party is a just method of resolving differences which have been created between nations.

Although I clearly wish to avoid even the appearance of desiring to profit by this occasion to raise points of litigation, I deem it my duty, nevertheless, to make clear that in the present crisis it is not Poland which is formulating demands and demanding concessions of any other States. It is, therefore, perfectly natural that Poland should hold aloof from any action of this kind, direct or indirect. I would like to close by expressing my ardent wish that your message of peace may contribute to a general appeasement which is so necessary to enable the nations once more to regain the blessed path of progress and civilisation.

184

127.

The following is the text of President Roosevelt's second appeal to Herr Hitler, dated August 25, 1939:—

I have this hour received from the President of Poland a reply to the message which I addressed to your Excellency and to him last night.

[The text of President Moscicki's reply is then given. President Roosevelt continues as follows]:—

Your Excellency has repeatedly stated that the aims and objects sought by the German Reich were just and reasonable.

In his reply to my message the President of Poland has made it plain that the Polish Government is willing, upon the basis set forth in my message, to agree to solve the controversy which has arisen between the Republic of Poland and the German Reich by direct negotiation or the process of conciliation.

Countless human lives can yet be saved and hope may still be restored that the nations of the modern world may even now construct the foundation for a peaceful and happier relationship, if you and the Government of the German Reich will agree to the pacific means of settlement accepted by the Government of Poland. All the world prays that Germany, too, will accept.

Broadcast Appeal by His Majesty the King of the Belgians in the name of the Heads of States of the Oslo Group of Powers on August 23, 1939, and Replies.

128.

(Translation.)   *The Appeal.*

The declaration which I am about to read is being made in the Palace of Brussels in the presence of the Foreign Ministers of the Oslo Group of States and in the name of the Heads of those States.

The world is living through a period of tension such that there is a risk that all normal collaboration between States will become impossible. The Great Powers are taking measures almost equivalent to the mobilisation of their armed forces. Have not the small Powers reason to fear that they will be victims in a subsequent conflict into which they will be dragged against their will in spite of their policy of indisputable independence and of their firm desire for neutrality? Are they not liable to become the subject of arrangements reached without their having been consulted?

Even if hostilities do not begin, the world is menaced by economic collapse. Mistrust and suspicion reign everywhere. Beneath our very eyes the camps are forming, armies are gathering and a fearful struggle is being prepared in Europe. Is our continent to commit suicide in a terrifying war at the end of which no nation could call itself victor or venquished, but in which the spiritual and material values created by centuries of civilisation would founder?

War psychosis is invading every home, and although conscious of the unimaginable catastrophe which a conflagration would mean for all mankind, public opinion abandons itself more and more to the idea that we are inevitably to be dragged into it. It is important to react against so fatal a spirit of resignation.

There is no people—we assert it with confidence—which would wish to send its children to death in order to take away from other nations that right to existence which it claims for itself.

It is true that all States do not have the same interests, but are there any interests which cannot be infinitely better reconciled before than after a war?

The consciousness of the world must be awakened. The worst can still be avoided, but time is short. The sequence of events may soon render all direct contact still more difficult.

Let there be no mistake. We know that the right to live must rest on a solid basis, and the peace that we desire is the peace in which the rights of all nations shall be respected. A lasting peace cannot be founded on force, but only on a moral order.

Does not wisdom order us to withstand the war of words, incitements and threats, and agree to discuss the problems before us? We herewith solemnly express the wish that the men who are responsible for the course of events should agree to submit their disputes and their claims to open negotiation carried out in a spirit of brotherly co-operation.

It is for this reason that in the name of His Majesty the King of Denmark, the President of the Republic of Finland, Her Royal Highness the Grand Duchess of Luxemburg, His Majesty the King of Norway, Her Majesty the Queen of the Netherlands, His Majesty the King of Sweden, and in my own name, each of us, acting in agreement with our respective Governments, issue this appeal. We express the hope that other heads of States will join their voices to ours in this same anxiety to maintain peace and safety for their peoples.

To-morrow hundreds of millions of men will be at one with us in their wish to stop the course of events leading to war. We can only hope that those in whose hands rests the fate of the world will respond to these sentiments, give effect to the desire which they have so often expressed that the disputes which separate them shall be settled in peace, and thereby avoid the catastrophe which threatens humanity.

186

Reply of His Majesty's Government.

Viscount Halifax to Sir R. Clive (Brussels).

(Telegraphic.)   *Foreign Office, August 24, 1939.*

His Majesty's Government welcome and are in full sympathy with the appeal issued by His Majesty the King of the Belgians on behalf of representatives of the Oslo Group of Powers assembled in conference at Brussels.

His Majesty's Government for their part have repeatedly expressed their desire to see all questions arising between nations settled by free negotiation, and they are at all times willing to do their utmost to contribute to the creation of conditions in which such negotiation might be carried to a successful and satisfactory conclusion.

Acquiescence in the imposition of settlements by force or threat of force can only hinder and thwart the efforts of those who strive to establish an international order of things in which peace may be maintained and justice done without violating the rights or independence of any sovereign State.

130.

Translation of the reply of the French Government of August 26, 1939.

The noble and generous appeal put forward by His Majesty the King of the Belgians in the name of the representatives of the Oslo Group of States assembled at Brussels has been welcomed by the French Government with the deepest sympathy. The contributions which France has made at all times to the cause of peace and her constant preoccupation to see peaceful methods set up for the settlement of all the problems which arise between peoples leaves no room for doubt as to the general views of the French Government. They remain ready to associate themselves with any initiative the object of which is to create an atmosphere favourable to a lessening in international tension. While resolved to accept no solution imposed by violence or threats, they believe that by their attitude they are contributing to the maintenance of peace and at the same time to the establishment in Europe and in the world of conditions assuring all States that their independence will be guaranteed and their most sacred rights respected.

President Roosevelt's reply of August 25, 1939.

I have read with great satisfaction Your Majesty's proclamation of the 23rd August, and your appeal for the maintenance of peace made in the name of the Oslo group of Powers. Your Majesty expressed the hope that other Heads of States might join their voices with yours in the same desire to preserve peace and safety for their peoples. I take this opportunity to assure you that the people of the United States and their Government cordially share the hopes and aspirations so eloquently expressed by Your Majesty.

132.

Translation of the Polish reply of August 25, 1939.

I have noted the noble speech of Your Majesty with profound admiration for the ideas which you have expressed. Poland has always defended the idea that power, if it is to last, cannot be based on the oppression of others. Similarly, Poland has always considered the best guarantee of peace to be the settlement of international disputes by the method of direct negotiations based on justice and respect for the rights and interests of those concerned.

133.

His Holiness The Pope's reply.

In his reply, which was in the form of an autograph letter, Pope Pius XII conveyed his gratitude to the King of the Belgians and expressed his sincere hope that the sentiments expressed by the King of the Belgians would be favourably received by the parties concerned.

Joint Offer of Mediation by His Majesty the King of the Belgians and Her Majesty the Queen of the Netherlands and Replies.

134.

Sir R. Clive to Viscount Halifax (received 11.30 p.m.)

(Telegraphic.) *Brussels, August 28, 1939.*

I have just been to see Prime Minister, who tells me he had also convoked French, German and Italian Ambassadors and Polish Minister for the following purpose:—

The King of the Belgians and the Queen of Holland wish jointly to offer their good offices in the hope of averting war.

Similar communication was being made at The Hague to the same five representatives.

I promised to telephone immediately to your Lordship.

135.

Reply of His Majesty's Government.

Viscount Halifax to Sir R. Clive (Brussels) and Sir N. Bland (The Hague).

(Telegraphic.)   *Foreign Office, August 31, 1939, 3.30 p.m.*

Your telegram of 28th August: Initiative of Belgian and Netherlands Sovereigns.

Please inform Belgian/Netherlands Government that His Majesty's Government have received with pleasure the intimation that the King of the Belgians and the Queen of the Netherlands wish jointly to offer their good offices in the interests of moderation in the present crisis, and in the hope of averting war. His Majesty's Government welcome this offer on the part of the two Sovereigns, and will be glad to take advantage of it should the occasion present itself. Meanwhile, they deeply appreciate the intentions which have prompted this initiative.

136.

Reply of the French Government.

In their reply the French Government welcomed with the greatest interest the offer of their good offices made by the two Sovereigns. For their part they were ready to support this initiative in any way possible and they sincerely wished it every success.

137.

Translation of communiqué recording reply of Italian Government.

"The Italian Government have taken careful note of the offer of their good offices made by Their Majesties the Queen of the Netherlands and the King of the Belgians. They deeply appreciate this initiative and request the Belgian Government to transmit on their behalf to the two Sovereigns their sincere gratitude."

138.

Reply of the Polish Government.

In their reply the Polish Government referred to the telegram from President Moscicki to President Roosevelt, in which the principle of mediation had already been accepted by Poland. The Polish Government further expressed their approval of the initiative taken by the two Sovereigns. They also emphasised that they were not for the moment prepared to make any more detailed statement, since none of the proposals of a similar nature had hitherto called forth any favourable response from the German Government.

Broadcast Appeal for Peace by His Holiness the Pope, August 24, 1939, and the Reply of His Majesty's Government.

139.

The Appeal.

(Translation.)

Once again a critical hour strikes for the great human family; an hour of tremendous deliberations, towards which our heart cannot be indifferent and from which our spiritual authority, which comes to us from God to lead souls in the ways of justice and of peace must not hold itself aloof.

Behold us then with all of you, who in this moment are carrying the burden of so great a responsibility, in order that through our voice you may hear the voice of that Christ from Whom the world received the most exalted example of living, and in whom millions and millions of souls repose their trust in a crisis in which His word alone is capable of mastering all the tumultuous disturbances of the earth.

Behold us with you, leaders of peoples, men of State and men of arms, writers, orators of the radio and of the public rostrum and all those others who have the power to influence the thought and action of their fellow-men for whose destiny they are responsible.

We, armed only with the word of Truth and standing above all public disputes and passions, speak to you in the name of God from "Whom all paternity in heaven and earth is named"—in the name of Jesus Christ, Our Lord, who desired that all men be brothers—in the name of the Holy Ghost, Gift of God most High, inexhaustible source of love in the hearts of men.

To-day, notwithstanding our repeated exhortations and our very particular interest, the fear of bloody international conflict becomes more excruciating; to-day, when the tension of minds seems to have arrived at such a pass as to make the outbreak of the awful scourge of war appear imminent, we direct with paternal feeling a new and more heartfelt appeal to those in power and to their peoples: to the former that, laying aside accusations, threats, causes of mutual distrust, they may attempt to resolve their present differences with the sole means suitable thereto, namely, by reciprocal and trusting agreements; to the latter that in calm tranquility, without disordered agitation they may encourage the peaceful efforts of those who govern them.

It is by force of reason and not by force of arms that Justice makes progress; and empires which are not founded on Justice are not blessed by God. Statesmanship emancipated from morality betrays those very ones who would have it so.

The danger is imminent but there is yet time.

Nothing is lost with peace; all may be with war. Let men return to mutual understanding. Let them begin negotiations anew. Conferring with goodwill and with respect for reciprocal rights they will find that to sincere and conscientious negotiators, an honourable solution is never precluded.

They will feel a sense of greatness—in the true sense of the word—if by silencing the voices of passion, be it collective or private, and by leaving to reason its rightful rule, they will have spared the blood of their fellow men and saved their country from ruin.

May the Almighty grant that the voice of this Father of the Christian family, of this Servant of servants, who bears amongst men, unworthily, indeed, but nevertheless really, the person, the voice and the authority of Jesus Christ, find in the minds and in the hearts of men a ready and willing reception.

May the strong hear us that they may not become weak through injustice, may the powerful hear us if they desire that their power be not a destruction but rather a protection for their peoples and a safeguard to tranquillity in public order and in labour.

We beseech them by the blood of Christ, whose conquering force in the world was His mildness in life and in death. And beseeching them we know and we feel that we have with us all those who are upright of heart; all those who hunger and thirst after justice—all those who already suffer every sorrow through the evils of life. We have with us the heart of mothers which beats as one with ours; the fathers who would be obliged to abandon their families; the lowly who labour and do not understand; the innocent upon whom weighs heavily the awful threat; the young men, generous knights of the purest and noblest ideals. And with us also is the soul of this ancient Europe which was the product of the faith and of Christian genius. With us all humanity seeks justice, bread, freedom; not steel which kills and destroys. With us that Christ, Who has made His one, solemn commandment—Love of One's Brother—the very substance of His religion and the promise of salvation for individuals and for nations.

Recalling finally that human efforts are of no avail without Divine assistance, we invite all to raise their eyes to Heaven and to beseech the Lord with fervent prayer that His divine grace descend in abundance upon this world in its upheaval, placate dissensions, reconcile hearts and evoke the resplendent dawn of a more serene future.

To this end and with this hope we impart to all, from the heart, our paternal Benediction.

140.

Viscount Halifax to Mr. Osborne (Holy See).

(Telegraphic.) *Foreign Office, August 25, 1939, 5.15 p.m.*

Please inform the Cardinal Secretary of State, or if it is practicable the Pope himself, that His Majesty's Government have much appreciated the moving and dignified appeal for peace which His Holiness broadcast to the world last night.

2. In my own broadcast yesterday evening I referred to the Pope's message, but I should wish His Holiness to know in a more direct manner of the response which his words have evoked in the hearts and minds not only of His Majesty's Government, but of the people of this country as a whole.

Further Appeal by His Holiness the Pope and action by His Majesty's Government.

141.

Mr. Osborne to Viscount Halifax (received 3.45 p.m.)

(Telegraphic.) *Holy See, August 31, 1939.*

Cardinal Secretary of State has just handed me a note of which the following is a translation:—

"The Pope is unwilling to abandon hope that pending negotiations may lead to a just pacific solution such as the whole world continues to pray for.

"His Holiness therefore, in the name of God, beseeches the German and Polish Governments to do all that is in their power to avoid any incident and to abstain from taking any step that might aggravate the present tension.

"His Holiness begs the British, French and Italian Governments to support his appeal."

Copies of the above were also handed to the Ambassadors of Germany, Poland, France and Italy. His Eminence also gave a copy to the Spanish Ambassador and is causing a copy to be conveyed to the United States Ambassador to the Quirinal.

*Viscount Halifax to Sir N. Henderson (Berlin) and
Sir H. Kennard (Warsaw).*

(Telegraphic.)   *Foreign Office, August 31, 1939, 10 p.m.*

Please make following communication to German/Polish Government:—

"His Majesty's Government have been informed of the Pope's appeal to your Government to do all that is in their power to avoid any incident and to abstain from taking any step that might aggravate the present tension.

"His Majesty's Government desire to support this appeal with all the earnestness at their command."

Similar instructions sent to His Majesty's Ambassador at Warsaw/Berlin.

143.

Efforts by the Italian Government.

*Sir P. Loraine to Viscount Halifax (received 3 a.m.,
September 5).*

(Telegraphic.)   *Rome, September 4, 1939.*

Following is translation of Stefani* communiqué issued to-night: —

"In view of aggravation of European situation on 31st August, Duce, while realising exceptional difficulties which then made pacific solution extremely problematic, wished to make final attempt to save European peace. With this object English and French Governments were informed that Duce, if he could have previous certainty of Franco-British adhesion and Polish participation assured by action in London and Paris, would have been able to summon an international conference for 5th September with object of reviewing clauses of Treaty of Versailles which are cause of present disturbance in life of Europe. Italian Government did not fail to emphasise necessity of extreme urgency of replying, but French and English Governments were not able to convey their answer until next day, 1st September. In the meantime, in night between 31st August and 1st September frontier incidents occurred which led Führer to initiate military operations against Poland. Replies reaching Italian Government being favourable in principle both on French and English side and great interest having been shown on French side despite military clash which had already

* The official Italian news agency.

taken place between Germany and Poland in a possible development of initiative of Duce, Italian Government on morning of 2nd September at 10 o'clock informed Chancellor Hitler *a titre d'information* that there was still possibility of summoning conference, preceded by armistice conference, which would have been designed to solve German-Polish conflict by peaceful means. Hitler replied to Duce, through our Ambassador to Berlin, that he did not reject *à priori* possibility of conference. He wished, however, to know by way of preliminary (*a*) if notes presented by French and British at Berlin had character of ultimatum, in which case negotiation would be useless; and (*b*) if he could count on a period of twenty-four hours to mature and take his decision on matter. Italian Government, getting again into contact with Governments of London and Paris at 2 *p.m.* on 2nd September, informed them of Führer's request. In late evening reply came from London and Paris affirmative [*sic*]* as regards two requests above, but adding that France and England, in view of new fact which had occurred between 31st August and 2nd September, viz., occupation of Polish territory by German forces, laid down as fundamental condition for participation in international conference evacuation of occupied territories. In these circumstances, Italian Government confined themselves again to informing Führer of this condition, adding that, unless German Government were of contrary opinion, they did not think they could take further action."

* See Nos. 109, 110 and 116. The communication from His Majesty's Government was in the nature of a warning and was not to be considered as an ultimatum. The Italian Government were so informed.

The Prime Minister's Broadcast Talk to the German People
on September 4, 1939.

144.

German People.—Your country and mine are now at war. Your Government has bombed and invaded the free and independent State of Poland, which this country is in honour bound to defend. Because your troops were not withdrawn in response to the Note which the British Government addressed to the German Government, war has followed.

With the horrors of war we are familiar. God knows this country has done everything possible to prevent this calamity. But now that the invasion of Poland by Germany has taken place, it has become inevitable.

You are told by your Government that you are fighting because Poland rejected your Leader's offer and resorted to force. What are the facts? The so-called "offer" was made to the Polish Ambassador in Berlin on Thursday evening, two hours before the announcement by your Government that it had been "rejected." So far from having been rejected, there had been no time even to consider it.

Your Government had previously demanded that a Polish representative should be sent to Berlin within twenty-four hours to conclude an agreement. At that time the 16 Points subsequently put forward had not even been communicated to the Polish Government. The Polish representative was expected to arrive within a fixed time to sign an agreement which he had not even seen. This is not negotiation. This is a dictate To such methods no self-respecting and powerful State could assent. Negotiations on a free and equal basis might well have settled the matter in dispute.

You may ask why Great Britain is concerned. We are concerned because we gave our word of honour to defend Poland against aggression. Why did we feel it necessary to pledge ourselves to defend this Eastern Power when our interests lie in the West, and when your Leader has said he has no interest to the West? The answer is—and I regret to have to say it—that nobody in this country any longer places any trust in your Leader's word.

He gave his word that he would respect the Locarno Treaty; he broke it. He gave his word that he neither wished nor intended to annex Austria; he broke it. He declared that he would not incorpor-

195

ate the Czechs in the Reich; he did so. He gave his word after Munich that he had no further territorial demands in Europe; he broke it. He gave his word that he wanted no Polish provinces; he broke it. He has sworn to you for years that he was the mortal enemy of Bolshevism; he is now its ally.

Can you wonder his word is, for us, not worth the paper it is written on?

The German-Soviet Pact was a cynical *volte face*, designed to shatter the Peace Front against aggression. This gamble failed. The Peace Front stands firm. Your Leader is now sacrificing you, the German people, to the still more monstrous gamble of a war to extricate himself from the impossible position into which he has led himself and you.

In this war we are not fighting against you, the German people, for whom we have no bitter feeling, but against a tyrannous and forsworn régime which has betrayed not only its own people but the whole of Western civilisation and all that you and we hold dear.

May God defend the right!

White Paper Supplement

Germany No. 1 (1939)

FINAL REPORT

BY THE RIGHT HONOURABLE

SIR NEVILE HENDERSON

G.C.M.G.

ON THE CIRCUMSTANCES LEADING TO THE TERMINATION OF HIS MISSION TO BERLIN

SEPTEMBER 20, 1939

*Presented by the Secretary of State for Foreign Affairs
to Parliament by Command of His Majesty*

TORONTO

THE MUSSON BOOK COMPANY LTD.

1 9 3 9

PRINTED AND PUBLISHED IN CANADA BY PERMISSION OF THE
CONTROLLER OF HIS MAJESTY'S STATIONERY OFFICE

Cmd. 6115

Final Report by the Right Honourable Sir Nevile Henderson, G.C.M.G., on the circumstances leading to the Termination of his Mission to Berlin, September 20, 1939.

145.

London, September 20, 1939.

My Lord,

Events moved with such rapidity during the last fortnight of my mission to Berlin that it proved impossible at the time to give any consecutive account of them. If I have the honour to do so now, while the facts are still fresh in my memory, it is with the hope that such an account may be both of immediate interest to your Lordship and serve a purpose from the point of view of historical accuracy.

2. Nevertheless, it is not these last minute manœuvres which have the real importance, except in so far as they confirm the principles and demonstrate the methods and technique of Herr Hitler and of Nazism. A brief description of the background to August, 1939, is consequently indispensable, if the events of the last few weeks are to be visualised in their proper perspective.

3. Herr Hitler and National Socialism are the products of the defeat of a great nation in war and its reaction against the confusion and distress which followed that defeat. National Socialism itself is a revolution and a conception of national philosophy. Contrary to democracy which implies the subordination of the State to the service of its citizens, Nazism prescribes the subordination of its citizens to the service of the State, an all embracing Moloch, and to the individual who rules that State.

4. So long as National Socialism remained an article for internal consumption, the outside world, according to its individual predilection, might criticise or sympathise or merely watch with anxiety. The government of Germany was the affair of the German people. It was not until the theory of German nationalism was extended beyond Germany's own frontiers that the Nazi philosophy exceeded the limits compatible with peace.

5. It would be idle to deny the great achievements of the man who restored to the German nation its self-respect and its disciplined orderliness. The tyrannical methods which were employed within Germany

itself to obtain this result were detestable, but were Germany's own concern. Many of Herr Hitler's social reforms, in spite of their complete disregard of personal liberty of thought, word or deed were on highly advanced democratic lines. The "Strength through Joy" movement, the care for the physical fitness of the nation, and, above all, the organisation of the labour camps, an idea which Herr Hitler once told me that he had borrowed from Bulgaria, are typical examples of a benevolent dictatorship. Nor can the appeal of Nazism with its slogans so attractive to a not over-discerning youth be ignored. Much of its legislation in this respect will survive in a newer and better world, in which Germany's amazing power of organisation and the great contributions which she has made in the past to the sciences, music, literature and the higher aims of civilisation and humanity will again play a leading part.

6. Nor was the unity of Great Germany in itself an ignoble ideal. It had long been the dream of some of the highest-minded of German thinkers, and it must be remembered that even in 1914, Germany was still immature as a political concept. In spite of the potential political danger for its weaker neighbours of a national philosophy which could so easily be distorted and extended beyond its due and legitimate frontiers, the unity of Great Germany was a reality which had to be faced no less than that other reality, the paramount economic importance of Germany in Eastern, Central and South-Eastern Europe. It was not the incorporation of Austria and the Sudeten Germans in the Reich which so much shocked public opinion in the world as the unscrupulous and hateful methods which Herr Hitler employed to precipitate an incorporation which would probably have peacefully come in due course of its own volition and in accordance with the established principle of self-determination.

7. Yet even those methods might have been endured in a world which had experienced 1914-1918 and which sought peace as an end in itself, if Herr Hitler had been willing to accord to others the rights which he claimed for Germany. Revolutions are like avalanches, which once set in motion cannot stop till they crash to destruction at the appointed end of their career. History alone will determine whether Herr Hitler could have diverted Nazism into normal channels, whether he was the victim of the movement which he had initiated, or whether it was his own megalomania which drove it beyond the limits which civilisation was prepared to tolerate.

8. Be that as it may, the true background to the events of August, 1939, was the occupation of Prague on the 15th March of this year, the callous destruction thereby of the hard and newly-won liberty of a free and independent people and Herr Hitler's deliberate violation by this act of the Munich Agreement which he had signed not quite six months before. In 1939, as in 1914, the origin of war with Germany has been

due to the deliberate tearing up by the latter of a scrap of paper. To the iniquities of a system which employed the barbarism of the middle ages in its persecution of the Jews, which subjected Roman Catholic priests and Protestant pastors alike to the inhumanities of the concentration camp for obedience to their religious faith, and which crushed out, in a fashion unparalleled in history, all individual liberty within the State itself, was added the violation not only of international agreements freely negotiated, but also of that principle of self-determination which Herr Hitler had invoked with such insistence so long as it suited his own purpose to do so. Up to last March the German ship of State had flown the German national flag, and in spite of the "sickening technique" of Nazism it was difficult not to concede to Germany the right both to control her own destiny and to benefit from those principles which were accorded to others. On the 15th March, by the ruthless suppression of the freedom of the Czechs, its captain hoisted the skull and crossbones of the pirate, cynically discarded his own theory of racial purity and appeared under his true colours as an unprincipled menace to European peace and liberty.

9. Two of the less attractive characteristics of the German are his inability either to see any side of a question except his own, or to understand the meaning of moderation. It would have been understandable to argue that a hostile Bohemia in the centre of Germany was an untenable proposition. But Herr Hitler could see no mean between rendering the Czechs innocuous as a potential enemy and destroying their liberty as an independent people. There is some surprising reason to believe that Herr Hitler himself was disagreeably and literally astonished at the reaction in Britain and the world generally, which was provoked by the occupation of Prague and his breach of faith with Mr. Chamberlain. But while he may have realised his tactical mistake, it did not deter him from prosecuting his further designs.

10. As I had reported to your Lordship, at the beginning of the year Germany's immediate objectives, apart from the complete political and economic domination of Czecho-Slovakia and the eventual restoration of German colonies, were Danzig and Memel. Herr Hitler felt that it would not add much to the general execration of his aggression and ill-faith in March if he settled these two problems simultaneously with Prague. The Democracies were, he thought, so averse to war that they would accept any *fait accompli*. They would be less disturbed if everything was done at once. Thereafter, the agitation would, he anticipated, gradually subside until, after consolidating his gains, he was once more in a position to strike again.

11. With this plan in view the Lithuanian Government was at once browbeaten into surrendering Memel. The same method was employed at Warsaw, but the Poles were made of sterner stuff. Negotiations had

been proceeding ever since Munich for a settlement of the Danzig and the Corridor question. After Prague, Herr Hitler decided that they must be abruptly concluded, and Herr von Ribbentrop peremptorily dictated to the Polish Ambassador the terms which Herr Hitler would be pleased to impose on the Polish Government. The reply of the latter was given on the 26th March and constituted a refusal to accept a Dictate, while expressing readiness to continue free and equal discussion. Alarmed at the threatening attitude adopted by the German Government in consequence of this refusal, the Polish Government mobilised part of its forces (the German army was already largely mobilised), and the British guarantee to Poland was given on the 31st March.

12. The Ides of March constituted in fact the parting of the ways and were directly responsible for everything which happened thereafter. Thenceforward no small nation in Europe could feel itself secure from some new adaptation of Nazi racial superiority and jungle law. The Polish guarantee was followed by unilateral guarantees on Britain's part to Greece and Roumania as well as by an attempt on the part of the British and French Governments to induce the U.S.S.R. to join in a peace front against aggression, ill-faith and oppression. The Nazi Government, for its part and with considerable success in Germany, represented this attempt as a renewal of the alleged pre-war British policy of encirclement. As a war-cry for the German people it was exceedingly effective up to the signature of the Russo-German non-aggression pact on the 23rd August. The rest of Nazi propaganda was on two entirely contradictory lines either of which was destined, according to the development of the situation, to serve Herr Hitler's purpose. The first spread the persistent report that Britain would never go to war for the sake of Danzig. It was calculated to undermine the confidence of the Poles and to shake the faith of the smaller Powers, as well as of the United States of America, in the determination of Britain to resist any further German aggression. The second represented Britain as resolved to make war at the first opportunity on Germany in any case and in order to crush her before she became a too formidable political and economic rival. Both were fallacies but the Germans are a credulous race and, since the first has failed, it is the latter argumentation which forms the basis of Germany's present war propaganda.

13. Up to the beginning of August, though the clouds were black and the peace front negotiations dragged on interminably, the situation remained serious but not immediately dangerous. Instead, however, of there being any sign of a relaxation of tension at Danzig the position there had gradually become more and more strained. From the end of March till the end of August all personal contact between Warsaw and Berlin was suspended. The remilitarisation of the Free City, alleged by the Germans to be purely defensive, but no less adaptable

for offensive purposes, had proceeded apace, and other measures had been taken indicative of a German intention to effect a sudden coup there. The Poles for their part, in view of the great increase in arms smuggling, had been obliged to strengthen their customs inspectors by a number of frontier guards. They had also taken certain economic counter-measures of a nature to prejudice the trade of the Free City.

14. What was, however, even more ominous were the extensive preparations which were being made by the Germans for the twenty-fifth celebration of the battle of Tannenberg on the 27th August, and a German warship was scheduled to visit Danzig at the same time and ostensibly for the same purpose. Early in July I drew your Lordship's attention to the menace involved by these equivocal preparations, which corresponded so closely to Hitler's usual technique of preparing for all eventualities, under cover of a plausible excuse.

15. The first mutterings of the storm were heard on the 4th August. At four posts on the Danzig-East Prussian frontier, the Polish Customs Inspectors were informed that they would not be permitted henceforward to carry out their duties. Alarmed at the gradual sapping of Polish rights and interests in the Free City, the Polish Commissioner General there was at once instructed to deliver a note to the Danzig Senate, warning the latter that the Polish Government would react in the strongest manner if the work of the inspectors was interfered with. The Senate subsequently denied that it had issued any instructions to the effect alleged but the German Government replied to what it described as the Polish ultimatum by a verbal note, which was handed by the State Secretary to the Polish Chargé d'Affaires at Berlin on the 9th August. The Polish Government was therein warned that any further demand addressed to the Free City in the nature of an ultimatum or containing threats of reprisals, would at once lead to an aggravation of Polish-German relations, the responsibility for which would fall on the Polish Government. The latter retorted on the following day by a similar verbal note, denying the judicial right of Germany to intervene in the affairs between Poland and the Free City, and warning in its turn the German Government that "any future intervention by the latter to the detriment of Polish rights and interests at Danzig would be considered as an act of aggression."

16. I have little doubt but that the latter phrase served more than anything else to produce that final brainstorm in Herr Hitler's mind on which the peace of the world depended, and upon which it always must have depended so long as the fate not only of Germany but also of Europe, rested in the hands of a single irresponsible individual.

17. The tragedy of any dictator is that as he goes on, his entourage steadily and inexorably deteriorates. For lack of freedom of utterance he loses the services of the best men. All opposition becomes intolerable to him. All those, therefore, who are bold enough to express opinions

contrary to his views are shed one by one, and he is in the end surrounded by mere yes-men, whose flattery and counsels are alone endurable to him. In my report on the events of 1938 I drew your Lordship's special attention to the far reaching and unfortunate results of the Blomberg marriage. I am more than ever convinced of the major disaster which that—in itself—minor incident involved, owing to the consequent elimination from Herr Hitler's entourage of the more moderate and independent of his advisers, such as Field Marshal von Blomberg himself, Baron von Neurath, Generals Fritsch, Beck, &c. After February of last year Herr Hitler became more and more shut off from external influences and a law unto himself.

18. People are apt, in my opinion, to exaggerate the malign influence of Herr von Ribbentrop, Dr. Goebbels, Herr Himmler and the rest. It was probably consistently sinister, not because of its suggestiveness (since Herr Hitler alone decided policy), nor because it merely applauded and encouraged, but because, if Herr Hitler appeared to hesitate, the extremists of the party at once proceeded to fabricate situations calculated to drive Herr Hitler into courses which even he at times shrank from risking. The simplest method of doing this was through the medium of a controlled Press. Thus what happened in September last year, was repeated in March this year, and again in August. Dr. Goebbels' propaganda machine was the ready tool of these extremists, who were afraid lest Herr Hitler should move too slowly in the prosecution of his own ultimate designs.

19. The 1938 stories of Czech atrocities against its German minority, were rehashed up almost verbatim in regard to the Poles. Some foundation there must necessarily have been for a proportion of these allegations in view of the state of excitable tension which existed between the two peoples. Excess of zeal on the part of individuals and minor officials there undoubtedly was—but the tales of ill-treatment, expropriation and murder were multiplied a hundredfold. How far Herr Hitler himself believed in the truth of these tales must be a matter for conjecture. Germans are prone in any case to convince themselves very readily of anything which they wish to believe. Certainly he behaved as if he did believe, and, even if one may give him the benefit of the doubt, these reports served to inflame his resentment to the pitch which he or his extremists desired.

20. Until the 8th August the campaign against the Poles had been relegated to the more discreet pages of the German press. Up to that date, public enemy No. 1 had been Great Britain and the alleged policy of encirclement. From that date, however, the stories of Polish atrocities began to take the leading place, and by the 17th August the campaign was in full swing.

21. Herr Hitler is a master of turning events to suit his own purpose, and the so-called ultimatum to the Danzig Senate of the 4th

August and the subsequent foreign press comments on a Danzig "climb down" gave him the opportunity which he was seeking. The Polish note of the 4th August provided an excuse for the German *note verbale* of the 9th August, which provoked in its turn the Polish reply of the 10th August. In the midst of these exchanges Dr. Burckhardt, High Commissioner of the League of Nations for Danzig flew to Berchtesgaden in a last effort to place the position at Danzig on a more satisfactory footing. He saw Herr Hitler on the 11th August, while Count Ciano and Herr von Ribbentrop were meeting at Salzburg.

22. Intransigent as he appears to have been at his interview with Dr. Burckhardt, there is little doubt in my mind that Herr Hitler would have been far more so had he at the time been in possession of the text of the final paragraph of the Polish reply of 10th August, which had only been communicated to the Ministry for Foreign Affairs at Berlin on that day. He was aware of it, however, when Count Ciano visited him at Berchtesgaden immediately after Dr. Burckhardt's departure, and it undoubtedly rendered unavailing the Italian Foreign Minister's laudable intention of pouring oil on the troubled waters. Once again, as in 1938, the inexorable fatality of the Greek tragedy was in evidence, and the coincidence of the Polish note of the 10th August with the Ciano visit was a striking example of it. Count Ciano returned to Italy and a day or so later the Italian Ambassador at Berlin was hurriedly summoned to Rome.

23. Herr Hitler's carefully calculated patience was, in fact, exhausted, and on the 18th August I telegraphed to your Lordship that I had come to the definite conclusion that, if peace was to be preserved, the present situation could not be allowed to continue and that the only alternative to war must be some immediate and mediatory action. In this connexion I repeated a suggestion which I had made some time previously, namely, that a personal letter should be addressed by the Prime Minister to Herr Hitler and be delivered by some emissary from London. Two days later I again telegraphed to the same effect, and stated my conviction that Herr Hitler had now finally decided upon some form of immediate action which would force the issue. I drew attention at the same time to the increased German military strength which had been assembled in East Prussia under cover of the Tannenberg anniversary and expressed my apprehension lest that celebration might prove the starting point for the action which Herr Hitler contemplated. I have little doubt but that such was Herr Hitler's original and premeditated intention.

24. On the 21st August information reached me that the long expected but carefully concealed German military concentrations were already in progress, and that instructions had been given to complete them by the 24th August. A report which reached me at that time

actually mentioned the 25th August as the date fixed for the German advance into Poland.

25. I shall return to this point later, but I must here refer to the bombshell which was exploded late in the evening of the 21st August by the announcement that negotiations had been concluded for the signature of a Russo-German non-aggression pact and that Herr von Ribbentrop would fly to Moscow on the 23rd to sign it.

26. The secret, which on the German side had been known to not more than a few persons, had been well kept. It had been realised that German counter-negotiations had been proceeding throughout the summer, but it was hoped that they had been abandoned after the actual arrival at Moscow of the French and British military missions. Comment on the subject is, however, outside the scope of this report, except in so far as it concerns the effect of this announcement on the German public. The first impression in Berlin was one of immense relief, partly at the removal of the dreaded Russian air menace, but more particularly because, in the minds of a public which had been led to believe by Goebbels propaganda that the British negotiations with the U.S.S.R. were really encirclement with a view to a preventive war, the conclusion of a Russo-German non-aggression pact meant that peace was assured, since Britain would not, it was told, fight for Danzig or Poland without Russian aid. Once more the faith of the German people in the ability of Herr Hitler to obtain his objective without war was reaffirmed. Its satisfaction was, however, short-lived and the deception considerable when it was realised that Britain's word to Poland did not depend on Russian support. Those who had fought the war of nazism against communism were furthermore puzzled by this complete *volte-face*. The Nazi theory of racial purity had been discarded in March and in August a second of its basic principles was thus equally relegated to the scrap-heap. To most Germans the old hereditary enemy is Russia, nor was their confidence in the sincerity of her good intentions towards Germany greatly fortified by this exhibition of Russian ill-faith towards the Western Democracies. Nevertheless, as a diplomatic *coup*, the Russo-German pact was a strikingly successful and surprising one. It is devoutly to be hoped that it may prove as Pyrrhic as are most diplomatic victories.

27. At the moment when Herr von Ribbentrop was preparing to fly to Moscow, I received shortly before 9 p.m. on the 22nd August your Lordship's instructions to convey without delay a personal letter from the Prime Minister to Herr Hitler. I at once got into communication with the Ministry for Foreign Affairs, and in the course of the night an interview was arranged for the following day. I left Berlin at 9.30 on the morning of the 23rd August accompanied by the State Secretary and Herr Hewel, in an aeroplane provided for me by the Ministry for Foreign Affairs.

28. I reached Salzburg about midday and I had my first audience with Herr Hitler at Berchtesgaden at 1 p.m. on the 23rd August in the presence of Baron von Weizsäcker and Herr Hewel. The correspondence, including the text of the Prime Minister's letter, of Herr Hitler's reply and my own telegraphic record of my two conversations with the Chancellor, is to be found in the Blue Book presented to Parliament and publishing the documents concerning German-Polish relations and the outbreak of hostilities between Great Britain and Germany on the 3rd September, 1939. (¹)

29. I need not say more here than that the three main points of the Prime Minister's letter were (1) insistence on the determination of His Majesty's Government to fulfil their obligations to Poland; (2) their readiness, if a peace atmosphere could be created, to discuss all the problems at issue between our two countries, and (3) their anxiety, during a period of truce, to see immediate direct discussion initiated between Germany and Poland in regard to the reciprocal treatment of minorities.

30. In Herr Hitler's reply of the 23rd August he declared that Great Britain's determination to support Poland could not modify his policy as expressed in the German verbal note to the Polish Government of the 9th August that he was prepared to accept even a long war rather than sacrifice German national interests and honour, and that, if Great Britain persisted in her own measures of mobilisation, he would at once order the mobilisation of the whole of the German forces.

31. At my first interview with him on that day, Herr Hitler was in a mood of extreme excitability. His language as regards the Poles and British responsibility for the Polish attitude was violent, recriminatory and exaggerated. He referred, for instance, to 100,000 German refugees from Poland, a figure which was at least five times greater than the reality. Again I cannot say whether he was persuaded or persuaded himself of the reality of these figures. At my second interview, when he handed me his reply, he had recovered his calm but was not less uncompromising. No longer, he told me, did he trust Mr. Chamberlain. He preferred war, he said, when he was 50 to when he was 55 or 60. He had himself always sought and believed in the possibility of friendship with England. He now realised, he said, that those who had argued the contrary had been right and nothing short of a complete change in British policy towards Germany could ever convince him of any sincere British desire for good relations. My last remark to him was that I could only deduce from his language that my mission to Germany had failed and that I bitterly regretted it.

32. I flew back from Berchtesgaden to Berlin the same evening. I had in fact little hope that either the Prime Minister's letter or my own language to Herr Hitler, however direct and straightforward,

(¹) Nos. 56, 57, 58, 60 (pages 98-103).

would give him pause. The Russian pact had, I felt, created in his opinion a situation which was favourable to his designs and I believed his mind to be definitely made up. Though he spoke of his artistic tastes and of his longing to satisfy them, I derived the impression that the corporal of the last war was even more anxious to prove what he could do as a conquering Generalissimo in the next.

33. Nevertheless the visit to Berchtesgaden may after all have postponed the disaster for a week. Herr von Ribbentrop flew back to Germany with the signed Russo-German Agreement and Herr Hitler returned to Berlin the night of the 24th August. I have some reason to believe—though I cannot confirm it—that the order for the German Army to advance into Poland was actually issued for the night of the 25th-26th August. It is difficult otherwise to find justification for the various orders and arrangements which came into force on the 26th and 27th August. In the afternoon of the 25th August itself all telephone communication between Berlin and London and Paris was unexpectedly cut off for several hours. The celebrations at Tannenberg were cancelled on the 26th and the Party Rally at Nuremberg on the 27th August; all Naval, Military and Air Attachés at Berlin were refused permission to leave the city without prior authority being obtained from the Ministry of War. All German airports were closed from that date, and the whole of Germany became a prohibited zone for all aircraft except the regular civil lines. All internal German air services were also suspended. Moreover as from the 27th a system for the rationing of food-stuffs and other commodities throughout Germany came into force. That this latter and — for the public — depressing measure should have been adopted prior to the outbreak of war can scarcely be explained, except on the assumption that war should actually have broken out on the 26th August.

34. The fact may well be, as I imagine it was, that Herr Hitler had had in consequence of the Prime Minister's letter one last hesitation and countermanded the orders to his Army, whereas the other arrangements were allowed to proceed unchecked. But it was not the horrors of war which deterred him. He had unlimited confidence in the magnificent army and air force which he had re-created and he was certainly not averse to putting them to the test so far as Poland was concerned. In two months, he told me, the war in the East would be ended and he would then, he said, hurl 160 divisions against the Western Front if England was so unwise as to oppose his plans. His hesitation was due rather to one final effort to detach Britain from Poland. Be that as it may, at about 12.45 on the 25th August, I received a message to the effect that Herr Hitler wished to receive me at the Chancellery at 1.30 p.m. At that meeting he made to me the verbal communication which is recorded in the Blue Book. (²)

(²) No. 68 (page 121).

35. Briefly put, Herr Hitler's proposals therein dealt with two groups of questions: (*a*) the immediate necessity of a settlement of the dispute between Germany and Poland, and (*b*) an eventual offer of friendship or alliance between Germany and Great Britain. My interview with Herr Hitler, at which Herr von Ribbentrop and Dr. Schmidt were also present, lasted on this occasion over an hour. The Chancellor spoke with calm and apparent sincerity. He described his proposals as a last effort, for conscience sake, to secure good relations with Great Britain, and he suggested that I should fly to London myself with them. I told his Excellency that, while I was fully prepared to consider this course, I felt it my duty to tell him quite clearly that my country could not possibly go back on its word to Poland, and that, however anxious we were for a better understanding with Germany, we could never reach one except on the basis of a negotiated settlement with Poland.

36. Whatever may have been the underlying motive of this final gesture on the part of the Chancellor, it was one which could not be ignored, and, with your Lordship's consent, I flew to London early the following morning (26th August), on a German plane which was courteously put at my disposal. Two days were spent by His Majesty's Government in giving the fullest and most careful consideration to Herr Hitler's message, and on the afternoon of the 28th August I flew back to Berlin with their reply.([3]) Therein, while the obligations of His Majesty's Government to Poland were reaffirmed, it was stated that the Polish Government were ready to enter into negotiations with the German Government for a reasonable solution of the matter in dispute on the basis of the safeguarding of Poland's essential interests, and of an international guarantee for the settlement eventually arrived at. His Majesty's Government accordingly proposed that the next step should be the initiation of direct discussions between the Polish and German Governments on that basis and the adoption of immediate steps to relieve the tension in the matter of the treatment of minorities. Furthermore, His Majesty's Government undertook to use all their influence with a view to contributing towards a solution which might be satisfactory to both parties and which would, they hoped, prepare the way for the negotiation of that wider and more complete understanding between Great Britain and Germany which both countries desired. Finally, after a reference to a limitation of armaments, His Majesty's Government pointed out that, whereas a just settlement of the Polish question might open the way to world peace, failure to do so would finally ruin the hopes of a better understanding between our countries and might well plunge the whole world into war.

37. Before continuing the record of events after my return to Berlin on the evening of the 28th August, it is necessary to give a

([3]) No. 74 (page 126).

brief account of what had happened after my meeting with the Chancellor at 1.30 on the 25th August. At 5 p.m. on that day Herr Hitler had received the French Ambassador and given him a letter for communication to M. Daladier. Its general tenour was a suggestion to France, with whom Germany was stated to have no quarrel, to abstain from further support of Poland. It received a dignified answer from the French Government, which was published on the 27th August. Appeals for peace were made at this time to both the German and Polish Governments as well as to other Powers by the Pope and the President of the United States of America. Though they received a favourable response from the Polish Government, they received scant consideration from Germany.

38. On the evening of the 25th August the Anglo-Polish Pact had been signed in London. Though it had been under negotiation for several months, its signature gave great offence to Herr Hitler, who was at first inclined to regard it as the reply of His Majesty's Government to his message to them. His immediate retort was the announcement on the morning of the 26th August that Herr Forster had been appointed Reichsoberhaupt, or Head of the State of Danzig. At the same time the German concentrations against Poland began to reach their final stage.

39. Thereafter there was a lull for two days pending my return to Germany with the reply of His Majesty's Government. I had left London at 5 p.m. on the 28th August, and at 10.30 p.m. I was received by Herr Hitler at the Chancellery and handed to him that reply, together with a German translation. I sent to your Lordship a full record of my conversation with the Chancellor the same night. (⁴)

40. On this occasion Herr Hitler was again friendly and reasonable and appeared to be not dissatisfied with the answer which I had brought to him. He observed, however, that he must study it carefully and would give me a written reply the next day.

41. I would mention incidentally that both that evening and the next, when I visited Herr Hitler again and was handed his reply, nothing was left undone to enhance the solemnity of the occasion. A considerable but quite expressionless crowd was waiting outside the Chancellery and a guard of honour awaited me in the courtyard of the main entrance. In view of what has been reported to the contrary, I desire to bear witness here to the fact that throughout the whole of those anxious weeks neither I nor my staff received anything but the utmost courtesy and civility from all Germans, except on one occasion to which I shall refer later.

(⁴) No. 75 (page 129).

42. Such information as reached me during the course of the day of the 29th August tended to represent the atmosphere as not unfavourable and to foreshadow Herr Hitler's readiness to open direct negotiations with the Poles. I was therefore somewhat disappointed on being summoned to the Chancellery at 7.15 that evening to find the Chancellor in a far less reasonable mood than on the previous evening. The German midday Press had reported the alleged murder of six German nationals in Poland, and this story, which was probably fabricated by the extremists in fear lest he was weakening, together with the news of the Polish general mobilisation, had probably upset him. I sensed in any case a distinctly more uncompromising attitude on Herr Hitler's part when he handed me his answer. I read it through carefully, and, though it reiterated his demand for the whole Corridor as well as Danzig, I made no comment till I reached the phrase at the end of it, in which, after a grudging acquiescence in direct discussions with the Poles solely by way of proof of Germany's sincerity in her desire for lasting friendship with Great Britain, it was stated that "the German Government counted upon the arrival in Berlin of a Polish Emissary with full powers on the following day, Wednesday, the 30th August." I pointed out to his Excellency that this phrase sounded very much like an ultimatum ("hatte den Klang eines Ultimatums"). This was strenuously and heatedly denied by Herr Hitler himself, supported by Herr von Ribbentrop. According to the former this sentence merely emphasized the urgency of the moment, not only on account of the risk of incidents when two mobilised armies were standing opposite one another, but also when Germans were being massacred in Poland. In this latter connection his Excellency asserted that "I did not care how many Germans were being slaughtered in Poland." This gratuitous impugnment of the humanity of His Majesty's Government and of myself provoked a heated retort on my part and the remainder of the interview was of a somewhat stormy character.

43. It was closed, however, by a brief and in my opinion quite honest harangue on Herr Hitler's part in regard to the genuineness of his constant endeavour to win Britain's friendship, of his respect for the British Empire, and of his liking for Englishmen generally.

44. I should like to state here, parenthetically but emphatically, that Herr Hitler's constant repetition of his desire for good relations with Great Britain was undoubtedly a sincere conviction. He will prove in the future a fascinating study for the historian and the biographer with psychological leanings. Widely different explanations will be propounded, and it would be out of place and time to comment at any length in this despatch on this aspect of Herr Hitler's mentality and character. But he combined, as I fancy many Germans do, admiration for the British race with envy of their achievements and hatred of their opposition to Germany's excessive aspirations. It is no

211

exaggeration to say that he assiduously courted Great Britain, both as representing the aristocracy and most successful of the Nordic races, and as constituting the only seriously dangerous obstacle to his own far-reaching plan of German domination in Europe. This is evident in *Mein Kampf,* and, in spite of what he regarded as the constant rebuffs which he received from the British side, he persisted in his endeavours up to the last moment. Geniuses are strange creatures, and Herr Hitler, among other paradoxes, is a mixture of long-headed calculation and violent and arrogant impulse provoked by resentment. The former drove him to seek Britain's friendship and the latter finally into war with her. Moreover, he believes his resentment to be entirely justified. He failed to realise why his military-cum-police tyranny should be repugnant to British ideals of individual and national freedom and liberty, or why he should not be allowed a free hand in Central and Eastern Europe to subjugate smaller and, as he regards them, inferior peoples to superior German rule and culture. He believed he could buy British acquiescence in his own far-reaching schemes by offers of alliance with and guarantees for the British Empire. Such acquiescence was indispensable to the success of his ambitions and he worked unceasingly to secure it. His great mistake was his complete failure to understand the inherent British sense of morality, humanity and freedom.

45. It must be mentioned here that the concluding passage of the Chancellor's reply to His Majesty's Government had contained a statement to the effect that the German Government would immediately draw up proposals for a solution of the Polish question which it would, if possible, place at the disposal of the British Government before the arrival of the Polish negotiator.

46. I had at once telegraphed to your Lordship the text of the German note, ([5]) and in the early hours of the morning of the 30th August (4 a.m.) I had already conveyed to the Ministry for Foreign Affairs your interim reply, to the effect that it would be carefully considered, but observing that it would be unreasonable to expect that His Majesty's Government could produce a Polish representative at Berlin within twenty-four hours, and that the German Government must not count on this.

47. Later in the course of the day, I received three messages for communication to the German Government. The first was a personal one from the Prime Minister to the Chancellor notifying the latter of the representations made to Warsaw in regard to the avoidance of frontier incidents, and begging the German Government to take similar precautions. (I transmitted this in the afternoon to its destination in a personal letter to the Minister for Foreign Affairs.) The second similarly notified the German Government of our counsels of restraint

([5]) No. 78 (page 136).

212

to Poland and asked for reciprocation on Germany's part. The third pointed out that the demand that a Polish Representative with full powers must come to Berlin to receive the German proposals was unreasonable and suggested that the German Government should follow the normal procedure of inviting the Polish Ambassador to call and of handing him the German proposals for transmission to Warsaw with a view to arrangements being made for the conduct of negotiations. This last communication also reminded the German Government that it had promised to communicate its detailed proposals to His Majesty's Government, who undertook, if they offered a reasonable basis, to do their best in Warsaw to facilitate negotiations. The good intentions of His Majesty's Government were, in fact, patently clear and had Herr Hitler honestly desired or preferred a pacific settlement all the arrangements to that end seemed to be in full swing.

48. I had arranged to see the Minister for Foreign Affairs at 11.30 p.m. to make these communications to him. Shortly before the appointed time I received in code the considered reply of His Majesty's Government to the German Note of the 29th August.(⁶) I was accordingly obliged to ask that my meeting with Herr von Ribbentrop should be postponed for half an hour, in order to give me the time to have this last message decyphered.

49. In the final passages of that communication His Majesty's Government, while fully recognising the need for speed in the initiation of discussions, urged that during the negotiations no aggressive military operations should take place on either side. They further expressed their confidence that they could secure such an undertaking from the Polish Government, if the German Government would give similar assurances. They also suggested a temporary *modus vivendi* at Danzig, such as would obviate the risk of incidents which might render German-Polish relations still more difficult.

50. I saw Herr von Ribbentrop at exactly midnight, before which hour the German Government had ostensibly counted on the arrival of a Polish emissary at Berlin. I say "ostensibly" since it seems hardly possible that it cannot have occurred to either Herr Hitler or his Minister for Foreign Affairs that it was utterly unreasonable to expect a Polish Plenipotentiary to present himself at Berlin without even knowing in advance the basis of the proposals about which he was expected to negotiate. It is conceivable that the Army Leaders had been representing to their Führer that even 24 hours' delay involved the risk of bad weather holding up the rapidity of the German advance into Poland, but, even so, it is difficult not to draw the conclusion that the proposals in themselves were but dust to be thrown in the eyes of the world with a view to its deception and were never intended to be taken seriously by the German Government itself.

(⁶) No. 89 (page 143).

51. Be that as it may, it is probable that Herr Hitler's mood in the hour when he had to decide between peace or war was not an amiable one. It was reflected in Herr von Ribbentrop, whose reception of me that evening was, from the outset, one of intense hostility, which increased in violence as I made each communication in turn. He kept leaping from his chair in a state of great excitement, and asking if I had anything more to say. I kept replying that I had, and, if my own attitude was no less unfriendly than his own, I cannot but say in all sincerity that I had every justification for it. When I told him that I would not fail to report his comments and remarks to my Government, he calmed down a little and said that they were his own, and that it was for Herr Hitler to decide. As for inviting the Polish Ambassador to come and see him, such a course would, he indignantly said, be utterly unthinkable and intolerable.

52. After I had finished making my various communications to him, he produced a lengthy document which he read out to me in German, or rather gabbled through to me as fast as he could, in a tone of the utmost annoyance. Of the sixteen articles in it I was able to gather the gist of six or seven, but it would have been quite impossible to guarantee even the exact accuracy of these without a careful study of the text itself. When he had finished, I accordingly asked him to let me see it. Herr von Ribbentrop refused categorically, threw the document with a contemptuous gesture on the table and said that it was now out of date ("überholt"), since no Polish Emissary had arrived at Berlin by midnight.

53. I observed that in that case the sentence in the German note of the 29th August to which I had drawn his and his Führer's attention on the preceding evening had, in fact, constituted an ultimatum in spite of their categorical denials. Herr von Ribbentrop's answer to that was that the idea of an ultimatum was a figment of my own imagination and creation.

54. I do not desire to stress the unpleasant nature of this interview. The hour was a critical one and Herr von Ribbentrop's excitability at such a moment was understandable. It seemed to me, however, that he was wilfully throwing away the last chance of a peaceful solution, and it was difficult to remain indifferent when faced with such a calamity. I would merely add that, contrary to what was subsequently published in the German press, I did not discuss a single detail of the German proposals with Herr von Ribbentrop, who flatly declined to do so. While it is true that they were read to me, it was in such a manner as to make them practically unintelligible.

55. I returned to His Majesty's Embassy that night with the feeling that the last hope for peace had vanished. I nevertheless saw the Polish Ambassador at 2 a.m., gave him a brief and studiously moderate account of my conversation with Herr von Ribbentrop, mentioned the

cession of Danzig and the plebiscite in the Corridor as the two main points in the German proposals, stated that so far as I could gather they were not on the whole too unreasonable, and suggested to him that he might recommend to his Government that they should propose at once a meeting between Field-Marshals Smigly-Rydz and Göring. I felt obliged to add that I could not conceive of the success of any negotiations if they were conducted with Herr von Ribbentrop.

56. Though M. Lipski undertook to make this suggestion to his Government, it would by then probably have been in any case too late. There was, in fact, for Herr Hitler only one conceivable alternative to brute force, and that was that a Polish Plenipotentiary should humbly come to him, after the manner of Dr. Schuschnigg or President Hacha, and sign on the dotted line to the greater glory of Adolf Hitler. And even that must happen at once. The Army was asking "Yes" or "No," since the success of its plans depended largely on the rapid occupation of Poland and the conclusion as soon as possible of the war on the Eastern front. Bad weather might otherwise intervene at any time and was likely to prove one of Poland's best defences against the highly mechanised German army. Moreover, a week had already been lost by Herr Hitler's hesitation on the 25th August.

57. I have no doubt that such and other considerations were present in Herr Hitler's mind on the night of the 30th August. I was consequently not surprised when I received in the early hours of the morning of the 31st reliable information that the actual decision had been taken to order the advance of the German Army by midday or 1 p.m. if no Polish Plenipotentiary had arrived before then. I believe this information to have been accurate, and I attribute the further brief respite which ensued to the twelfth-hour efforts of the Italian Government to restrain Herr Hitler from war.

58. I had in the meantime obtained from another source more definite, if unauthorised, details of the German proposals, and these I at once communicated through the Counsellor of His Majesty's Embassy to the Polish Ambassador, who spent that morning on the telephone to Warsaw. About the middle of the day I had transmitted to the Ministry for Foreign Affairs a further message from His Majesty's Government to the German Government notifying them that the Polish Government were taking steps to establish contact with them through the Polish Ambassador at Berlin, and asking them to agree to an immediate provisional *modus vivendi* at Danzig, for which purpose M. Burckhardt was suggested as intermediary. To this communication I never received any reply. There was, however, a further delay of some 12 hours. The Polish Government had authorised their Ambassador to establish contact with Herr von Ribbentrop, and Herr Hitler waited to see what message M. Lipski would bring. The question, in fact, was whether his qualifications would be those of a Plenipo-

tentiary empowered by the Polish Government to conduct and conclude negotiations or not. On no other terms was Hitler prepared to postpone action. His army was ready and Poland must be taught a lesson. She must crawl or get her whipping.

59. During the day there had been much activity on the part of Field-Marshal Göring. I think there can be no doubt that Field-Marshal Göring himself would have preferred a peaceful solution, but in matters such as these it was Herr Hitler's decision which alone counted; and whatever Field-Marshal Göring himself might feel, he was merely the loyal and submissive servant of his master. Moreover, he had come down definitely on the side of peace a year before and it may have been difficult for him to adopt this course a second time. He invited me, however, to come and see him that afternoon, and I did so at 5 p.m. in company of Sir G. Ogilvie-Forbes. Inasmuch as I had heard that the text of the proposals which Herr von Ribbentrop had refused to give me was to be announced that evening, my first remark was to point out to the Field-Marshal that this procedure would probably and finally wreck the last prospect of peace and to beg him to do his utmost to prevent their publication. Field-Marshal Göring's reply was that he could not intervene, and that the German Government felt obliged to broadcast their proposals to the world in order to prove their "good faith".

60. Instead he talked for the best part of two hours of the iniquities of the Poles and about Herr Hitler's and his own desire for friendship with England, and of the benefit to the world in general and the advantage to England in particular of such a friendship. It was a conversation which led nowhere and I could not help feeling that his remarks, which from his point of view were perfectly genuine but which I had heard often before, were chiefly intended for the edification of his listeners. I augured the worst from the fact that he was in a position at such a moment to give me so much of his time. He had a few days before been made president of the new German Defence Council for the Reich (or War Cabinet) and he could scarcely have afforded at such a moment to spare time in conversation if it did not mean that everything down to the last detail was now ready for action.

61. Incidentally the composition of that council was evidence of Herr Hitler's acumen. He had selected for it all the most respectable of the Nazi leaders, such as Herr Frick, Dr. Lammers, Dr. Funk, who might be counted upon, with Field-Marshal Göring himself the most popular of them all with the general public, to inspire the confidence of the German people. The worst extremists and the most unpopular with the people were omitted from it. To them was to be confided the less enviable task of dealing with the neutrals, of organising the Interior and of ruthlessly repressing any internal discontent. My general

216

impression of this last talk with Field-Marshal Göring was, in fact, that it constituted a final but forlorn effort on his part to detach Britain from the Poles. Nevertheless the Field-Marshal seemed sincere when, having been called to the telephone, he returned to tell us that M. Lipski was on his way to see Herr von Ribbentrop. He seemed to hope that, provided contact was only established, war might after all prove unnecessary. The meeting between the Polish Ambassador proved, however, quite futile. M. Lipski stated that he was acting solely in his capacity as an Ambassador without plenary powers to *discuss or to negotiate, and handed to the Minister for Foreign Affairs a brief communication to the effect that the Polish Government were weighing favourably the proposal of His Majesty's Government for direct discussion and that a formal answer in this matter would be communicated to the German Government in the immediate future. He did not ask for the German proposals and Herr von Ribbentrop did not offer to give them to him. Their meeting lasted but a few minutes.

62. Early in the morning I had rung up the State Secretary and, after pointing out that the German Government had promised to communicate these proposals to His Majesty's Government, and how helpless I was without the authorised text of them, had asked him to suggest to Herr von Ribbentrop once more that they should be communicated to me. I heard no more from Baron von Weizsäcker until late in the evening, when I received a message asking me to call upon him at 9.15 p.m. Similar messages had been sent to the French Ambassador and to the United States Chargé d'Affaires, giving them appointments for 9.30 and 9.45 respectively. I accordingly called on Baron von Weizsäcker at the hour named and received from him the text of the proposals, together with an explanatory statement. (⁷) As both these documents had already been broadcast at 9 p.m. I asked the Secretary of State what was the point now of making these communications to me. Baron von Weizsäcker observed that he was merely carrying out his instructions and that he could make no further statement to me. I could only infer from this reply that Herr Hitler had taken his final decision. I accordingly drafted that night a telegram to your Lordship to the effect that it would be quite useless for me to make any further suggestions since they would now only be outstripped by events and that the only course remaining to us was to show our inflexible determination to resist force by force.

63. In point of fact the advance into Poland had been ordered that night, and in the early hours of the 1st September, without any declaration of war the German army crossed the frontier and the German Air Force proceeded to bomb the Polish aerodromes and lines of communications.

(⁷) No. 98. (page 149).

64. In accordance with Herr Hitler's usual technique everything was done by the German authorities to prove to the German public that it was the Poles who had been the aggressors instead of the aggressed. Cynical notices were communicated at 6 a.m. to His Majesty's Embassy notifying me that the Bay of Danzig was closed both to navigation and to flying in view of the possibility of military operations "against hostile attacks by Polish naval forces or by Polish aircraft." Field-Marshal Göring also sent me a message to say that the Poles had begun the war by blowing up the bridge across the Vistula at Dirchau, while Herr Hitler himself issued a proclamation to the German army, declaring that the Polish State had refused the settlement which he offered and had appealed to arms, that the Germans in Poland were being persecuted by a bloody terror, and that the Poles were no longer willing to respect the frontier of the German Reich. Every German newspaper repeated the lie that it was the Poles who had begun the fighting. Finally at 10.30 a.m. Herr Hitler met the Reichstag which had been summoned for that hour, and similarly announced to the assembled Delegates that he had been "forced to take up arms in defence of the Reich." The die had in fact been cast and never can there have been or ever be a case of more deliberate and carefully planned aggression.

65. Late that evening I was instructed by your Lordship to notify the German Government that the latter by their action had created conditions which called for the implementation by the Governments of the United Kingdom and France of their undertaking to come to Poland's assistance, and that, unless His Majesty's Government received satisfactory assurances that the German Government had suspended all aggressive action and would be prepared to withdraw its forces from Polish territory, His Majesty's Government would, without hesitation, fulfil their obligations to Poland. I was instructed at the same time to request an immediate reply, and was authorised, if asked, to explain that this communication was in the nature of a warning, and was not to be considered as an ultimatum.

66. I handed this communication in writing to the Minister for Foreign Affairs at 9.30 p.m. that evening. Herr von Ribbentrop received it without other comment than that the sole blame rested on the Poles, that it was they who had first mobilised and who had first invaded Germany with troops of the regular army. He made no enquiry as to the nature of the communication which he merely said that he must submit to the Führer. I said that I realised that this would be necessary, and that I would be available at whatever hour he might be in a position to give me the Reichschancellor's reply. The French Ambassador, who had been instructed to make a similar communication, did so immediately after me and received a reply on the same lines.

67. Earlier in the afternoon of that day, in accordance with your Lordship's instructions, I had officially requested the United States Chargé d'Affaires to be good enough to take charge of British interests in the event of war. All cyphers and confidential documents were burnt, and the whole of the Staff left their normal residences and were concentrated in the Adlon Hotel next door or in the Embassy itself. All the arrangements were carried out with a maximum of efficiency and a minimum of confusion, which did the utmost credit to the organisation and competency of the very excellent Staff of His Majesty's Embassy. The chief responsibility for this rested upon Mr. Holman, as Head of the Chancery.

68. The 2nd September was a day of suspense. The Poles were, it was reported, putting up a brave resistance in the face of surprise and overwhelming numbers, and in spite of the vast superiority of the German air force and mechanised forces. No reply was received from the German Government throughout the day to the British and French warnings.

69. On the other hand, the Italian Government was making one more effort to save the situation. The Italian Ambassador had come to see me at midday on his way to the Ministry for Foreign Affairs. Signor Attolico told me that he must know one thing immediately. Was the communication which I had made the previous evening to Herr von Ribbentrop an ultimatum or not? I told his Excellency that I had been authorised to tell the Minister for Foreign Affairs if he had asked me—which he had not done—that it was not an ultimatum but a warning. I mentioned to Signor Attolico that I understood that the Italian Government had put forward a suggestion for the cessation of hostilities and the immediate summoning of a conference of the interested Powers. In this connection I said that I felt bound to express the opinion that such a proposal would never be entertained unless at the same time all the German troops were withdrawn from Polish territory.

70. The Ambassador retorted that I could not speak for my Government. I admitted that fact, but said that I could not imagine the possibility of ourselves, and much less of the Poles, agreeing to any lesser course. I do not know what reply, if any, was given by the German Government to this proposal. But I should like to put on record here that no one ever worked harder for peace than did Signor Attolico not only this year but last year also. He was entirely selfless in this his earnest endeavour.

71. There were, in fact, for Herr Hitler only two solutions: the use of force, or the achievement of his aims by the display of force. "If you wish to obtain your objective by force, you must be strong; if you wish to obtain them by negotiation, you must be stronger still." That was a remark which he made to a foreign Statesman who

219

visited him this year, and it expresses in the concisest possible form the Hitler technique. It was exactly that which he displayed in September, 1938. He was no more bluffing then than he was bluffing in August, 1939. Up to the middle of August this year the fear of a war on two fronts, with Russia hostile or at least unfriendly, might possibly have deterred him and his military advisers from action against Poland. There was no Eastern front to give him cause for hesitation in 1938, and he could have counted then on Hungarian as well as Polish support in his nefarious plans for the dismemberment of Czecho-Slovakia. But for Munich he would without a shadow of doubt have invaded that country on the 29th September last year, just as surely as he invaded Poland on the 1st September this year, and the war would have come eleven months earlier. In both cases the methods employed were identical: the gradual mobilisation of the German army over a period of months and its secret concentration at the appointed positions, whence the advance could begin at almost any moment and within a very few hours.

72. So it was again in 1939. If he could have secured his objectives by this display of force he might have been content for the moment, with all the additional prestige which another bloodless success would have procured for him with his own people. But it would only have been to start again once the world had recovered from the shock, and even his own people were beginning to be tired of these repeated crises. Millions of Germans had begun to long for a more peaceful existence. Guns instead of butter were becoming more and more unpopular except with the younger generation, and Hitler may well have wondered what might happen to his Nazi revolution if its momentum were allowed to stop. Moreover the financial and economic position of Germany was such that things could scarcely continue as they were without some form of explosion, internal or external. Of the two alternatives the most attractive from the point of view of his growing personal ambitions, and those of the clique which was nearest to him, was war.

73. It is scarcely credible that he would have acted as he did if bloody war, rather than a bloodless victory, had not seemed the fairer prospect for him. He had always meant to teach the Poles a lesson for what he regarded as their base ingratitude in refusing the "generous" demands which he had made to them in March. His only manœuvres since that date were with the object of creating circumstances favourable to his plans or of inducing Britain and France to abandon their Polish ally and to leave him a free hand in Central and Eastern Europe.

74. To this end, encouraged by Herr von Ribbentrop, who apparently advised him up to the last moment that Britain would not fight, he worked unceasingly. In the course of one of the five inter-

views which I had with him during those last few days, I remarked to him that it was he who was ungenerous to the Poles, in view of the advantages which his treaty of 1934 with Pilsudski had brought him. Herr Hitler denied that that treaty had ever been of any benefit to Germany and asserted that it had merely been unpopular with the Germans. It was a remark which was typical of Herr Hitler's capacity to ignore everything which he might have said, promised or done in the past as soon as it had become contrary to views for the present or the future.

75. One of Herr Hitler's greatest drawbacks is that, except for two official visits to Italy, he has never travelled abroad. For his knowledge of British mentality he consequently relied on Herr von Ribbentrop as an ex-Ambassador to Britain, who spoke both French and English, and who had spent some years in Canada, and whom he regarded as a man of the world. If report be true Herr von Ribbentrop gave him consistently false counsels in regard to England, while his successes in other spheres induced Herr Hitler to regard him more and more as a second Bismarck, a conviction which Herr von Ribbentrop probably shared to the full.

76. Even the most absolute Dictator is susceptible to the influence of his surroundings. Nevertheless Herr Hitler's decisions, his calculations, and his opportunisms were his own. As Field-Marshal Göring once said to me, "when a decision has to be taken, none of us count more than the stones on which we are standing. It is the Führer alone who decides." If anything did count, it was the opinion of his Military Advisers. I have always believed that it was they who, in the interests of Germany's strategical security, recommended the establishment of the Protectorate over Bohemia. And again this August, it was they, I fancy, who told Herr Hitler that further delay would be fatal lest the seasonal bad weather in Poland might upset their calculations for her swift overthrow. The army grudged him even the week between the 25th August and the 1st September which his last attempt to secure British neutrality or at least goodwill had cost it.

77. Yet even so the advice of his soldiers was probably merely cover for the prosecution of Hitler's own plans. His impatience and precipitate action on that last day of August can scarcely have been other than premeditated. All through the summer he had been waiting on events to turn in his favour and had been making his preparations to seize the opportunity, when it was offered to him. The Russian pact appeared to give him the advantage which he was seeking and thereafter there was no time to lose, if mud was not to be added to Poland's allies.

78. When therefore the Polish Government delayed 48 hours in sending its Plenipotentiary to beg for terms at Berlin and even then

sent only an Ambassador without plenary powers, Herr Hitler in spite of the expressed readiness of Poland to enter into direct negotiations, finally made up his mind not to keep his army waiting any longer. The order for the advance into Poland was probably given immediately after M. Lipski's interview with Herr von Ribbentrop at 6.30 p.m. on the 31st August.

79. Late in the afternoon of the 2nd September I communicated to the Secretary of State for the information of the German Government the verbatim report of the Prime Minister's speech in the House of Commons on that date. Therein Mr. Chamberlain stated that while His Majesty's Government could not agree to the proposal of the Italian Government for a conference while Poland was being subjected to invasion, they would be willing, if the German forces were withdrawn from Polish territory, to regard the position as being the same as before the forces had crossed the frontier. It was the last chance of avoiding the great catastrophe of war at the last minute, but the German Government remained silent.

80. In the early hours (4 a.m.) of the 3rd September I was accordingly instructed by your Lordship to arrange for a meeting with the Minister for Foreign Affairs at 9 a.m. There was some difficulty in establishing contact with the Ministry at that hour, but I was finally informed that Dr. Schmidt was authorised by the Minister to accept on his Excellency's behalf any communication which I might make to him. I accordingly handed to Dr. Schmidt at 9 a.m. precisely the final ultimatum from His Majesty's Government, pointing out that over 24 hours had elapsed since I had requested an immediate answer to our warning communication of the 1st September, that since then the attacks on Poland had been intensified, and that, unless satisfactory assurances were received by His Majesty's Government before 11 a.m. British summer time of the suspension of all aggressive action against Poland and of the withdrawal of the German forces from that country, a state of war would exist between our two countries as from that hour.

81. Dr. Schmidt received this communication and undertook to deliver it immediately to his Chief. As no reply from the German Government was vouchsafed by 11 a.m., the German Representative in London was informed in due course at that hour that a state of war existed between Britain and Germany. By 10 minutes past 11 a.m. every British consular officer in Germany had been advised by the staff of His Majesty's Embassy at Berlin that this was the case.

82. Shortly after 11 a.m. I received a final message from Herr von Ribbentrop asking me to call upon him at once. I did so at 11.30 and he handed me this time a lengthy document to read, beginning with a refusal on the part of the German people to accept any demands in the nature of an ultimatum made by the British Government, and

stating that any aggressive action by England would be answered with the same weapons and the same form. The rest of the document was pure propaganda with a view to attempting to prove to the German people and the world generally that it was Britain alone who was to blame for everything which had happened. My only comment on reading this completely false representation of events was: "It would be left to history to judge where the blame really lay." Herr von Ribbentrop's answer was to the effect that history had already proved the facts and that nobody had striven harder for peace and good relations with England than Herr Hitler himself. His last remark to me was that he wished me personally good, to which I could only reply that I deeply regretted the failure of all my efforts for peace, but that I bore no grudge against the German people. Thereafter I saw no further German official except the member of the Protocol, who accompanied our special train as far as Rotterdam. My last official communication to the German Government was a note which I presented on the instructions of His Majesty's Government enquiring whether the German Government would observe the provisions of the Geneva Protocol of 1925 prohibiting the use in war of asphyxiating, poisonous or other gases and of bacteriological methods of warfare—I understand that the German Government have since replied through the Swiss Minister in London giving the required assurance on the understanding that His Majesty's Government would similarly observe the provisions of the Protocol.

83. The French Ambassador had presented at noon a similar ultimatum to the German Government to expire at 5 p.m. For a few hours after 11 a.m. the telephonic lines of His Majesty's Embassy at Berlin continued to function, but about 4 p.m. all telephonic lines were cut off and both the Staff at the Adlon Hotel and the Embassy itself was isolated from all external contact. Members of my staff, however, had visited the Protocol at 11 a.m. with a view to arranging for our departure. They were treated with every civility and consideration and were informed that a special train would be placed at our disposal the following morning.

84. Our only contact thereafter with the outside world was through the American Embassy. Its aid and help was invaluable. No trouble was too great for the Chargé d'Affaires, Mr. Alexander Kirk, and the members of his staff. They did everything that was possible to smooth over the difficulties of those last 24 hours, and our pleasantest recollection of them is our appreciation of the great sympathy and willing assistance which we received from the American Embassy.

85. The French Embassy left Berlin at 9 a.m. the following morning, Monday, the 4th September. The British Embassy followed in a special train, leaving the Charlottenberg station at 11.20 a.m. The whole party consisted of 30 men, 7 women and 2 dogs. A small

crowd collected round the Embassy before our departure, but unlike 1914 it evinced no single sign of hostility. Mr. Kirk rendered me one more last service by driving me to the station in his own car. The streets of Berlin were practically deserted and there was nothing to indicate the beginning of a war which is to decide whether force is to be the sole arbiter in international affairs; whether international instruments solemnly and freely entered into are to be modified, not by negotiation, but by mere unilateral repudiation; whether there is to be any faith in future in written contracts; whether the fate of a great nation and the peace of the world is to rest in the future in the hands of one man; whether small nations are to have any rights against the pretensions of States more powerful than themselves; in a word, whether government of the people by the people for the people is to continue in this world, or whether it is to be replaced by the arbitrary will and ambition of single individuals regardless of the peoples' will.

86. Our journey through Germany, if prolonged, was uneventful. At the various stations at which we stopped there was some curiosity but no evidence of hostility. We reached Rheine, a small station some 20 kilom. from the German frontier, at about 6 p.m. on the Monday evening. There our train was detained for nearly twenty hours pending the safe arrival in Dutch territorial waters of the German mission from London. We eventually left Rheine at 1.30 p.m. on Tuesday and were received with great hospitality at the Dutch frontier. We reached Rotterdam that evening, and after spending a night at The Hague and one on board the Dutch steamer *Batavier V*, left Rotterdam in the early hours of Thursday morning, the 6th September. We arrived at Gravesend about 6 p.m. that evening.

I have, &c.

NEVILE HENDERSON.

224